A Whole Country in Commotion

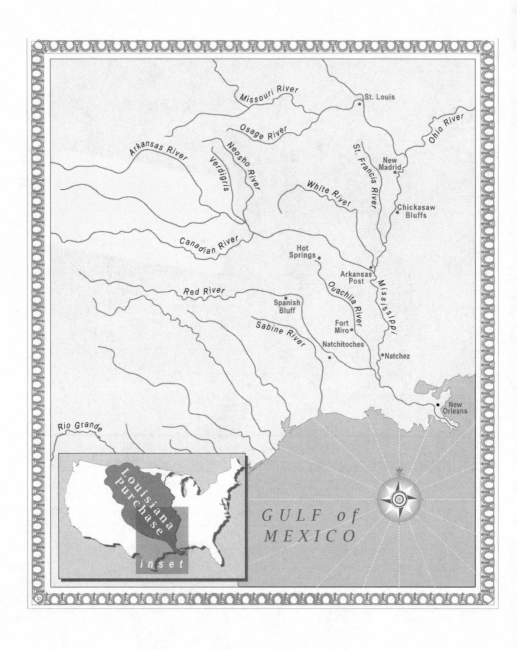

A Whole Country
IN
Commotion

*The Louisiana Purchase
and the American Southwest*

**EDITED BY PATRICK G. WILLIAMS,
S. CHARLES BOLTON, AND
JEANNIE M. WHAYNE**

The University of Arkansas Press
Fayetteville
2005

09   08   07   06   05   5   4   3   2   1

Designed by Ellen Beeler

⊗ The paper used in this publication meets the minimum requirements of the
American National Standard for Permanence of Paper for Printed Library
Materials Z39.48-1984.

This project is supported in part by the Blair Center of Southern Politics and Society.

Library of Congress Cataloging-in-Publication Data

A whole country in commotion : the Louisiana Purchase and the American
   Southwest / edited by Patrick G. Williams, S. Charles Bolton, and Jeannie M.
   Whayne.
      p. cm.
   Includes bibliographical references and index.
   ISBN 1-55728-784-8 (pbk. : alk. paper)
   1. Louisiana Purchase. 2. Frontier and pioneer life—Southwest, Old.
   3. Southwest, Old—History—19th century. 4. Southwest, Old—Ethnic
   relations. 5. Louisiana—History—To 1803. 6. Louisiana—History—
   1803–1865. 7. Arkansas—History—19th century. I. Williams, Patrick G.,
   1957– II. Bolton, S. Charles. III. Whayne, Jeannie M.
   E333.W47 2005
   976'.03—dc22

                                                                  2004025295

Contents

PART THREE: Remembering the Purchase Era

Contributors

S. CHARLES BOLTON is professor of history at the University of Arkansas at Little Rock. He is author of *Territorial Ambition* (1993) and *Arkansas, 1800–1860* (1998).

KATHLEEN DUVAL is assistant professor of history at the University of North Carolina, Chapel Hill.

DAN FLORES is A. B. Hammond Professor of History at the University of Montana and a specialist in American environmental history. He is the author most recently of *Horizontal Yellow* (1999) and *The Natural West* (2001) and edited *Southern Counterpart to Lewis & Clark: The Freeman & Custis Expedition of 1806* (2002).

LYNN FOSTER is professor of law at the University of Arkansas at Little Rock William H. Bowen School of Law.

JOSEPH PATRICK KEY is assistant professor of history at Arkansas State University.

CHARLES F. ROBINSON II is associate professor of history at the University of Arkansas and author of *Dangerous Liaisons* (2003).

GEORGE SABO III is research station archeologist at the Arkansas Archeological Survey and a professor of anthropology at the University of Arkansas. He is coauthor of *Arkansas: A Narrative History* (2002) and author of *Paths of Our Children: Historic Indians of Arkansas* (rev. ed., 2002).

ELLIOTT WEST is Alumni Distinguished Professor of History at the University of Arkansas and author of *The Contested Plains* (1998), *The Way to the West* (1995), and *Growing Up with the Country* (1989).

JEANNIE M. WHAYNE is professor of history at the University of Arkansas, director of the Arkansas Center for Oral and Visual History, editor of the *Arkansas Historical Quarterly,* and secretary-treasurer of the Arkansas Historical Association. She is author of *A New Plantation South* (1996) and coauthor of *Arkansas: A Narrative History* (2002).

PATRICK G. WILLIAMS is associate editor of the *Arkansas Historical Quarterly* and assistant professor of history at the University of Arkansas.

Acknowledgments

The editors of this volume wish to thank *Montana: The Magazine of Western History* for allowing us to reprint a revised version of Dan Flores's "A Very Different Story: Exploring the Southwest from Monticello with the Freeman and Custis Expedition of 1806" (*Montana* 50 [Spring 2000]: 2–17). We would also like to acknowledge the *Arkansas Historical Quarterly* for allowing us to reprint five essays that were previously published by that journal. These essays were revised for inclusion in this volume by their authors, Kathleen DuVal, S. Charles Bolton, Joseph Patrick Key, Lynn Foster, and George Sabo III. Sabo's work was published in the Winter 2003 issue of the journal, while the others appeared in the Autumn 2003 issue. The editors express a special thanks to Michael Pierce for his editorial work on these five essays. We are grateful to Thomas R. Paradise of the University of Arkansas for preparing the map for this volume.

The editors are also particularly grateful to those who participated in and sponsored the Louisiana Purchase Conference held on the University of Arkansas campus November 19–20, 2003. A similar conference had been held at the Butler Center for Arkansas Studies at the Central Arkansas Library System in Little Rock the previous May, and Bobby Roberts, Tom Dillard, and Cary Cox encouraged the convening of one in Fayetteville. We thank the Arkansas Secretary of State's Office and the Louisiana Purchase Bicentennial Committee for providing funds. Their contributions, together with that of the Hartman Hotz Lecture Series in Law and Liberal Arts at the University of Arkansas, made the conference possible. A special thanks also goes to the Blair Center of Southern Politics and Society, which is dedicated to fostering political scholarship, public service, and the study of southern politics, history, and culture. The Timothy P. Donovan Lecture Series, a fund supported by the University of Arkansas History Department, sponsored one of the lectures, as did the Department of Anthropology's Stigler Memorial Anthropology Lecture Fund.

S. Charles Bolton wishes to thank Conevery Bolton Valencius and the *Arkansas Historical Quarterly*'s anonymous referee, who read an earlier version of the essay that appears in this volume.

Dan Flores wishes to thank the A. B. Hammond Endowment for Western History at the University of Montana for its travel and financial assistance.

Kathleen DuVal thanks S. Charles Bolton, Alan Taylor, Bob Moore, Dan Richter, an anonymous reader for the *Arkansas Historical Quarterly*, and the University of Pennsylvania History Department, where she presented a version of the essay that appears in this volume.

Lynn Foster is indebted to Judge Morris S. Arnold, the foremost authority on colonial Arkansas, and Prof. S. Charles Bolton of the University of Arkansas at Little Rock History Department, both of whom reviewed the manuscript and suggested various changes. Lynn Morrow and Greg Bast of the Missouri State Archives allowed access to the General Court Records and generously made photocopies of several case files. Linda Pine and the staff of the UALR Archives also supplied photocopies. Foster also thanks Russell Baker at the Arkansas History Commission, Kathryn Fitzhugh at the UALR/Pulaski County Law Library, and Matt Wells for his fine work on the record books of the territorial courts. Work on the Arkansas Territorial Records and Briefs Collection was made possible by a grant from the Donaghey Foundation.

Joseph Patrick Key thanks S. Charles Bolton, Elliott West, and the anonymous reader for the *Arkansas Historical Quarterly*, who read an earlier version of the essay contained in this volume.

Charles F. Robinson II thanks Patrick G. Williams for his editorial assistance and Jeannie M. Whayne for inviting him to be a participant.

George Sabo III wishes to thank the members of the Caddo community who patiently and generously shared their knowledge of the Turkey Dance traditions, including Cecile Elkins Carter, LaCreda Weller Daugomah, John and Mary Lou Downing Davis, George and Billie Ruth Hoff, Frances Cussen Kodaseet, Marilyn Murrow, Ed and Donna Smith Spaulding, and Charlene Wright. Errors that remain despite this kind assistance are the author's responsibility.

Elliott West thanks Patrick G. Williams, James Ronda, Ray Wood, Jeannie M. Whayne, Charles F. Robinson II, Joseph Patrick Key, and Dan Flores.

Jeannie M. Whayne wishes to thank Patrick G. Williams, Morris S. Arnold, S. Charles Bolton, Elliott West, Daniel Usner, and Kathleen DuVal.

Introduction

Patrick G. Williams

"This expedition seems to have thrown their whole Country into commotion."
—*Peter Custis, 1806*

The U.S. government chose to mark the bicentennial of the Louisiana Purchase with a postage stamp showing the signing of the treaty by which France ceded the enormous territory to the United States and some new nickels evoking Meriwether Lewis and William Clark's exploration of a portion of that territory. An epic moment and an epic episode, surely, but these official images fail to capture the full range of commotion attending the purchase. The Louisiana Purchase brought much touted benefits to the young nation, doubling its size and transforming the Mississippi River from a contested boundary to a securely American artery of commerce. Yet it also created turmoil along the territory's fringes and brought wrenching change to many Americans both west and east of the river.

This volume hopes to do a better job at examining these latter aspects of the purchase. Rather than lavishing attention on the details of the "noble bargain" struck between the United States and France, many of its essays attend to the more complexly multilateral negotiations among peoples, nations, and empires that preceded and followed the actual transfer of territory. The cast of characters accordingly expands beyond Thomas Jefferson's slaveholding republic and Napoleon's empire of *liberté*—and beyond Lewis, Clark, Sacagawea, and York—to include the increasingly ramshackle Spanish colonial apparatus, Indian peoples west of the Mississippi and eastern Indians moving west, métis and mestizos of the southern borderlands, and interlopers of assorted European backgrounds. Readers might also find lingering just offstage the black Jacobins of St.

Domingue and even, as Elliott West has discussed elsewhere, the anopheles mosquito.[1] The essays in part two of this volume concern the manifold transformations wrought *within* the Louisiana territory as these assorted actors encountered, worked upon, and, in some cases, worked over one another—reorderings of populations, livelihoods, cultures, systems of justice, and even kinship and gender roles. Ironically, perhaps, these species of commotion came most immediately and dramatically to a portion of the territory well south of the path paddled by the party celebrated whenever our new nickels come up tails.

In considering the international dimensions of the purchase, the essays in part one, "West by Southwest: The Louisiana Purchase and American Expansion," make the point that even though Louisiana came to the United States not by conquest but by uncoerced sale, it was no unchallenged or uncomplicated bit of business, at least as far as other players in North America's continental politics were concerned. The purchase vastly extended the nation's frontier with British Canada, but the treaty with the French did little to locate that boundary—and the United States and England were far from being best friends. Within ten years of the purchase, the nation would again be at war with Britain, in part because Americans understood England to be supporting Indians in their resistance to white American expansion *east* of the Mississippi. Thirty years after that, sabers rattled over the fixing of U.S.-British boundaries in the Pacific Northwest. But while Lewis and Clark tramped well beyond any sensible boundary to the old French claim, the greatest commotion American probing caused with imperial powers came not with England, but with Spain.

The Spanish had long been wary of the United States' westward course of empire, and the purchase, as the essays by Elliott West and Dan Flores show, brought American citizens far deeper into what had always been contested ground. An impossibly long but dangerously unfixed new border was now established much closer to Spain's valued Mexican possessions. Troops sent out by Spain to contain the American claim to the interior never caught up with Lewis and Clark, but Spanish opposition did hem in the two expeditions dispatched by Jefferson to explore the southern reaches of the purchase territory: that of George Hunter and William Dunbar up the Ouachita River, which is described in Jeannie Whayne's "A Shifting Middle Ground," and that of Thomas Freeman and Peter Custis up the Red River, of which Dan Flores has become the leading authority. While Lewis and Clark reached the Pacific shore, neither of the southern parties would or could venture more than several hundred miles into the politically sensitive southwestern borderlands. The Freeman-Custis expedition, in fact, took place amid what seemed like a budding border war with Spain (the "commotion" to which Custis refers).

Both expeditions also moved cautiously out of fear of stirring up commotion with the Osages, an expansionist people who, as Kathleen DuVal shows in her essay could in the short term probably bring as much power to bear in the Louisiana territory as any U.S. expansionist or European power could. Not only the Osages but also a whole constellation of Indian peoples and polities would have their own roles to play in the politics and diplomacy of the purchase. Both the United States' and Spain's thinking about Louisiana would be profoundly affected by the relations each wished to establish or needed to maintain with the native peoples of the American interior. U.S. encroachment could well disrupt trade and security *within* the remnant of Spain's North American empire, for example, by intruding upon what modus vivendi royal officials had arrived at with such key players on the southern plains as the Taovaya-Wichitas and Comanches.[2] Yet even when Spain had formally governed Louisiana, as DuVal demonstrates, it had never managed to harmonize its own interests with the varied interests of the different groups of Indians there, making any prospect of joint Spanish-Indian resistance to American expansionism rather dim. The United States had problems of its own harmonizing its interests and that of the Indians. S. Charles Bolton's contribution to this volume, "Jeffersonian Indian Removal and the Emergence of Arkansas Territory," illustrates the degree to which the American drawing of political boundaries within the Louisiana territory was shaped by the Jefferson administration's interest in moving eastern Indians across the Mississippi. Yet this desire never really meshed with the nation's interest in securing the trade, friendship, or acquiescence of the *native* native peoples of Louisiana territory, who did not necessarily welcome Indian newcomers. The bloody messes this made for, however, came largely at Indians' rather than the United States' expense.

Spooked by the Osages and more directly abbreviated by Spanish resistance, what Dan Flores has called the southern counterparts to the Lewis and Clark expedition have largely disappeared from memory. Yet in addition to illustrating how contested the U.S. claim to the purchase territory proved to be, the Dunbar-Hunter and Freeman-Custis expeditions possess another emblematic quality. Like Meriwether Lewis and William Clark, Virginian Peter Custis had blue blood running through his veins. The other three principals of southwestern exploration—William Dunbar, George Hunter, and Thomas Freeman—were, by contrast, all European immigrants. Many other immigrants would follow in their wake, the Trans-Mississippi West ultimately becoming one of the United States' most ethnically diverse regions. And, as Dan Flores and Elliott West pointedly observe in considering the trajectory of American expansion, both naturalized and native-born American settlers came most rapidly and in greatest number to the portion of the purchase scouted by the immigrant explorers, rather than following the trails blazed by Lewis and Clark. This left the southwestern precincts of the Louisiana country an especially rich ethnic stew as white Americans, their black slaves, and European immigrants settled among an already variegated population of Spanish and French Creoles, métis, and Indians.

To explore the many sorts of commotion this migration would bring to the region, part two of this volume, "Transforming the Territory," takes a closer look at that portion of Louisiana that would become the state of Arkansas. As Jeannie Whayne shows, even in this sparsely settled scrap of French and Spanish Louisiana, native populations had already been touched by distant influences. For generations before 1803, Indians and whites, though in small numbers, had established what Whayne, following Richard White, sees as a "middle ground" of economic and cultural accommodation that allowed both groups to participate in an international trade in animal products. An Indian called Captain Jacobs, who Dunbar and Hunter encountered in 1804, may have been the archetypal Arkansawyer of the "colonial" period—a native man with a European name and vermilion painted around his eyes. After the purchase, however, two distinct streams of westward movement would shake that middle ground. One was increased Indian immigration to Arkansas. Bolton's essay describes how, well in advance of the Trail of Tears, a good portion of the Cherokee nation moved west, directed by "Jeffersonian persuasion" to that bit of the purchase territory that would become Arkansas. Other eastern peoples joined them. This westward migration of Indians occasioned conflict with native peoples long established in the region as the immigrants intruded upon hunting grounds and even usurped the natives' role in existing trade networks. Indeed, much of the blood spilled in the wake of the purchase would be Indian blood shed by other Indians, such as in the Osages' murderous fights with Cherokees.

Yet it was a second and ultimately much larger westward movement that finally washed away Arkansas's "middle ground." White farmers flooded in, and they viewed Indians in Arkansas, however recent their vintage, not as the trading and sexual partners they had been in the colonial era but as pests to be cleared from potentially valuable land. This led to a removal of peoples only recently arrived west of the Mississippi as thoroughgoing and absolute as what was visited upon longtime residents like the Osages. Arkansas would take its present shape during the 1820s in a bout of ethnic cleansing that saw the western portion of Arkansas Territory (the bulk of present-day Oklahoma) ceded to Native Americans to create an Indian-free eastern zone.

Joseph Key's essay, "'Outcasts upon the World,'" plumbs this demographic sea change—in which white Americans and their black bondsmen quickly came to outnumber immigrant and native Indians—by tracing its effect upon a single people of the purchase territory, the Quapaws of southeastern Arkansas. No longer perched on the border of empires and republics, the Quapaws lost their strategic place in the diplomacy of the lower Mississippi valley. And as agriculture began to dominate the economy, they lost their similarly strategic place in regional trade. But the transformation worked by the Louisiana Purchase worked at other, very intimate, levels, such as in reconfiguring gender roles. The sort of farming that the federal government urged upon Indians as the means and measure of acculturation required men to work as women traditionally had in Quapaw culture.

The Louisiana Purchase also brought considerable commotion to whites already resident in Arkansas—and not simply because a hunting-and-trading economy gave way to an agricultural-and-pastoral one. The workings of justice would be transformed as U.S. systems of law replaced those of France and Spain in the region. By examining recently unearthed court records from Arkansas Post, Lynn Foster shows how messy a thing this could be in frontier portions of the purchase territory in the first decade of American rule. For even as U.S. citizens streamed into Arkansas, few settled in any one spot in great enough number that an American legal apparatus of judges, juries, prosecutors, and attorneys for the defense could be maintained without dismaying interruptions and some pretty hair-raising conflicts of interest.

Ultimately, the essays by Key, Bolton, and Charles Robinson are of a piece in reminding us that the demographic transformation of the southern portion of the Louisiana territory would in large measure be the product of forced migration: not only the removal of Indians but also the transport of African American slaves from the southeastern and border states to the richer and more abundant lands of the lower Mississippi valley and the Southwest. The Louisiana Purchase came exactly ten years after Eli Whitney's introduction of the cotton gin gave African American slavery a relentless expansionism all its own. Whitney's "engine" made cotton growing a potentially profitable pursuit in vast stretches of the southern interior, and the purchase extended that interior (as far as U.S. citizens were concerned) far to the west. One can only shudder at the commotion caused among black families as tens of thousands of eastern slaves were sold across the Mississippi or carried there by ambitious masters. One estimate numbers twenty-six thousand slaves from the Chesapeake states as exported to Louisiana, Arkansas, and Missouri between 1810 and 1820 alone.[3] Although little noted in official commemorations of the bicentennial, this forced migration was familiar enough to nineteenth-century Americans to become a staple in popular culture. Yankee readers dabbed their eyes at the sad fate of a Kentuckian, Uncle Tom, moved to Louisiana; Americans North and South hummed Stephen Foster's "My Old Kentucky Home."[4] If African Americans had no reason to cheer acquisition of Louisiana, neither, Charles Robinson tells us, did the black Louisianans already residing in the territory. The legal status of slaves and free people of color in a republic of liberty, equality, and representative government was, if anything, lowlier than that enjoyed by those of African descent in the ossifying colonial structures of France and Spain.

The lesson of Robinson's essay, then, is that Americans' just pride in the Louisiana Purchase and its legacy might best be tempered by the sense that its cost far exceeded the fifteen million dollars forked over to the French. From beginning to end, the story of the purchase has slavery at its heart. As is well known, Napoleon's ambitions for Louisiana went to smash, and the territory became the object of a French fire sale, when an army sent to reimpose slavery in St. Domingue was destroyed by black Haitians and mosquito-borne illness.[5] Jefferson spoke of the Louisiana Purchase "enlarging the empire of liberty," but the first three states carved out of the territory embraced slavery. And Congress's final bit of decision making about the future of slavery in the purchase territory—Stephen Douglas's Kansas-Nebraska Act of 1854—blew the American political system to smithereens, yielding civil war in a few short years.

If the essays in part one offer readers an opportunity to consider the international aspects of the Louisiana Purchase beyond the exchanges of French and American diplomats, and those in part two address the consequences of the purchase beyond its setting the stage for Lewis and Clark's bold journey, George Sabo's concluding piece shows us that there are other means of remembering the purchase era than through scholarly essays—or reenactors, postage stamps, and nickels. One of the original peoples of the territory, the Caddos, dance, sing, and drum.

Dancing Caddos and Elliott West's perorational invocation of Howlin' Wolf, who forged his delta sound on both sides of the Mississippi, allow us to close this introduction on a more uplifting note. Both point toward a cause for celebration overlooked in much of the bicentennial hoopla. The southern portions of the Louisiana Purchase would come to constitute a good deal of that crucible out of which flowed one of the United States' most bounteous gifts to the world: its folk and popular music. If Americans need to take stock of the troubles, messes, and hardships made by the Louisiana Purchase, they might at the same time revel in the joyous commotion that would issue from the juke joints, dancehalls, and choir lofts of New Orleans, Helena, West Memphis, Kansas City, and St. Louis.

PART ONE

West

BY

Southwest

*The Louisiana Purchase
and American Expansion*

Lewis and Clark: Kidnappers

ELLIOTT WEST

A prominent historian recently commented that Americans do not have much use for history, but they sure like anniversaries.[1] Nowhere is that better shown than in the celebratory frenzy over the Lewis and Clark expedition, which began poling its way up the Missouri River from St. Louis in the spring of 1804. Well before the two hundredth anniversary of the Corps of Discovery had even arrived, there had already been dozens of symposia and lecture series, impressive new visitor centers, truckloads of new books, and several television and film documentaries.

What is especially striking about this public outpouring is the contrast between it and the popular response a century ago. In 1903–4, Americans also were in a cheering, flag-waving mood, but their focus was not the centennial of Lewis and Clark's journey. It was the Louisiana Purchase. The exploration to the Pacific, all but unavoidable in the media today, had largely faded from public awareness. When the city fathers of

St. Louis were planning the exposition of 1904 in celebration of the purchase, they decided to stress their local connection to that grand event by dusting off this mostly forgotten sidelight, the expedition to the Northwest that began and ended in their city. Oregon also got in on the act, erecting as its official site on the fair grounds a replica of Fort Clatsop, the expedition's 1805 winter quarters, above which fluttered a special Lewis and Clark flag.[2] Looking back, that signaled the reemergence of Lewis and Clark into the American consciousness, their first tentative step toward their current celebrity.

The contrast between 1903 and 2003 raises intriguing questions. We should ask, for instance, why the expedition has so caught the public's fancy. The answers can teach us plenty about national mythologies and current beliefs and values. The prime lesson, however, should be how scandalously we have come to neglect what we were whooping and hollering about a hundred years ago. This is not to say we should necessarily be celebrating the Louisiana Purchase, at least not with the unalloyed praise heard in 1904. Native Americans, Hispanic Americans, and (as Charles Robinson argues in chapter 7) African Americans have good reasons to look back on the doubling of the national domain as an event of grim foreboding for their people. The point, rather, is that the historical consequences of the purchase, for good and ill, were incomparably greater than those of Lewis and Clark and their trek to the Pacific.

The Louisiana Purchase was one of the two or three most significant events in nineteenth-century American history. It is difficult to imagine the geographical shape, human makeup, and historical trajectory of the United States had the purchase not occurred. And yet it is possible to get the impression today that its main importance lay in its giving purpose to the expedition that was in fact a tiny blip on the national timeline.

Thus the title of this chapter. Lewis and Clark, as they have emerged in collective memory, have effectively kidnapped the Louisiana Purchase. The purchase, as an episode of influence, should be standing tall before us, commanding our attention and showing us how it shaped our national past. But instead Lewis and Clark have grabbed it, tied and gagged it, tossed it into their trunk, and driven off in their own direction. For the most part, we have followed along.

Fully rescuing the Louisiana Purchase from the Captains of Discovery is far too ambitious a task for any one short essay. Instead the hope here is to make a few modest suggestions, sprinkled with a few modest examples, about the neglected significance of the purchase. The more particular focus will be the influence of the purchase on westward expansion. More specifically still, the argument will be that when we give the episode its due, our attention will naturally shift directions. Once we recognize the significance of the purchase, we will also see the importance of the American South in westward expansion.

A few facts are incontestable. The Louisiana Purchase was a trigger to American expansion to the Pacific; less than fifty years after the transaction, we had acquired all of the "Lower Forty-eight" save the bit of southern Arizona we would buy from Mexico a few years later. That expansion brought the United States the stuff of national power—resources ranging from gold and silver to copper and timber to grasslands and fertile soil, outlets onto the vast Pacific Rim, room for a rapidly growing population. These connections, at least, are familiar to anyone with a rudimentary understanding of American history. And yet there is only the fuzziest popular appreciation of the particulars of these connections—a step-by-step understanding, that is, of how the purchase led to our acquisition of the Far West.

Part of the reason again is our fascination with Lewis and Clark. Because *they* are so intimately connected to the purchase in popular perception, we are subtly encouraged to picture the energy of national expansion as taking the same direction as the famous expedition. The president of the national commission on the Louisiana Purchase summed it up at the St. Louis Exposition: The Corps of Discovery were a "hardy band of pioneers which blazed the way to the Pacific coast and established American supremacy there."[3] At work here is a principle well known to any magician: what people think is happening depends on where people are looking. We know the purchase led to expansion, and we associate the purchase with Lewis and Clark, so we assume the forces propelling us to the Pacific were acted out roughly along the northwesterly direction taken by the corps—up the Missouri River, over the northern Rockies, and on to the northern Pacific coast. No wonder then that we suffer a disconnect between the purchase and the particulars of national growth, for it would be nearly forty years before anything of much significance to expansion happened on that northwestward bias.

The course of expansion was not west and *north* but west and *south*. It was out of Mississippi and Louisiana and toward Texas and New Mexico that America's outward energies were projected. That energy was released immediately, and it gathered strength over the next quarter century. Once we recognize the southwesterly thrust of national growth, the particulars quickly fall into place and unfold in a sequence that seems obvious.

Begin with the fact that Lewis and Clark's expedition was only one of four sent into the purchase during the Jefferson administration. The other three all were directed toward the southwest. In mid-October 1804, as Lewis and Clark approached their winter camp at the Mandan villages in present-day North Dakota, an expedition led by Dr. George Hunter and William Dunbar left Natchez, Mississippi, to begin their foray up the Red and Ouachita Rivers into Arkansas. In early May 1806, as the Corps of Discovery had just begun their return from their second winter at the mouth of the Columbia River, a party led by Thomas Freeman and Peter Custis set off from Concordia Parish in Louisiana up the Red River. The following July, as Lewis and Clark descended Lolo Pass on the eastern slope of the Rockies, Zebulon Pike departed St. Louis for Nebraska, the first leg of a journey that would take him up the Arkansas River and on to a fateful rendezvous in present-day southern Colorado.

Simply remembering those three southwesterly expeditions should help us realize that official attention was focused intently on the southern reaches of the purchase. President Jefferson looked in that direction, if for no other reason, to determine just what those southern reaches were. On the question of boundaries, the treaty that transferred greater Louisiana was vague in the extreme. It merely said that the United States was acquiring from France whatever France had acquired from Spain in 1800. When pressed on just what that was, Talleyrand famously answered: "I can give you no direction. You have made a noble bargain for yourself, and I suppose you will make the most of it." While the comment is familiar, Jefferson's response is less so: he quickly took the French minister up on his suggestion. Where the purchase started was clear—the Mississippi River. But where did it stop on the far side? Jefferson set in motion efforts to find out. His first instruction to Lewis and Clark was to trace the Missouri River to its source. Reckoning the northernmost reach of the river presumably would roughly establish how far north the expanded nation now reached.

Jefferson asked the same question about the southern part of the purchase, but his actions in that direction were different. While he took a wait-and-see posture on the northern boundary, content to make his claim there after hearing what the corps found, to the southwest the president quickly began to push American claims aggressively outward. In September 1803 he wrote an astonishing document, "The Limits and Bounds of Louisiana."[4] Here he claimed solemnly that the newly acquired territory stretched all the way to the Rio Grande. Even with charity his argument can at best be called tortured. In 1684, two years after his trip down the

Mississippi River to its mouth, Robert Cavalier Sieur de la Salle had led an expedition that landed on the Texas coast at Matagorda Bay and set up a ramshackle fort. The episode turned into a full-blown disaster, ending with La Salle murdered, most of his men dead, a handful of others trekking overland to Illinois, and the few who remained near Matagorda eventually arrested by Spain. No matter, Jefferson wrote: La Salle's landing and his crude fort gave France claim to the entire Gulf Coast down to the Rio Bravo (Rio Grande). With the Louisiana Purchase, those claims now belonged to the United States.

Obviously the boundaries of the purchase were very much up for grabs. Beyond that, Jefferson's outrageous bid tells us that he was willing to push hard to expand those borders, and the direction that he pushed tells us that he was particularly concerned about the southern border. Why? And why not a similar concern to the north? The British had for many years been an economic presence on the upper Missouri River. Their agents had worked with the Mandans and others—indeed, there were British traders in the villages where Lewis and Clark wintered. Jefferson meant to counteract their influence, and a greater worry was the indication that England might soon establish a commercial outpost in the Pacific Northwest. In fact it was Alexander Mackenzie's recommendation for such a venture that prodded the president to organize the expedition to the Columbia River. Still, the British presence on the northern border (wherever that was) was thin and relatively unthreatening. At the time, at least, not much was at stake. In 1802 the French minister of marine and colonies had written to his superiors that the northern portion of greater Louisiana "contains little more than uninhabited forests or Indian tribes, and the necessity of fixing a boundary never yet has been felt there."[5] Jefferson seems to have held much the same opinion.

The southern boundary was another matter entirely. The Old World presence there was not England but Spain. In the realm of Atlantic power, Spain was far less formidable than England, but Jefferson's focus was not on the larger Atlantic world but on what was now his nation's far western edge. The Spanish were there in numbers. They had established towns and military outposts in Texas and New Mexico and had shown a willingness to send forces of considerable size in response to perceived challenges from their north. On that point Spain had traded greater Louisiana to France in 1800 precisely because Spain was alarmed by the potential expansion of the United States toward the southwest. Napoleon, master of Europe and in command of the continent's most feared army, would be far more effective in standing firm against the young republic's anticipated push toward Texas. France's sale of Louisiana to the United States, the nation that the trade was meant to protect *against,* was a breathtaking betrayal of Spanish interests. Spain in fact argued to Jefferson that the purchase should be voided because its deal with Napoleon stated that if France wanted to get rid of its new possession, Louisiana could only be given back to the Spanish. When the president ignored the demand, Spain backed down, not out of doubts over its legal position but because it feared that if the point were pursued, the United States would simply seize the territory and perhaps push even farther.[6] Jefferson's astonishing claim to land all the way to the Rio Grande confirmed Spain's fears of pressure from its ambitious northern neighbor.

In short, the president's aggressive stance on the question of the southern boundary could not have been better designed to arouse suspicions and insecurities that had long been building among the Spanish. His actions quickly became part of a looming diplomatic showdown. In stark contrast to the vague, long-term worries about the northern portion of the purchase, the situation at the southern end was volatile and simmering.

Lewis and Clark themselves in fact were instructed to gather information that would bear directly on the rising tensions to the south. In the instructions he gave Lewis in June 1804, Jefferson included a subtle but revealing emphasis when telling him what to look for while exploring the upper Missouri River region. While the expedition's main route would be up the Missouri, the president wrote,

> yet you will endeavor to inform yourself, by inquiry, of the
> character and extent of the country watered by its branches,
> and especially on its southern side. The . . . Rio Bravo [Rio
> Grande], which runs to the Gulf of Mexico, and the . . . Rio
> Colorado, which runs into the Gulf of California, are under-
> stood to be the principal streams heading opposite to the waters
> of the Missouri, and running southwardly. Whether the dividing
> grounds between the Missouri and them are mountains or flat
> lands, what are their distance from the Missouri, the character
> of the intermediate country, and the people inhabiting it, are
> worthy of particular inquiry. The northern waters of the
> Missouri are less to be inquired after.[7]

Pay special attention, Jefferson stressed, to the region south of the Missouri, particularly its rivers. The president's keen interest sprang from the common (but mistaken) belief that many of the great rivers of the

West—he mentions the Missouri, Colorado, and Rio Grande—arose close together on a highland roughly in the area of the central Rocky Mountains.[8] Rivers being the main avenues of travel and commerce, whoever controlled that highland would have fullest access to the Far West. Specifically Jefferson seemed to hope that an ascent of the Missouri would position Americans to move easily to the head of the Rio Grande and the Colorado, rivers Jefferson knew flowed through Spain's northern frontier. Strange as it seems from what we know of the actual lay of the land, Jefferson's hope was that the upper Missouri might be the gateway to the Spanish Southwest. Thus his instructions: ask about those rivers "running southwardly," about how close their headwaters were to the Missouri's, and about the terrain separating them and the peoples living there. Those geographical basics, he wrote with considerable understatement, "are worthy of particular inquiry."

The Spanish, meanwhile, were well aware of the hungry interest of the young nation now leaning hard against their northern border. One of the constants of Spanish rule in fact had been an extreme sensitivity to any threat against its frontier. Losing command of Texas and New Mexico would likely endanger their far more valuable holdings in Mexico. For decades that concern had made the outer zone of their northern rim a place of jab and parry with European rivals, especially the French. La Salle's disastrous foray into Texas, now the basis for Jefferson's expansive claim, was an early example of a contest that continued over the next decades. In the 1720s, for instance, the contested area was the central Great Plains. The French made overtures to extend their influence by opening trade, including that of firearms, with tribes there. The effort included a trip by Etienne de Veniard, Sieur de Bourgmont up the Missouri and Kansas Rivers in 1724 to a spot close to the present site of Wichita, Kansas, roughly the point where Coronado had pushed farthest to the northwest 180 years earlier. Bourgmont invited a delegation of Indians to visit France, where they met with Louis XV, danced on the stage of the Paris Opera, and shot a large number of the royal peacocks on the royal estates.[9] Four years earlier Spain had responded to rumors of the French thrust into the northeastern edge of its orbit of influence. Pedro de Villasur led more than a hundred men into that area to reinforce his nation's presence. Along the Platte River in present-day Nebraska, he reached a village of Pawnees and Otoes who apparently had indeed been recently courted by the French. The Indians fell on Villasur's camp, killing him and all but a dozen of his men.[10] Guiding Villasur was Jean L'Archeveque. As a teenager he had accompanied La Salle to Texas, had helped plan his murder, and had been arrested by the Spanish. In time he gravitated to New Mexico, married well, and by 1720 had emerged as a seasoned go-between with plains tribes. His odyssey and death by the indirect hand of his mother country sums up nicely the shifting tides of imperial influence in this vast, contentious continental interior.

In one sense the arrival of the United States on New Spain's northern border merely introduced a new contender, one more source of worry. But all parties understood that this new player was fundamentally different. France's intrusion had been for the purposes of trade, worrisome enough but something that Spain could counter with its available power. American interests included trade, but the commerce in furs, skins, and other animal products would be the opening wedge of a more powerful and enduring threat. England's colonies, particularly those of the South, had evolved into an expansive agrarian society. Its exploitative farming methods and a birth rate that would surpass any in the world today combined to create a voracious appetite for new land. On the eve of the American Revolution, that expansive pressure breached the Appalachians. By the 1790s it was advancing along a broad front, but an especially aggressive salient came out of the Carolinas and Virginia through Tennessee and Kentucky. It was fueled partly by the faith that moving westward necessarily would mean improved circumstances. An observer among the crowds pushing across the Appalachians in 1795 wrote of the result: "Ask these Pilgrims what they expect when they git to Kentuckey the Answer is Land. have you any. No, but I expect I can git it. have you anything to pay for land, No. did you Ever see the Country. No but Every Body says its good land. . . . here is hundreds Traveling hundreds of Miles, they Know not for what Nor Whither, except its to Kentuckey."[11]

To the north of the Ohio River, another wave of farming families was rolling westward through Ohio, then on to Indiana and Illinois, but the southern thrust was in one way more expansive. As the Ohio valley frontier crossed the Mississippi into the newly acquired territory of the purchase, it would run up against the geography and climate of the Great Plains, which Americans could not exploit with their current methods of farming. This northern salient, that is, would reach its natural limits while still in American territory. Not so in the South. The thrust through Tennessee and Kentucky would naturally curve toward the territories of Missouri, Arkansas, and Louisiana. Beyond them lay Spanish Texas. Its eastern portion of piney woods and prairies was well suited for the agrarian styles of the southern frontier.

These two points—American expansion's southern thrust toward the exceptionally inviting country of eastern Texas and Spain's determination to defend that country—explain the diplomatic clash immediately evident after the Louisiana Purchase. Both sides understood the dynamic. In October 1803 Secretary of State James Madison wrote to Charles Pinckney, American minister to Spain: "What is it that Spain dreads? She dreads, it is presumed, the growing power of this country, and the direction of it against her possessions within its reach. Can she annihilate this power? No. Can she sensibly retard its growth? No."[12] Several years earlier Manuel de Godoy, chief advisor to the Spanish king, was reading reports from northern New Spain on the gathering threat from American expansion, with advice to establish posts to oppose it. At one point he scribbled in the margin, "No es posible poner las puertas al campo."[13] The literal translation is, "It is not possible to place gates in a field," but a more accurate version would be: "You are saying we should put up gates—gates with no fences—in an open field. What's the point?" Whoever is meant to be kept out will simply go around the gates, simply bypass any undermanned posts the Spanish might set up. De Godoy shrewdly understood the nature of the threat and his limited chances of effectively coping with it. That threat, Madison knew, was the expansive agrarian energies of the United States and their projection out of the South toward the southwest. "Can [Spain] annihilate this power?" Madison asked, "Can she sensibly retard its growth?" De Godoy had already given the answer: "No es posible."

Nonetheless Spain tried gamely to meet the challenge. The Lewis and Clark expedition shows this to have been the case but directs our attention to the south rather than the northwest. Spanish authorities learned that the Captains of Discovery would be making their way up the Missouri, and encouraged by that great scoundrel of the day, James Wilkinson, the nation's highest-ranking military officer as well as a paid spy for Spain, they hoped to turn them back or arrest them. No fewer than three military parties, possibly four, were dispatched northward to intercept Lewis and Clark.[14]

Meanwhile there were those other three expeditions into the purchase region, all of them much closer along the border of New Spain. They had one thing in common: their interest centered on the Red River. The Hunter-Dunbar party ascended the lower Red, originally with the intent of following it farther but diverted up a tributary, the Ouachita, into Arkansas as far as the hot springs later touted as a healing spa. Their detour is a revelation to us today. As Jeannie Whayne illuminates in chapter 4, the expedition's journals and the letters of John Treat show a mingling of native and European influence, an active zone of trade—and a portion of the border already tilting toward changes that the purchase would soon accelerate. The Freeman-Custis expedition pushed up the Red to a point in present Bowie County, Texas. Zebulon Pike's far longer journey never took him to the Red, but his ostensible purpose was to reach its upper watershed by a long, looping route through the central plains to the eastern slope of the Rockies.

The common concern with the Red River is explained by its emergence as the prime candidate, roughly at least, as the southern boundary of the purchase. However serious Jefferson had been in reaching out to the Rio Grande, his claim was shaky at best and beyond his power to enforce. A sturdier argument was that the purchase was defined by its watersheds. The contention was that La Salle's descent of the Mississippi in 1682 gave France claim to all lands drained by all rivers and their tributaries flowing into the Mississippi. The eastern watershed subsequently had passed from France to England to the United States. The western had gone from France to Spain, back to France in 1800, then to the United States three years later. The purchase thus would be defined on the west by the highlands from which all waters flowed east. The northern and southern boundaries would be the farthest drainages that emptied eventually into the Mississippi. Jefferson's instructions to Lewis and Clark worked from this assumption. The size of the Missouri, he reasoned correctly, taught that it must flow from the far northern interior. Find this river's source, he told Lewis, and we will have a rough guide to how far north and west the United States now extends. On the return trip Lewis moved up the Marias River on the supposition, also correct, that it was the tributary that arose farthest to the north, and so its headwaters should be the reckoning point of American national extent. "The northern waters of the Missouri are less to be inquired after," Jefferson had written to Lewis, but this interest was cooler relative only to the president's heated curiosity about rivers flowing toward New Spain. Inquiry toward the north *was* in order. Knowing the course of northern waters would tell him where the United States now stopped and British territory began.

As with the Missouri and the north, establishing a firm claim to the purchase's southern boundary would require tracing the course of the Red, the southernmost of the Mississippi's western tributaries. Mapping the watershed would lay down the U.S. national boundary, or at least the claim to it. But this border was far more contested than that with

Canada. Claims to land west of the Mississippi were based only partly on prior exploration such as La Salle's. There was also prior occupation. Especially in question was the country along the lower Red River and to the southwest of it. Spain and France had long jockeyed for position here. Officially each could claim settlements; less formally, French and Spanish had met, mingled, and intermarried through this region for generations. Just where France's possessions stopped and Spain's took up in 1763, when Louisiana went from one to the other, was to say the least an unsettled question. The issue was just as fuzzy in 1800 when Louisiana went back to France, and thus it remained open when the United States acquired, in the words of the treaty, whatever France had received from Spain. The give and take is confusing, but it boils down to this: the border between the United States and New Spain was yet to be determined, and determining it was partly a matter of exploration and settlement.

Sending out parties to trace the Red River thus was a confrontational act. American officials might say they were merely surveying the new border, but that begged the question of just where that border was. Spanish officials also feared that many Americans considered the national boundary, wherever it was, a jumping off place for some expansionist enterprise. The Pike expedition was evidence that their fears were fully justified.[15] Pike was not sent by President Jefferson but by the same man who had urged the Spanish to intercept Lewis and Clark—Gen. James Wilkinson, revolutionary veteran, ranking officer in the U.S. Army, and commander of forces in the lower Mississippi. With Vice President Aaron Burr, Wilkinson was up to his nose in arguably the most famous conspiracy in American history. The Burr Conspiracy's exact goals remain unclear, but they clearly involved a military foray out of Louisiana to seize some part of Spanish Texas. There are strong indications that Pike's expedition may have been meant, at least in part, to reconnoiter Spanish strength and positions in the Southwest. Whatever his instructions, reconnoitering the Spanish position is what Pike ended up doing. His official mission was to find the upper Red River, but after he followed the Arkansas River upstream to the Rockies, he did not move southward along their face, the logical strategy of looking for a river he assumed flowed from the mountains. Instead he *crossed* the mountains. On the far side he found a river he said he thought was the Red, then built a fortification and waited. Pike was not at the Red, however, but was on the river Jefferson had claimed was the new southwestern border, the Rio Grande. A Spanish force, yet another one sent on rumors of American forays into the region, found and arrested Pike and his men, took them first to Santa Fe and then to Chihuahua, and finally sent them back to Louisiana.

The mysteries around the Pike expedition and the Burr Conspiracy pull us so strongly into their details that we easily miss the larger context. Whatever Burr, Wilkinson, and Pike were up to, it is hard to imagine an episode that illustrates more sensationally how the Louisiana Purchase instantly spurred already vigorous expansionist ambitions; how those ambitions took a decidedly southwesterly direction; how the Spanish, who stood to lose the most from that thrust, responded with their own vigor; and how all this was building quickly toward one of the republic's early diplomatic crises. The purchase offered an obvious and alluring outlet for pressures from the land hunger felt keenly on the southern frontier. Burr and Wilkinson's scheme, regardless of particulars, assumed a warm interest among settlers in Kentucky, Tennessee, Mississippi, and lower Louisiana for some venture offering opportunities to the southwest. Spain dreaded, as Madison put it, America's growing power (the phrase has a nice double meaning: the nation's increasing influence and the potency of its increase) and where that power was aimed.

Pike's arrest was part of a much broader Spanish response to what they saw correctly as the most aggressive challenge ever against their northern lands. Already noted were the parties sent to intercept Lewis and Clark. Another strategy was to reinforce connections with Indians and to try to firm up a native barrier against U.S. expansion. In previous generations native peoples, not Europeans, had been the real power brokers in this region (as Kathleen DuVal convincingly describes in chapter 3). The Osages in particular had been the force to reckon with, and it was concern over their resistance, at least as much as Spain's, that persuaded Jefferson to redirect the Hunter-Dunbar expedition from the Red up the Ouachita. It followed that courting the Osages would be a key to counteracting the Spanish strategy. This in fact was one motive behind the Pike expedition. He began his journey by returning a few Osages, taken earlier by the Spanish, to their homes in villages close to the present western border of Missouri. On delivering them a member of Pike's party asked Osage chiefs: "Who did this? Was it the Spaniards? No. The French? No. Had either of those people been governors of the country, your relatives might have rotted in captivity, and you never would have seen them; but the Americans stretched forth their handes, and they are returned to you! What can you do in return for all this goodness? Nothing; all your lives would not suffice to repay their goodness."[16] His next stop was Nebraska's Republican River, where he visited villages of another of the area's more powerful groups, the Pawnees. There he learned that only weeks earlier the Pawnees had received an extraordinary delegation from the Southwest. Lt. Fecundo Melgares had led about five hundred men and more than two thousand horses and mules out of Santa Fe, down the Red River, and northward across the central plains to the Pawnees. Some hived off along the way, but the impressive column that arrived among the Pawnees was obviously meant to present a formidable appearance— more than six hundred mounted cavalry, and with them gifts of flags and medals and word that other Spaniards soon would arrive to build a town near the villages. Melgares's purpose was in part to block the Freeman-Custis party should it choose to continue up the Red. His second goal in marching on the Pawnees may have been to reach the Missouri and intercept Lewis and Clark, who in fact were then descending the river and at one point came within 150 miles of the Spanish command. Pike believed Melgares had come to stop him. The Pawnee chief, Pike wrote, reported that "it was the *will of the Spaniards that we should not proceed* [emphasis in the original]."[17] But proceed the Americans did, marching off toward New Spain by following the wide track of beaten earth left by Melgares's column.

Freeman and Custis, meanwhile, were leading their men up the Red River.[18] Of the four expeditions this one abraded most directly against the core of the country contested by Spain and the United States, the lower Red and the land southwest of it. Not coincidentally, it evoked the strongest Spanish response. As Freeman and Custis fought their way through the "great raft," a logjam more than a hundred miles long, Nemesio de Salcedo y Salcedo, New Spain's commandant of internal provinces, dispatched a large force from Nacogdoches to the point along the Red later named Spanish Bluff, roughly twenty miles northwest of present-day Texarkana. On July 28, 1806, Freeman and Custis reached the spot, encountered the nearly two hundred cavalry and foot soldiers, and turned back. By the end of August, they were back in Natchitoches, Louisiana.

The great showdown came in what today is western Louisiana, country long contested between Spain and France, now the one part of the vast purchase where Spanish and American populations came together in significant numbers.[19] In the weeks after the return of Freeman and Custis, more than a thousand Spanish troops faced about fifteen hundred American militia under Wilkinson's command across the disputed ground between the Sabine River on the west, claimed by the United States as the boundary, and Louisiana's Arroyo Hondo on the east, claimed by Spain as the proper border. For a while the two nations flirted with war. Jefferson secured a two-million-dollar appropriation and at one point drew up a tentative treaty of military alliance with England to settle the matter in his favor. In the end both sides backed away. In November 1806, agents of Spain and the United States signed an agreement making the land between the Sabine and the Arroyo Hondo neutral territory.

Remembering these events, all but forgotten in today's surveys of early American diplomatic history, can help correct the distorted view of the Louisiana Purchase and its role in westward expansion. Specifically they compel us to shift our attention toward the southern end of the great purchase and away from the direction we are currently encouraged to look, the northwest. The event that draws our attention so powerfully northwestward, the Lewis and Clark expedition, was indeed an extraordinary story full of insights into the nature of North American history during the early republic. But in both the short and the long run, the expedition's consequences were limited, nothing like those unfolding to the south along the border between the United States and the competitor uppermost in the minds of American leaders, New Spain. What happened there is worth studying if for no other reason than for its place in the history of our foreign relations. The showdown with Spain was one of America's sharpest diplomatic crises between the Revolution and the War of 1812, yet it gets at most a glance in the historical overviews of the period. But paying closer attention to these events, and understanding better their context and the forces behind them, offers more than that.

The Louisiana Purchase was the trigger to the nation's continent-wide expansion, and not just in the rather abstract sense of projecting the national imagination toward the Pacific. The events clustered around the Spanish crisis of 1803–6 led quickly to others that unfolded in an unbroken sequence ending with the American acquisition of the entire Far West by 1848. The steps of expansion fall roughly into three periods. The first, from 1806 to 1820, saw a dramatic expansion of the southern frontier, especially after 1815, and various attempts to penetrate eastern Texas from lower Louisiana across the line established by the showdown of 1806. On three occasions (1812–13, 1817, and 1819) filibustering expeditions tried unsuccessfully to carve Texas away from Spain. Defusing the immediate crisis of 1806 obviously did little to blunt the desire to push westward out of the lower Mississippi valley.

The second phase, from 1819 to 1836, began with two events, one seeming to stabilize matters, the other opening new possibilities. The Adams-Onís Treaty of 1819 finally established the southern boundary of the Louisiana Purchase. The United States surrendered Jefferson's flimsy claim to Texas in return for a border drawn up the Sabine River to the thirty-second meridian, north to the Red River, up the Red to the one hundredth meridian, north again to the Arkansas, and then upstream to its headwaters at the Continental Divide (at present Leadville, Colorado). Soon afterward Mexico declared its independence from Spain. In a move that seems (and in retrospect was) self-defeating, Mexico took a far friendlier stance toward those U.S. interests pressing against its north-eastern border. The Santa Fe trade was opened to Missouri merchants. Within a few years dozens of wagons, and eventually hundreds, were shuttling between the Missouri River and New Mexico. More remark-ably, Texas was thrown open to American settlers from the southern fron-tier. The observer of Kentucky pilgrims quoted above ("Ask . . . what they expect when they git to Kentuckey the Answer is Land") was Moses Austin. He settled in Missouri, and on the eve of Mexican independence, he had persuaded Spanish authorities to let him settle hundreds of Americans on the potentially rich cotton lands of central Texas. Austin died soon afterward, but his son Stephen confirmed the arrangement with the new Mexican government. As Mexico approved several more such empresario grants, the population in Texas rose dramatically, with the great majority of the new arrivals from the American South. The idea was to turn the southern frontier's expansive force, Madison's unimpedable "growing power," back upon itself. Settlers would be admitted only if they gave the assurance that they would assume Mexican citizenship, live by the laws and customs of their new nation, and convert to Roman Catholicism. Thus transformed into reliable citizens, the Texans would do what the Spanish had been unable to do: create an effective human bar-rier against the tide of the southern frontier. The result, we know now, was rather different. Although Austin and the other empresarios made a mostly honest effort to meet the terms of the arrangement, the differences in laws and customs, the distance from the seat of power in Mexico, and the instability of the Mexican government all fed a growing dissatisfac-tion among the settlers. Mexico tried to suspend immigration in 1830, but the result instead was an influx of illegal settlers who were even less under the control of the empresarios and even more inclined to resist Mexican authority. The population in the province had ballooned to thirty thousand by 1836, the year the Texans forced the issue and won de facto independence.

Thirty years after the showdown on the Louisiana-Texas border, the country Spain meant to protect in that episode, Texas, had been lost to

American interests. U.S. expansion from the southern frontier had over-whelmed all barriers, albeit with the aid of Mexico's miscalculated poli-cies. By then American interests were also well entrenched in New Mexico. Through the fur trade and commerce between Santa Fe and Missouri, men like Charles Bent and Lucien Maxwell had married into the Mexican social and political power structure while maintaining close connections along the U.S. border. They established positions of influence that later would leverage American power in the Southwest. Something similar had happened farther to the west among American merchants in Southern California.

Notice what had, and more importantly what had not, happened toward the northwest by 1836. Lewis and Clark's expedition was an immediate stimulus to the fur trade, which established a modest American presence in the northern part of the purchase and in the Pacific Northwest. The most ambitious move by fur-trading interests, however, John Jacob Astor's attempt to found a permanent trading outpost at the mouth of the Columbia River, aborted on the eve of the War of 1812, and there was no serious attempt to follow up later. The fur trade did encourage a vigorous exploration of the Far West, but except for the discovery of what would be the immigrants' great gateway westward, South Pass, the most signifi-cant trailblazing was south of the forty-second parallel, routes across the Great Basin and the Desert Southwest. Little was done to follow up on any beginnings to the northwest, essentially because there was not yet any expansionist pressure aimed in that direction. By 1836, the American presence in the region visited by Lewis and Clark consisted of a few posts and a handful of missionaries.

During the third stage of southwestern expansion, from 1836 to 1848, expansionist interests from the northern frontier finally emerged. Most notable were farmers from north of the Ohio drawn to the central valley of California, where, amazingly, Mexico had approved another empresario grant for John Sutter, and to the rich Willamette River valley in the Oregon country north of California, a region claimed by both the United States and Great Britain but open to American settlers under an agreement of joint occupation. Overland traffic from the Missouri valley to California and Oregon grew from thirteen persons in 1841 to nearly nineteen thousand in 1848.[20] Mercantile interests in cities of the Northeast also showed a growing interest in ports on the Pacific, particu-larly the magnificent harbor at San Francisco.

Pressures out of the South continued too. Texans claimed the entire length of the Rio Grande as their border and so insisted that half of present New Mexico was theirs. They tried and failed to seize Santa Fe, where American-born merchants and landowners enhanced their influence. A similar scenario continued to unfold in Southern California. Between 1836 and 1845, Texas experienced the most rapid rate of increase in population, both free and slave, in the slaveholding South. Any doubts about whether Texas could maintain its independence had vanished by 1844 when champions of slavery expansion launched a successful effort in Washington to invite the Lone Star Republic to seek statehood. That, plus the breathtakingly inept diplomacy that convinced many Mexicans that the United States was determined to annex their nation and extend southern slavery to its peoples, brought the final crisis. More than four decades of expansionist energy toward the southwest, plus the far more recent desire for Oregon and California farmland and Pacific ports, ended with the Mexican War, the Treaty of Guadalupe Hidalgo, and the Mexican Cession.

Once recognized, the steps that connect the Louisiana Purchase to the nation's long reach westward are obvious. When viewed backward they seem almost choreographed. The purchase was born of a concern for the lower Mississippi valley. It immediately inflamed the southern frontier's expansionist sentiments and provoked the first of several crises with whoever stood in the way. These events triggered others, which triggered their own, all falling together to carry the United States from the Mississippi River to the Pacific in less than half a century. The flow was relentlessly from east to west across the south, yet that regional focus, and consequently the role of the purchase in expansion itself, has largely been lost to public view.

There are, however, a few oblique recognitions, one of which is in Arkansas. Sixty miles east of Little Rock, Interstate 40 intersects U.S. Highway 49. Driving southeastward along that highway, from the small town of Brinkley to Helena and the Mississippi River, a traveler will have no doubt which region he is entering. This is the South. Cotton fields spread out on either side of the road. The summer air grows muggier as the miles unroll, the trees grow taller, and, sadly, the towns seem increasingly impoverished the nearer the car gets to the economic disaster zone of the delta. This is blues country, as one of the masters, Howlin' Wolf (Chester Burnett), reminds us:

First I'm gonna stop at the whiskey store,
Gonna buy me a jug of wine,
First I'm gonna stop at the whiskey store,

Gonna buy me a jug of wine,
  I'm gonna hit the highway
They call Highway Forty-nine.

A bit more than twenty miles beyond Brinkley, where the boundaries of Phillips, Lee, and Monroe Counties converge, a gravel road leads off to the left. At its end is a parking lot and the start of a boardwalk into a lovely swamp, and at the end of that walkway, shaded by cypress and oak and rising out of dark water thick with duckweed, is a large stone inset with a plaque. It marks the initial survey point of the Louisiana Purchase. Government surveyors Prospect Robbins and Joseph Brown met here when Robbins plotted a meridian due north from the mouth of the Arkansas River and Brown plotted a parallel west from the mouth of the St. Francis River. From that spot they began laying out the classic American grid of ranges, townships, and sections, and all the other surveys in the purchase built on theirs, north to Canada and west to the Continental Divide.

The Louisiana Purchase is anchored in a southern swamp. And so it should be with our historical attention. Our appreciation of this pivotal moment should be rooted in the South and should look out from there along the southern pathway that became a road of empire.

2

Jefferson's Grand Expedition and the Mystery of the Red River

DAN FLORES

No one has ever accused Thomas Jefferson of being uncomplicated or easy to cipher. As much as historians have grappled with his
political legacy, his contradictory stance on social justice, or his vision for
the great western country that the Louisiana Purchase folded into
America's destiny, Jefferson has remained the Great American Enigma.
Part of this has to do with the pragmatism that colored most of his decisions, but he also possessed a certain risk-taking impulse. The man who
was willing to speak in favor of the occasional revolution was the same
individual who could push the envelope of possibility in such matters as
exploring the West. Sometimes, as with a Lewis and Clark expedition
whose presence in the American imagination is presently in full soar, these
gambles paid off. But when they did not, Jefferson was fully capable of
turning his back.

For the better part of fifteen years, I have been trying to untangle what Jefferson intended with his actions vis-à-vis the other—and compared to Lewis and Clark, today virtually invisible—exploration he personally launched into the Louisiana territory. I do not here mean either of the Zebulon Pike probes, though most people familiar with Jeffersonian-era exploration would assume that. Like his earlier search for the source of the Mississippi, Pike's 1806–7 overland expedition to the southern Rockies was a mission launched by the American military—by Gen. James Wilkinson, in fact—and not Thomas Jefferson. Other than being pointed in the same general direction as Lewis and Clark, it shared little in common with their probe in either intent or preparation. Nor do I mean the brief expedition of William Dunbar and Dr. George Hunter to the Ouachita Mountains of present-day Arkansas in 1804–5, even though this one preceded even Lewis and Clark in reporting back from the Louisiana territory and made its two leaders famous enough in their time that no less than John James Audubon would later speak reverently of Hunter as that "renowned *Man* of Jefferson."[1] Although that expedition did originate with Jefferson and his intent not to leave out the southern parts of the Louisiana Purchase in the master plan for exploring the West, the Dunbar and Hunter probe as executed was merely a trial balloon for the "Grand Excursion"—the southwestern counterpart to Lewis and Clark—Jefferson had in mind all along.

It is the historical fate of the latter expedition, directed in the field by a civilian engineer-surveyor named Thomas Freeman, assisted by Meriwether Lewis's personal friend Capt. Richard Sparks of Virginia along with young Peter Custis, the first academically trained American naturalist to examine the West, that is most intriguing. And frankly, while hard digging and a good bit of luck have adorned that event in every manner of factual dress that history had not known before, I still find aspects of the episode puzzling, even troubling.

Not so mystifying is the expedition's invisibility in the *popular* American imagination, though. Unless multicultural history in the twenty-first century shapes the writing of the American past far more than at present and the fate of Jefferson's southwestern exploration comes to be celebrated by southwestern Hispanos as one of their great early successes in *resisting* U.S. imperialism, there should be no doubts why Lewis and Clark's history is worthy of a Ken Burns film and not even a single roadside historical marker exists to remind the American public of Freeman and Custis.

The answer to that one is simple, and it has to do with the truism that the winners write the version of events later generations celebrate. In contrast to the nationalistic pride, tapped so effectively by Stephen Ambrose–style history, that adheres to the remarkable success of the Lewis and Clark expedition's traverse of the continent, failure was the legacy of Jefferson's southwestern exploration. Intended originally to chart the entire lengths of both the Red and Arkansas Rivers, the south-western expedition failed even to achieve its last-minute, more limited objective of exploring the Red River only. What brought it to a halt after four months and an ascent of only half the river's length had nothing to do with daunted courage on the part of its leaders or a disinclination to "procede on" in the face of nature's obstacles (and there were some big ones). Jefferson's second Lewis and Clark expedition was intercepted, blocked, and turned around on the Red River by a Spanish force four times its size. In the face of Spanish resolve he may have underestimated (and—perhaps—certain individuals encouraged him to underestimate), Jefferson had taken a risk that backfired.

That a failed exploration, confronted and forced to "retrograde" by a foreign power, should fade in the American memory is not a surprise, of course. But since the intent of Jeffersonian exploration was always at least nominally scientific discovery (and the letter of instruction Jefferson gave Thomas Freeman at their private White House dinner in November 1805 called for precisely the kind of broad-ranging examination Meriwether Lewis had been directed to conduct), it has always been puzzling that an exploration that did, after all, have a look at almost seven hundred miles of landscape unfamiliar to Americans somehow ended up *erased* from history at every level. What is the explanation for this, and what does it tell us about the process of selective historical memory in our national story? Given the growing fascination with Lewis and Clark on the two hundredth anniversary of their grand expedition, perhaps it is worthwhile to take another look—a refresher, if you will—at their southwestern counterparts, whose story in professional history has come to be attached to Lewis and Clark in something of the manner of a tail flapping along after a kite.

The genesis of the U.S. exploration of the Southwest lay, no question, in the goals Jefferson expressed with respect to the Lewis and Clark expedition. While a probe along the line of the Missouri and Columbia river systems would resolve the question of a commercial Northwest Passage and clarify the extent of U.S. holdings as specified by the Louisiana Purchase, more than anything else exploring parties in the West would establish an American presence on the land and a claim that Jefferson hoped both competing imperial powers and indigenous peoples would acknowledge. Additionally—and the issue was unquestionably important to Jefferson—western exploration represented an official government support of Enlightenment science aimed directly at part of the earth where European plant collectors and naturalists had only nibbled. There was a whole fascinating world out there beyond his Blue Ridge Mountains about which Jefferson's mind wondered restlessly.

But the Lewis and Clark expedition would leave these missions unfulfilled for an enormous stretch of the Louisiana territory, and that was hardly Jefferson's intent. Indeed, he seems from the first to have regarded an American expedition across the southern reaches of Louisiana as nearly equal in importance to his Missouri/Columbia exploration. In 1803, in an exchange of letters with Meriwether Lewis (intended in part to cool Lewis's ardor for making a quick probe toward New Mexico from his winter camp in Missouri), the president explained his larger plan this way:

> The object of your mission is single, the direct water communication from sea to sea formed by the bed of the Missouri & perhaps the Oregon [the Columbia]. . . . I have proposed in conversation, & it seems generally to be assented to, that Congress shall appropriate 10, or 12,000 D. for exploring the principal waters of the Missisipi & Missouri. In that case I should send a party up the Red River to it's [sic] head, then cross over to the head of the Arcansa, & come down that. . . . This will be attempted distinctly from your mission.[2]

Once Lewis and Clark were underway in the spring of 1804, then, Jefferson devoted the time and energy he had for exploration to assembling and launching what he and all the principals came to regard as the southwestern counterpart to the Lewis and Clark expedition. Nearly two years of detailed planning and preparation, much of it devoted to a search for personnel for the journey, and a congressional budget of five thousand dollars (which happened to be twice the original appropriation for Lewis and Clark), finally poised the president's "Grand Expedition" for a scientific strike into the heart of the Southwest in April 1806. With Lewis and Clark then crossing the Bitterroot Mountains bound for St. Louis and home, one triumph seemed ready to proceed on the heels of the other.

But why specifically the Red and Arkansas Rivers? Aside from the geographic symmetry offered by aiming a second western expedition at the most southerly tributaries of the Mississippi, the reasons as Jefferson saw them for venturing into the sunlit spaces of the Southwest were compelling. For one, there was the matter of the boundaries of the Louisiana Purchase. The agreement that transferred Louisiana to the United States had left the boundaries of the province vague, specifying only that the lines of demarcation were to be the same as when France had controlled the region. But while France had legally owned Louisiana since the 1800 Treaty of San Iledefonso with Spain, her officials had not assumed direction of the province. And before Spain had won undisputed claim to the whole Southwest with France's exit from North America in 1763, the two powers had failed to delineate their possessions on the continent clearly. In 1687 the French explorer La Salle, seeking to found a colony at the mouth of the Mississippi, had missed that river and made landfall along what is now the Texas Gulf Coast southwest of present-day Galveston. La Salle's "colony" was an accident that had almost immediately collapsed; in the long run it had little effect other than to inspire Spanish interest in Texas. The French had gone on to establish permanent settlements among the Caddo Indians at Natchitoches along the Red River in 1714 and at New Orleans along the Mississippi in 1718. With century-old settlements already in New Mexico, Spain had responded with the presidio/mission of Los Adaes (present-day Robeline, Louisiana) in 1716 and San Antonio in 1718. Over the ensuing decades, French traders following the likes of Luis de St. Denis and especially Bénard de La Harpe—who founded a post several hundred miles up the Red in 1719—used the Red and Arkansas Rivers to penetrate far into the southwestern interior. Indeed, many interested in the region knew that in 1739 Pierre and Paul Mallet had reached Santa Fe, then descended a river (everyone assumed it was the Red) back to French Louisiana.

Jefferson's research into the matter of boundaries in his own library led him to a startling conclusion. In 1803, in a widely read treatise he called "The Limits and Bounds of Louisiana," the president argued that La Salle's appearance on the Texas coast had established a French claim that meant that the Rio Grande should actually be the western boundary of the Louisiana territory! This startling conclusion at once made Jeffersonian exploration to the southwest far more threatening to other North American powers than the Lewis and Clark probe. Spanish diplomat Pedro Cevallos quickly responded that the American pronouncement was "absurd reasoning! which does not merit to be refuted."[3] But the president's ambitious (if poorly supported) claim now threw Spanish possession of both Texas and New Mexico into dispute. While the matter of just which southwestern river properly should be the international boundary would eventually get resolved in the Adams-Onís Treaty of 1819, Jefferson's Rio Grande argument did have the important consequence of turning the Red River—where French activity was far better documented—into a reasonable compromise and a suitable venue for American exploration.

In the actual world of southwestern geography, though, how feasible —in fact—*was* an exploration that would ascend the Red and descend the Arkansas? Where would the Red River lead American explorers? The truth, despite the longstanding Euro-American settlements in New Mexico and Louisiana, was that only the Indians and a handful of traders knew the surprising answer to that question. Jefferson and everyone else in the U.S. government assumed that major rivers head in mountain ranges, and that given its lower course and size, the Red must have its origins somewhere in the southern ranges of the "Stony Mountains," at the foot of which lay a tantalizing destination: Santa Fe. Indeed, these assumptions seemed corroborated by the most recent maps, particularly Alexander von Humboldt's not-yet-published *Carte Generale du Royaume de la Nouvelle Espagne,* which Humboldt presented to Jefferson during a visit to Washington in 1804. Based on manuscripts in Mexico City, this map mistakenly identifies the Pecos River—which heads in the Sangre de Cristo Range east of Santa Fe but flows south to the Rio Grande—as the upper reaches of the river the French called "Rivière Rouge" (Red River) in Louisiana.[4] And in his private conversations, Jefferson left no room for doubt that the Grand Expedition was aimed at Santa Fe.

What the Jefferson administration lacked was the kind of information about southwestern geography that existed in the heads of late-eighteenth-century travelers Pierre ("Pedro") Vial, Jose Mares, and Francisco Fragoso, who with Indian guides had made a series of journeys in the 1780s and 1790s that attempted to link the Spanish settlements of St. Louis, Natchitoches, and San Antonio with distant Santa Fe. Geographic details like the actual courses of the rivers they followed seem to have eluded even Spanish officials. But what did catch their attention was Vial's claim in 1793 that it was possible to make the journey between St. Louis and Santa Fe in twenty-five days. That put the expansive, republican Americans far too close for comfort.[5]

Information about the Red River did make it back to Washington via Gen. James Wilkinson, who would emerge as one of the principal proponents (for reasons all his own) of southwestern exploration. In July 1804, with Lewis and Clark underway and Jefferson's focus redirected toward the exploration of southern Louisiana, Wilkinson submitted to Secretary of War Henry Dearborn a twenty-two-page letter calculated to excite "the Presidential Eye" about the Southwest, mentioning volcanoes and other marvels of the "natural History of this Wonderful Country." Among Wilkinson's information was a description of the upper Red River country that combined reality with confusion:

> About 20 leagues above [the Wichita Indian villages,] the Red River forks, the right descending from the Northward and the left from the westward . . . , it appears that the right branch . . . takes its source west of a Ridge of mountains, in the East side of which the Arkansas and Ouichita or Black River head.
>
> The left branch which is reputed to be the longest is said to have its source in the East side of a height, the top of which presents an open plain, so extensive as to require the Indians four days in crossing it. . . . west of this high plain my informants report certain waters which run to the Southward/ probably those of the Rio Bravo/ and beyond these they report a ridge of high mountains extending North and South.[6]

What this document conveys was someone's (perhaps horse trader and smuggler Philip Nolan's) firsthand knowledge of the upper Red, though embroidered with secondhand assumptions. It accurately portrayed to the Jefferson administration—and for the first time—the existence of the Llano Estacado, the great southwestern escarpment and plateau on which the Red River headed, well beyond which lay the southward-running Pecos River and the Sangre de Cristo front of New Mexico. While this ought to have raised doubts that the main arm of the Red would lead American explorers to the Rockies, Wilkinson's muddled account of the North Fork probably alleviated those doubts. It is true, as the document asserts, that the North Fork of the Red flows through a "Ridge of mountains." But the reality is that this range is the Wichita Mountains of present-day southwestern Oklahoma, not the Rockies. And the Arkansas River, of course, does not head in the Wichitas either but rises 350 miles northwest of there, in the heart of present-day Colorado.

In historical hindsight, then, Jefferson's fascination with the river he called, "next to the Missouri, the most interesting water of the Mississippi," seems to have been ill starred from the first.[7] However diplomatically correct a choice it appeared to be, it was not going to lead his explorers where he thought it would to fulfill his geographic objectives with respect to the Southwest. And unlike the Missouri, the Red would bring Americans threateningly near to Spanish settlements and make them dangerously accessible to Spanish presidios. And yet, given Jefferson's interest in natural history—as well as the economic potential of opening a trade route between Louisiana and New Mexico—his risk-taking inclinations caused him to persist in planning his next expedition as information about the Red continued to come in between 1804 and 1806.

To be sure, the evidence that fascinating things were there to be discovered in the Southwest *was* tantalizing. In response to Jefferson's call for knowledge about the region, the New York naturalist Samuel Mitchill reported to the president that the Red was said to be navigable for one thousand miles above the town of Natchitoches, penetrating westward into a country of immense and rich prairies. Alligators, buffalo, tigers, wolves, and "innumerable herds" of wild mustangs abounded, Mitchill said, along with a luxuriant growth of indigenous fruits and many unknown species of both plants and animals.

Another effusive source of information for Jefferson was the renowned Scottish expatriate scientist Sir William Dunbar of Natchez, who spoke of the Red's long course, its medicinal plants, and its sources in mountains of pure or partial salt. Dunbar also dangled "wonderful stories of wonderful productions," among them trader accounts of unicorns (!) and giant water serpents (probably garbled stories of the horned water serpent of Pueblo mythology). And there were vague tales of huge masses of metal—in reality meteorites—venerated by the Indians and assumed to be silver ore.[8] Critically, from Dr. John Sibley, his Indian agent at Natchitoches, Jefferson learned that as gateway to New Mexico, the upper Red was controlled by the horticultural "Panis" (Wichitas), under their forceful leader Awahakei, and the buffalo-hunting "Hietan" (Comanche) bands. These Indians, who had fond memories of the days when Spanish and French traders had competed for their friendship, were openly expressing interest in the Americans, Sibley reported.[9]

In April 1804, with Lewis and Clark still involved in preparations for casting off up the Missouri, Jefferson began taking steps to make his southwestern expedition a reality. On the fourteenth, while at home in Monticello, the president sat down to compose a seven-page letter of instruction for southwestern exploration, which he left unaddressed since he had not yet selected a leader for the probe. Unpublished until 1984, Jefferson based this missive closely on his June 20, 1803, letter of instruction to Meriwether Lewis, a document that scholars have long praised as a classic expression of Enlightenment scientific instruction. The south-western version differed from Lewis's letter in discussing routes, of course, and assigned a greater diplomatic burden in winning the Indian tribes of the Spanish border over to the Americans. Like Lewis, the as-yet-named leader of this expedition was enjoined to emphasize the United States' peaceable intentions and interest in trade, but these instructions seem tailored to a more competitive situation, economically and diplomatically. Jefferson directed the southwestern explorers to advance to the Indians the dubious proposition that Spain had ceded its claims to the entire western watershed of the Mississippi and to stress the United States' wish "to carry on commerce with them on terms more reasonable and advantageous for them than any other nation ever did." The letter also included a line that had its origins with the Lewis and Clark instructions, but that would prove far more significant in the Southwest: "if at any time a superior force authorized or not authorized by a nation should be arrayed against your further passage and inflexibly determined to arrest it, you must decline its further pursuit and return."[10]

That done, the president commenced the next logical step: the search for an addressee. First, however, he wrote William Dunbar in Natchez, successfully enlisting the Mississippi scientist's help in organizing the expedition and mentioning that Dr. George Hunter, a Philadelphia chemist, had agreed to become the naturalist for the southwestern tour. Although he did not realize it then, Jefferson had set in motion what in effect would become a trial run for his major expedition. Hunter did not arrive at Dunbar's plantation until late July 1804, and during the interim, ominous warnings from Spain (which had refused a passport request for the explorers) and from a disaffected band of Osages along the Arkansas River convinced Jefferson to delay the Grand Expedition and instead send Dunbar and Hunter on a quick reconnaissance of the Ouachita River, a lower tributary of the Red, as a kind of shakedown run for the larger operation.

That autumn and winter, then, Dunbar and Hunter led fifteen men in a rapid ascent of the Ouachita into the pine-clad mountains of present-day Arkansas. The short, careful journey was without mishap except for an accidental gunshot wound to Hunter and the total failure of the boat he had designed and brought down from Pittsburgh. But their official report was published in the congressional documents and in several reprints and serialized in 1806 in the administration's favorite newspaper, *The National Intelligencer*.[11] The Dunbar-Hunter exploration has only recently begun to reclaim some of the attention it garnered at the time, having become the subject of a modern documentary.[12]

The Dunbar and Hunter probe had important consequences for Jefferson's Grand Expedition. For one, it prompted Hunter (who was in his fifties) to decline the more arduous expedition. For another, it led Dunbar to argue, citing the prospect of difficult mountain portages and continued hostile displays by the Osages, that the planned descent of the Arkansas River ought to be dropped and that the southwestern expedition ought to focus all its energies on the more interesting river, the Red. Jefferson's focus from the first had been the Red rather than the Arkansas, and he agreed to this alteration of objectives in May 1805. Over the ensuing year, as Spanish officials issued ominous pronouncements about the Grand Expedition, Dunbar would have second thoughts about this decision. But Jefferson was unwavering. It was the Red River he wanted his party to explore, and Dunbar reluctantly acquiesced.

May 1805, and still no Jeffersonian party on the Red. The reason, Lewis and Clark aficionados ought to note, had everything to do with the difficulty of finding young men who possessed leadership skills, a woodsman's physique, and sufficient scientific education to command such a party. Indeed, the frustrations of evaluating and rejecting at least five candidates in order to find another Meriwether Lewis would lead Dunbar to write the administration in exasperation: "I am surprised that young men of talents unencumbered by family affairs are not found in numbers with you who are solicitous to go upon so inviting an expedition."[13]

The sixth candidate, and the one to win Jefferson's personal blessing as the leader of his southwestern probe, today has the distinction of being early American history's least-known explorer. Indeed, until recently, most major works on American exploration confused him with a New Orleans military officer with the same surname. But Thomas Freeman was not a military officer, and he was not a Louisianan. He was in fact an Irishman who had come to America in 1784 and who had employed his considerable skills as a civil engineer and surveyor on various government projects, including laying out Washington, D.C. Freeman had important connections across the political spectrum in Jeffersonian America, from James Wilkinson to Alexander Hamilton. But it seems to have been his friend Robert Patterson, the mathematician at the University of Pennsylvania who had tutored Meriwether Lewis, who brought the young man to Jefferson's attention in the fall of 1805. So on November 16, 1805, it was Thomas Freeman who dined privately with the president at the White House, and had the honor of seeing Jefferson finally inscribe the name of an addressee—"To Thomas Freeman Esquire"—across that long-inert letter of southwestern-exploring instruction.[14]

In Freeman, Jefferson had found a leader with superior scientific skills who had optimism and vigor on his side. As Freeman wrote to his friend John McKee shortly after dining with the president, he well understood the hazards of "travel in the Neighborhood of *St. Afee.* . . . [A] Great many difficulties, and some personal danger will attend the expedition, but, I will—'Stick or go through.' The more danger the more honor."[15] Now, could the administration find a naturalist similarly willing to hazard life and limb on such a dangerous assignment?

Given that the president considered many of the famous names in American natural history, and given Jefferson's goal of selecting the first trained American naturalist to explore the West, the search certainly ought to be a better known episode in Jefferson-era science. Those invited to apply, or who made application, to take "the department of Natural History in the voyage up the Red River" included the erratic genius Constantine Rafinesque, the internationally known author William Bartram (sixty-five years old when Jefferson extended the invitation), and an eager Alexander Wilson, soon to be recognized as the founder of American ornithology with his nine-volume *American Ornithology* (1808–14). Through Bartram, Wilson had been in contact with Jefferson about matters ornithological since March 1805. He learned of the Red River exploration from the president's offer to Bartram, and on February 6, 1806, the two of them wrote him encouraging Wilson's appointment as naturalist. Wilson eagerly awaited a reply through much of that winter, leading him finally to wonder whether Jefferson failed to respond to his letter about "our Journey" because he "expects a brush with the Spaniards" and telling a friend that "very probably the design of sending parties through Louisiana will be suspended." By late April, Wilson had decided to accept a position working on an encyclopedia.[16]

Jefferson in fact already had a naturalist by February 1806. The selection had fallen to twenty-five-year-old Peter Custis, a medical student from a well-connected family back in Jefferson's home county, who was then studying with America's top academic naturalist, Benjamin Smith Barton, at the University of Pennsylvania.[17] When Jefferson personally selected Capt. Richard Sparks, familiar to him via Meriwether Lewis as "one of the best woodsmen, bush fighters, & hunters in the army," to head the military contingent, the search for leaders was complete.[18]

All was haste now in procuring guides and laying in supplies so that the Grand Expedition could enter the river soon enough to navigate their pair of specially designed barges as far as the Wichita villages, from whence they planned to explore upriver by horseback. In addition to various microscopes, thermometers, and three sextants, scientific supplies included a nautical almanac for 1806 and a high-quality chronometer for establishing longitudes, a portable barometer for taking elevations, and an achromatic telescope of either 60x or 75x power to fix latitudes by observing the eclipses of Jupiter's moons. The party also had a camera obscura to produce topographic images, though they never seem to have used it. For natural-history work, Custis brought his shotgun, plant presses, and various traps and preservation equipment, plus reference volumes by Le Page DuPratz, Jefferson, Bartram, Humphrey Marshall, Thomas Walter, and his mentor, Barton. But he primarily relied on Linnaeus's four-volume *Systema Naturae* and the single-volume world compendium *Systema Vegetabilium* (which unfortunately saved space by eliminating information on geographic ranges) for vertebrate and botanical classification.[19]

By mid-April 1806, the bulk of the exploring party had assembled in Natchez and was conducting its last round of outfitting at Fort Adams and at Dunbar's plantation, The Forest. Lt. Enoch Humphreys at Fort Adams was so eager to accompany the expedition that he volunteered to go without pay; he was added to the party as assistant astronomer. Muster rolls from 1806 indicate that among the two noncommissioned officers and seventeen privates attached to the expedition were Joseph Parsons, Samuel Reed, Eliphalet Kelsey, John Martin, Edward Mooney, Nimrod Fletcher, and Doughty Nicholson, men carefully selected for their "general good health & . . . robust temperaments." As with Lewis and Clark, there was a single black man in the southwestern party. Unlike York, his name remains unknown.[20]

When President Jefferson's expedition into the Southwest finally entered the mouth of the Red River on May 1, it anticipated a year-long probe penetrating some thirteen hundred river miles into the interior. But despite high spirits and "perfect harmony," the party could not miss the warning signs along the Spanish border. As Custis would phrase it in his journal, "This expedition seems to have thrown their whole Country into commotion."[21]

But the American explorers could not have grasped the full dimensions of the maelstrom they were entering. Spanish unease about the soft underbelly its Provincias Internas presented to the world was a century old in 1806, and it had not mellowed with age. New Spain's colonial officers in Texas and New Mexico were veterans of the eighteenth-century game of finding interloping French traders. More recently they had taken to arresting and even killing Americans like Philip Nolan, shot for the sin of mustanging in the Texas outback in 1801.[22] In March 1804, when Spain initially learned from its slippery contact, Gen. James Wilkinson, that Jefferson was planning an exploration of the Missouri, the Council for the Fortification and Defense of the Indies concluded that the Crown should defend a boundary running from the Gulf of Mexico to Los Adaes (well within present-day Louisiana) and on to the Red River—and from there northward to the far bank of the Missouri.

While the council hardly needed urging to react against U.S. exploration, it got it in no uncertain terms from Wilkinson: Since any weakness would give the key to the continent to Spain's "most dangerous neighbor and the revolutionary spirit of the times," the general warned Spanish officials to "detach a sufficient body of chasseurs to intercept Captain Lewis and his party . . . and force them to retire or take them prisoners." In the Southwest, Spain should "drive back every illegal usurpation toward the region of Texas" and block all American probes on the rivers, else "they will very quickly explore the right path which will lead them to the capital of Santa Fe."[23]

Who knows what Wilkinson was up to? Historians in fact have widely divergent opinions. My own perspective is that given Wilkinson's encouragement of Jefferson in his western explorations, his simultaneous secret reports urging Spain to capture those same parties, and his association with Aaron Burr's shadowy southwestern conspiracy, the cynical but logical answer is that the man was a reprehensible individual who wanted to provoke a confrontation and probably a war—something to lay open the Provincias Internas to his and Burr's exploitation. Just how manipulated New Spain's officials were is questionable, but they did make at least three attempts to have a Pedro Vial–led party intercept Lewis and Clark. Each time, distance and Indians foiled Vial's efforts at interception. Speculation about the possible result *if* Vial had been successful once led Donald Jackson to pen an essay, "What If the Spaniards Had Captured Lewis and Clark?" Perhaps the best way to answer that is to look at what *did* happen with Freeman and Custis.[24]

The Red River was not nearly so distant from Spanish power as the Missouri. When Spanish boundary commissioner the Marques de Caso Calvo learned from Wilkinson in the early summer of 1804 that Jefferson was planning an expedition into the Southwest, he wrote the governor of Texas that this "daring undertaking" must be frustrated, that Spain had to be willing to "divert and even to destroy such expeditions." Amid the rumors during the fall of 1805, Provincias Internas commandant Nemesio de Salcedo y Salcedo decided that war with the revolutionary Americans was "already fact."[25] When word reached him that Jefferson had proved stubborn enough to launch an exploration over Spain's objections, Salcedo got active in a hurry. He dispatched not one but two bodies of troops to intercept Freeman and Custis. One, commanded by his ramrod-straight adjutant inspector of troops, Francisco Viana, he sent from Nacogdoches to confront the Americans on the lower river. The other, referred to proudly by Zebulon Pike (who mistakenly thought he was its target) as "the most important ever carried on from the Province of New Mexico," was the insurance policy. Commanded by Lt. Fecundo Melgares, it left Santa Fe bound for the Red in early June.[26]

With that, time and the summer of 1806 merely waited out the rendezvous of the opposing forces. When Jefferson's Grand Expedition arrived in Natchitoches, the last American outpost on the Red, and heard of the ominous troop movements, the two questions its members must have been asking themselves were, "How far are we going to get?" and "Will I live through this?" Nonetheless, this was the president's own mission and now also the largest exploring party of the age, having been brought up to fifty men and seven boats with the addition in Natchitoches of twenty more troops. New party members included Spanish interpreter Lt. John Joseph DuForest, métis guide François Grappe, and Lucas Talapoon, an Indian or métis whose skills in Plains Indian sign language had thrilled the American scientific community in 1800.[27] So once they posted their reports and Custis wrote his mentor, Barton, summarizing his natural-history work thus far, the explorers reentered the Red River on June 2. Freeman's "stick or go through" motto was about to be tested.

When confronting only nature, the party could make good on the motto. Within a week the American explorers found themselves in a watery maze, the channel blocked by a remarkable phenomena of the Red River's natural ecology. The chaos of debris before them was the Great Raft, an ancient and massive logjam. Possibly five centuries old, it had exerted a tremendous influence on the environment and history of the Red River valley. Over the centuries, as its lower end rotted away and the upper continued to accumulate drift, the raft had slithered upriver like some immense brown serpent. By 1806 it dammed the channel for one hundred miles. The only way around it by that time was a tortuous, twisting detour through its creation, the Great Swamp. Lying east of the clogged channel, these lowlands rerouted the brick-colored waters through a world of cypress, Spanish moss, and neo-tropical wildlife. For Custis, the Great Swamp was botanical treasure. For everyone else, it was misery, "fourteen days of incessant fatigue, toil and danger, doubt and uncertainty," as Freeman put it.

Beyond the Great Raft, Freeman found his first opportunity to try out his diplomatic skills on the Indians whose country they now entered. Claimed by both Spain and the United States, this was actually Cado-doquia, the ancestral lands of an ancient but reduced population of mound builders known as the Caddo Confederacy. Camping adjacent to an Alabama-Coushatta (Creek) village on a bluff above the river, from June 29 until July 11 the Americans treated with Dehahuit, hereditary chief of the Caddos, and forty of his principal men. While Freeman presented U.S. flags and successfully solicited Caddo endorsement of the expedition, Custis was free to observe Creek ceremonies and Caddoan customs and skills (their talents with the bow put him in mind of stories from the *Iliad*) and to post a twenty-six-specimen botanical collection downriver. For young Custis, the beautiful Red River valley seemed "the Paradise of America," the naturalist's Eden that Jefferson had promised.

In his letter of instruction, Jefferson had made it clear that he valued whatever information his explorers could gather, no matter how far they traveled. The image of Freeman and Custis that I particularly savor is the one of their proceeding upstream in July 1806, busily gathering information on the river valley, fully aware that a Spanish force four times their number was shadowing them in the undulating hills to the west. Guided now by the Caddos Cut Finger and Grand Ozages, the party engaged in a series of minor adventures. On the nineteenth they visited the former site of the Lower Kadohadacho village, and with the Indian guides Freeman ascended Cha'Kani'Na, the Medicine Mount of Caddoan creation myth. By the twenty-second they had rounded the Great Bend of the Red and were now heading due west, visiting two more abandoned Caddo village sites. On the twenty-seventh—portentously—the Caddos told them that they had reached the former location of La Harpe's post, the most westerly of the French settlements along the Red River. Distressingly too, after going two weeks without a summer thunderstorm, the water in the Red had become alarmingly shallow for their barges (1806, it turns out, may have been one of the single driest years in the climate history of the Southwest).[28]

The Spanish army's movements were equally direct and purposeful. After angrily cutting down the American flag he found flying in Dehahuit's Caddo village, Viana marched his force north to the Red, taking a position on an eminence known since as Spanish Bluff, a few miles east of the present-day Oklahoma line. As he later wrote his superiors, he knew "the irremediable damage that would result to this Province if the union is accomplished of the Expedition of the United States with the faithless Taboayases [Wichita] Indians, and the Comanches." Therefore, he would confront the Americans above the old French post and "where the territory of the Taboayases begins," for "this territory is ours."[29]

That no violent encounter occurred was the result of the actions of three individuals: Viana's firm and even polite refusal to allow the Americans to pass on the afternoon of July 28, Captain Sparks's skilled deployment of the outnumbered Americans into a defensive perimeter, and Freeman's mature assessment of his situation. Therefore, on July 30, 1806, having ascended the Red River some 615 miles to the edge of the blackland prairies, though still only halfway to the great mystery of the Red's sources, Freeman finally stuck. Jefferson's Grand Expedition into the Southwest had encountered "the other" in the American wilderness and, rather than proceeding on, had been forced to do the unthinkable— fall back.

For a total expenditure of $8,700, what had the United States realized from this aborted ascent of the Red River?[30] Compared to the results of the Lewis and Clark expedition, or even the geographical knowledge provided by Zebulon Pike's overland trek into the southern Rockies later that fall and winter, the cost/benefit returns must have seemed paltry. While Freeman's astronomical readings produced by far the most precise maps to emerge from Jeffersonian exploration, he had barely penetrated into unknown territory and had failed particularly to resolve the question of the Red's sources. The official map of the expedition was a beautiful study done by Nicholas King in 1807. But though it appeared on Anthony Nau's *The First Part of Captn. Pike's Chart of the Internal Part of Louisiana* (1807), when William Clark's map of the West was published in 1814, the Freeman and Custis route was cropped out by a printer.[31]

These meager geographic results—and Spain's spirited reaction, of course—reduced Jefferson's 1807 consolation plan of sending Freeman to explore the Arkansas to a nonstarter in Congress and effectively brought to a conclusion the vision of exploring the Southwest that the president had entertained at least since 1804. As a "favorite of government," Freeman was rewarded with the post of surveyor general of the country south of Tennessee, a position he occupied until his death in 1821.[32] Shortly thereafter, the War Department turned over his detailed daily journal of the Red River expedition to Edwin James, chronicler of the

Stephen Long expedition, which in 1819–20 had also targeted the Red River. Freeman's valuable journal subsequently vanished, most likely destroyed when James had all his papers burned upon his death.[33] Were Freeman's journal or other materials to turn up, however, as have so many materials from the Lewis and Clark expedition (namely, the Whitehouse journal, Charles Floyd's brief journal, the John Ordway journal, Lewis and Clark's so-called Eastern Journal, Clark's field notes, and Lewis's astronomy notebook), undoubtedly there would be renewed interest in the Red River operation.[34]

Custis's work, if anything, turned out to be even more ill starred. In fact I have come to believe that one of the major reasons the Red River expedition almost immediately disappeared into a black hole even of scientific memory had much to do with Custis's failure to follow up on his investigations. In truth his four reports from the expedition (which I discovered in the National Archives in 1982) and his extant specimens (which turned up among the Lewis and Clark specimens at the Philadelphia Academy of Natural History the same year) constitute an extraordinary encyclopedia of early Red River ecology. Custis catalogued a total of 267 species, recognizing 22 as new and proposing seven new scientific names. And his specimens collection concentrated particularly on ethnobotanical plants used by the Indians and on species indicating the party's approach to the semi-arid western prairies.

Today Custis's reports provide a time-travel view of a Red River "wilderness" extensively shaped by both the Indian and previous European presence.[35] Yet he ended up getting virtually no credit for his observations during his lifetime. Although he did produce an article for *The Philadelphia Medical and Physical Journal* on the natural history of the Red below Natchitoches, Custis spent most of 1807 completing his doctorate and searching for a suitable position.[36] His mentor, Benjamin Smith Barton, among many other projects had accepted the task of identifying Lewis and Clark's specimens and apparently was stretched too thin to help Custis work up the many remaining—and most interesting—of his discoveries for publication.

Unpublished discoveries were nothing, however, to the disaster of the "official report" of the expedition. In 1807 the Jefferson administration produced a small run of Nicholas King's redacted version of the explorers' journals, *An Account of the Red River in Louisiana*. Precursor to Nicholas Biddle's 1814 rewrite of the Lewis and Clark journals, King's version of the Red River probe showed just how far government science had to go. *An Account* was a total embarrassment, with its horrific mangling of Custis's

Latin binomials and descriptions.[37] By 1808 Custis had retreated to New Bern, North Carolina, where he established a medical practice, successively married the daughters of two fellow physicians, gave the name Linnaeus to one of his sons, and never wrote another word about natural history. Known in Carolina society as "highly popular," though counterintuitively also as "somewhat blunt and caustic in his manner, and [in] the life of all social companies in which he appeared," Peter Custis died there on May 1, 1842, the longest lived of any of the leaders in whom Jefferson had vested his frustrated hopes to explore the Southwest.[38]

Although Jefferson's letters do not reveal the extent of his disappointment about his southwestern expedition, the president's public reaction was clear enough. Donald Jackson has called the exploration "a headstrong decision that put in danger the lives of Americans pursuing an impossible goal," and it does in fact appear that the consequences of his own stubbornness embarrassed Jefferson.[39] Too, there was the undercurrent of public suspicion that he had known about and privately approved the Burr Conspiracy. And at least one prominent newspaper would later editorialize, perhaps a little sensationally, that the ferment with Spain in 1806 was *not* caused by Burr, as the administration tried to insist, but by Jefferson's "secret expeditions, secret orders, and secret plans" of exploration.[40]

There was another truth involved too, though Jefferson died never having grasped it. The river Jefferson had targeted for his southern counterpart to Lewis and Clark would never, after all, have led his explorers where he thought he was sending them. Even had they evaded Spain's forces, the Red would not have taken the Americans into the soaring peaks of the Stony Mountains or into the thicket of trade possibilities and revolution in New Mexico. Instead, it would have pitched them atop the great remote tableland Hispanic traders called El Llano Estacado— a runeless slate in the middle of nowhere (an outcome that intrigued me into including in my 1999 book a novella called "The River That Flowed from Nowhere," a fictional story that imagines Freeman and Custis continuing up the Red River into a Southwest beyond all of Thomas Jefferson's fantasies).[41]

In fact, unlike the Missouri and Columbia, or the Arkansas, Rio Grande, and even the Colorado, the Red continued to shimmer and dance like some high-plains mirage beyond reach of official American exploration for another seventy years. In 1807 Pike found the Rio Grande where he thought the Red should have been. Thirteen years later explorer Stephen Long was flabbergasted when the "Red River" he followed eastward from the southern Rockies somehow transmogrified itself into the

Canadian. In 1852 Capt. Randolph Marcy finally entered the maze of striped badlands and seven-hundred-foot-deep canyons sluiced by the Red's exit from the Llano Estacado. But Marcy's romantic descriptions and drawings of the "head-sources" have turned out to represent Tule Canyon, a sheer side-gorge one hundred miles short of the river's actual headwaters.[42]

And so the coda to Pres. Thomas Jefferson's dream of southwestern exploration: It was not until 1876 that U.S. Army lieutenant Ernest Ruffner finally spent two months exploring and mapping the multihued desert canyonlands—so strikingly different from the snow-clad mountains Americans had imagined—that give rise to a river Jefferson had targeted seventy-two years earlier as "next to the Missouri, the most interesting water of the Mississippi."[43]

As for exploration historian Donald Jackson's question—what if the Spaniards had captured Lewis and Clark?—I think the Freeman and Custis expedition provides an answer that might give different insights into, and a renewed appreciation for, the Lewis and Clark story. The fate of the Grand Expedition seems to argue that America's destiny in the West did not really rest on successful Jeffersonian exploration. Despite the failure of Freeman and Custis, U.S. traders carrying American goods (and even American flags) still intruded themselves among the Indians of the Southwest in the years immediately following.[44] The Red River (at least to the one-hundredth parallel) did finally become the boundary between Spain and the United States in 1819. Mexico did gain its independence by 1821. And American expansionist policies in the three decades after Jefferson still brought Texas, New Mexico, and the Spanish Southwest into the United States. Had Spain similarly intercepted Lewis and Clark, the American West would have lost an epic story, no question. But the analogy provided by Freeman and Custis in the Southwest argues that even without Lewis and Clark, the history of the Northwest likely would have turned out just about the same as it did. In other words, in the Big Picture, other currents of history were far more powerful than Jeffersonian explorers.

3

Could Louisiana Have Become an Hispano-Indian Republic?

KATHLEEN DUVAL

After 1800 the fortunes of both Spaniards and Native Americans in the North American West changed dramatically. Spain evacuated the vast Louisiana territory in 1803. As described in the first two chapters, the Spanish managed to hem in the most ambitious American claims to the Southwest in the years immediately following the Louisiana Purchase, but within twenty years Spain had been driven from the region entirely as Mexico won its independence. By the end of the 1840s, the United States had in turn seized Texas and much of the rest of the Southwest from Mexico. More tragically, Anglo-Americans pushed Native Americans off their homelands and into Indian Territory or onto reservations that represented only a tiny fraction of the lands the Indians had once occupied.

We tend to think of the United States in the nineteenth century as a juggernaut, but what if Europeans and Indians in the Trans-Mississippi West had banded together? Could they have changed history by blocking

United States expansion not only beyond the Red River but also into the Louisiana territory itself? Could Louisiana, Arkansas, and Missouri be part of Mexico now, or the Spanish-speaking or French-speaking "Republic of Louisiana," or an Osage-dominated or pan-Indian nation, bordered on the east by the United States and the south and west by Mexico, with its own representatives at the United Nations? Those possibilities sound far fetched in the twenty-first century. But Tecumseh and other Indian leaders in the Ohio valley built a powerful pan-Indian alliance, eventually supported and armed by the British, in the early nineteenth century. West of the Mississippi, there were Spaniards and Indians who in the late eighteenth century had conceived of a similar collaboration against the United States.

It is not simply in retrospect that the Louisiana Purchase is understood as a crucial step in American expansion. Spain had fought against Britain during the American Revolution, but by the end of the war, officials in Spanish North America already had reason to worry about the new republic with which they were sharing the continent. In 1783 neither Spaniards nor Indians who had fought in the war were invited to participate in negotiating the Treaty of Paris. As part of the treaty, the British surrendered what would become Tennessee, Mississippi, and Alabama to the United States. Congress quickly began surveying these lands and selling them off. But it was Spain's troops that during the war had seized much of this region from the British. With good reason, Spanish officials worried about the "unmeasured ambition of a new and vigorous people, hostile to all subjection, advancing and multiplying . . . with a prodigious rapidity," as the Spanish governor of Louisiana, François Luis Hector, the Barón de Carondelet, put it. The Spanish predicted that this expansionist people's next acquisition would be Louisiana, which spanned the entire western Mississippi valley, from present-day Louisiana to Minnesota in the north and the Rockies in the west.[1]

Likewise Louisiana's native peoples heard rumors of a new kind of European, one who came in unprecedented numbers, trampled Indian land rights, and called themselves "Virginians," "Pennsylvanians," and "Americans." During the 1780s Iroquois, Shawnee, Cherokee, Chickasaw, and Choctaw speakers from the east toured Louisiana, telling tales of an "ambitious" "plague of locusts" that was streaming across the Appalachians. The visitors warned Louisiana Indians that their lands would be next consumed by this host.[2]

If the Indians and Europeans of Louisiana had banded together, they could have assembled ten thousand men to defend against the expanding United States, more if they had recruited Indians and Frenchmen in the contested regions just east of the Mississippi. So why didn't they? The peoples west of the Mississippi failed to resist Anglo-American expansion because of their own historical relationships within the region. No united front, they were instead a barely coexisting collection of peoples who did not necessarily trust one another any more than they trusted the United States.

Their failure to unite had clear precedent. Most of the people in Louisiana had in fact contemplated joint military action against another expansionist people, the Osage Indians, themselves residents of the purchase territory. While it may be difficult now to conceive of the Osages as possessing the kind of power that the United States held over the fate of the continent, most people in the late-eighteenth-century Arkansas, Missouri, and Red River valleys saw the Osages as the greatest threat to their land and lives. In the early 1790s Spanish administrators, French hunters and traders, Quapaws, Caddos, Shawnees, and Chickasaws had tried to join together to fight the Osages but had failed because of each group's refusal to subordinate its own interests to the joint effort. Subsequent proposals for a coalition against the United States faced the same organizational difficulties, compounded by a new sense of frustration with one another after ten years of failures against the Osages.

The Osages had dominated their neighbors south of the Missouri River for almost a century. By the mid-eighteenth century, they numbered nearly ten thousand, while fewer than fifteen hundred Quapaws and perhaps two thousand Caddoan peoples lived along the Arkansas River. All of these groups greatly outnumbered the fewer than one hundred Europeans there.[3] After French traders arrived with guns and ammunition in the late seventeenth century, the Osages had become the best-armed people in Louisiana. Osage hunters then began to expand their ranges in search of more items that they could trade to the French—deer, buffalo, horses, and captives to sell as slaves. They moved southwest across the Arkansas River at the expense of Caddoan and Wichita peoples with inferior access to arms. To maintain their technological advantage, the Osages plundered and occasionally killed French traders who attempted to ascend the Missouri, Arkansas, and Red Rivers to trade arms to their enemies. Louisiana became part of the Spanish empire in 1763, but the situation on the ground did not change much. Most traders and even many officials in the Spanish hierarchy in Louisiana remained Frenchmen. And the Osages continued their expansion.[4]

By the second half of the eighteenth century, expansion had made the Osages many enemies. French traders feared for their lives when they went upriver. The Caddoan and Wichita peoples had fled south, losing their homelands without escaping attacks from the Osages, who simply extended their raids. Along the lower Arkansas River, the Quapaw Indians often clashed with the Osages. Shawnees, Chickasaws, and other peoples from east of the Mississippi wanted to hunt and even settle across the river as game diminished and the number of Anglo-Americans increased in the east, but Osage attacks made Louisiana a dangerous place for these outsiders. Finally the Spanish officials who had to hear all of their neighbors' complaints about Osage violence would very much have liked to establish control over that troublesome people. These groups all wanted to bring down the Osages, but conflicting interests prevented them from forming an effective coalition against them.

The desire of Spanish officials to crack down on Osage violence dated from early in their tenure in Louisiana. In 1779 then-governor Bernardo de Gálvez declared that "it is not right" that the Osages should receive generous annual presents from the king "and then, in return, commit atrocities against his subjects."[5] But the Spanish had been distracted by their battles against Britain during the American Revolution and against the Apaches in the west. After war ended on these fronts, Governor Carondelet instructed the Arkansas commandant in 1792 to arm the Quapaws, Caddos, and other nations, as well as white hunters, to fight the Osages in order to "finish with them once and for all."[6] He proclaimed that "any subject of His Majesty, or individual of the other nations, white or red, may overrun the Great and Little Osages, kill them and destroy their families, as they are disturbers of the prosperity of all the nations." The governor believed it necessary "to humiliate or destroy those barbarians," who were the enemy of all Spain's friends.[7] In 1793 Carondelet ordered "a general expedition against the Osages" from Arkansas, St. Louis, New Madrid, and Natchitoches led by the Quapaws.[8]

Spain's allies in this proposed war had some conditions that had to be met before they would fight, however. To begin with, the Indians insisted that European traders had to stop providing the Osages with weapons and ammunition; otherwise, war against this heavily armed foe would be suicidal. They demanded that officials first enforce trade sanctions. The government did agree to prohibit trade with the Osages, but it proved difficult to make good on this pledge. The ban angered French traders and merchants, who made tremendous profits from the Osage trade. Influential St. Louis merchants lobbied hard to reinstate trade.[9] The Spanish commandants of local posts generally agreed with these merchants. Commandants made money from licensing traders, and when commerce was forbidden, traders did not buy licenses.

Even after the ban stopped official trade, illicit traffic between unlicensed traders and the Osages continued unabated along the Missouri and, especially, the Arkansas Rivers. For example, an Osage woman testified that ten barges of goods had arrived at the Osage villages in the summer of 1792 despite the prohibition.[10] Commerce with the Osages was simply too valuable for traders to relinquish. During the 1790s, the Arkansas Post trade with the Osages alone was worth four times the local settlers' entire agricultural output.[11] Osage trade was similarly important to St. Louis, where the lieutenant governor in 1790 called their business the best at the post.[12] Colonists dependent on the fur trade were not likely to stop dealing with their most profitable partner.

Even if the Spanish could have stopped all traders from *willingly* supplying the Osages, some still would have supplied them against their will by having their goods stolen. When official commerce slowed, the Osages increased their raids on those dealing with other Indian nations. To reach the Caddos, the Pawnees, or the Missouri Indians, traders had to travel past Osage lands. If these men were abiding by trade sanctions, Osage warriors were likely to stop them and strip them of all their goods. The Osages had still another source of European goods, British traders from Canada, who eagerly did business behind the back of their Spanish enemy throughout the 1790s.[13]

Spain's Indian allies were disgusted at the ineffective embargo. In 1793 a Chickasaw man named Thomas conveyed the frustration of many Osage enemies when he reminded the Spanish that they had "forbidden the white men to carry goods into their [Osage] villages" so that the Chickasaws and other Indians could strike them without fear. Yet, Thomas charged, the Osages were "well clad in new blankets" and well supplied with new guns—goods were pouring into their villages. Thomas explained that St. Louis traders "take guns, powder, and ball to the Osages and buy from them all this booty which they steal from the Spaniards and red men on the rivers and . . . they kill all the whites of Natchitoches and Arkansas and all the red men of this region who cannot hunt without being killed or plundered by the Osages." He concluded, "Ah, my father, if the great chief of New Orleans had all those who carry goods to the Osages killed, there would be no one to carry [them] and . . . we could plan to attack their village."[14]

When the Spanish reprimanded their allies for not fighting the Osages, Thomas and others responded by blaming colonial officials for allowing traders to give an enemy the goods that only allies deserved. Indians would fight the Osages, Thomas said, if Europeans would stop giving them weapons. According to a Miami chief named Pacane, Europeans were only following their own interests and love of money.[15] Such complaints pervaded Spanish relations with Indians throughout the late eighteenth century. Thomas's and Pacane's accusations in the 1790s echoed a charge made by a Caddo chief more than ten years before that the Spanish refused to "treat the Osages as enemies."[16] But with fewer than a thousand troops spread over all of Louisiana—about one soldier for every two hundred square miles—Spanish officials could do little to enforce the embargo.[17]

Thomas, Pacane, and other chiefs charged that this failure to enforce the trade ban was part of a larger pattern wherein officials claimed weakness in order to avoid fulfilling their alliance obligations. When the Spanish first arrived in Louisiana, they had described to Indians the wealth and power of the Spanish empire. As a result, their Indian allies expected Spanish troops to fight alongside them against the Osages, and they expected ample supplies for the war, including guns, ammunition, and food. But the Spanish could no more meet the Indians' expectation of material aid than meet the demand for an end to the Osage trade. Spain did not have troops to spare and could not afford the supplies necessary to guarantee their allies' participation. One can imagine the growing reluctance among warriors after Lt. Gov. Zenon Trudeau informed them: "war having been declared at their solicitation," they could "expect nothing of us" except munitions "indispensably necessary . . . for each expedition."[18]

To the Spanish, it was perfectly reasonable to supply only guns, powder, and balls, and only when a large party was going on a campaign. After all, the Indian enemies of the Osages were the ones calling for their destruction. But to the Chickasaws, the Caddos, and their allies, if the Spanish wanted them to fight a war without colonial troops, against enemies armed with European weapons, they had better supply rations and give them enough arms so that they could not only win battles but also defend themselves against the inevitable Osage reprisals.

Unsurprisingly, war did not ensue. When Trudeau attempted to organize an attack on the Osages returning from their summer hunt in 1793, only one hundred warriors gathered in St. Louis. Most nations sent their regrets. Some from the east explained that the Americans would march against them if they left home. Some cited hostilities with native peoples other than the Osages, claiming that they could not leave their wives and children alone because the tribes with which they were already at war "might easily attack and destroy their families" in the warriors' absence.[19]

Along the Arkansas River, the Quapaws had their own history of frustrating the Spanish with their "inability" to confront the Osages. In an earlier attempt in 1786 to stop Osage raiding there, Arkansas commandant Jacobo Du Breuil dejectedly reported that Quapaw warriors had "abandoned the whites" with whom they were pursuing Osage raiders.[20] In response to Du Breuil's report, then-governor Esteban Miró agreed that the Quapaws "have not conducted themselves on this occasion with the activity and zeal that I expected of them after the fine words and promises they made here to be ready whenever we might need them. It is necessary for you to reprimand them severely, and bring them to see that they do not know their own true interest, and that in protecting the Osage they are protecting a viper which will gnaw their entrails."[21]

How the Quapaws responded to this advice is not recorded, but they did not change their policy regarding the Osages. They knew their "own true interest" better than Miró. Still, throughout the 1780s and 1790s, the Quapaws kept promising to fight the Osages in order to get what supplies the Spanish offered and to prevent a rupture with their European friends. Two months after the incident of which Du Breuil complained, Spanish officials in Natchitoches stated that the Quapaw great chief was leading a multitribal anti-Osage offensive, but it never materialized.[22] In 1789 three parties of Quapaws set out against the Osages but returned "without having found any."[23]

The Quapaws, like other Indians, clearly understood that the potential harm from engaging the Osages without full Spanish support outweighed the benefits. Therefore, native groups generally, while sustaining a rhetoric of belligerence, tacitly declined to make war. By the time of the attempted offensive of 1793, Trudeau explained to Governor Carondelet that all the tribes were technically "at war" with the Osages but that "one does not see any of them killing more than two Osages in a year; and they will never succeed in destroying them."[24] By the time the Spanish decided to organize a full-scale offensive against the Osages, most of their likely allies had already adopted a policy of limited self-defense.

Spain's Native American allies believed that the Spanish role in their alliance was not only to supply but also to organize their multiparty Osage war. If the Spanish did not fulfill that latter duty, their allies would not do it for them. When their colonial agent instructed the Shawnees to "prepare themselves for an expedition against the Osages" and to "set a time and a meeting place with all the nations of the lower part of the river and of Mexico," Shawnee leaders replied that they were eager to fight but "that it was not up to them to fix a time, but to their father to set it for his children."[25] Without full support from colonial officials, Louisiana's native peoples might occasionally skirmish to defend themselves or to support their own interests but no more.

If local French settlers had sided with them, the Indians might have been more willing to endanger their own lives, but French Louisianans were reluctant to plunge into an Osage war, even though they regularly suffered from Osage attacks. Ste. Genevieve offers one example of this reluctance to challenge a powerful enemy. In a joint letter to the governor in 1790, residents complained that the Osages continually pillaged their town and "take our Horses, kill our Cattle, plunder the French and Indian Hunters," and generally made life there dangerous and unprofitable. The petitioners demanded that the governor punish these "Bandits."[26] But when war loomed in 1793, Ste. Genevieve's residents had second thoughts. As Trudeau explained to the governor, "fear makes them want peace." They had stopped going out to work in their fields for fear of Osage reprisals, and they certainly did not volunteer to fight.[27]

As European traders, native allies, and their own lack of supplies undermined Spanish officials' plans, the Osages themselves disarmed the Spaniards by coming to the negotiating table. Governor Gálvez's 1786 orders on Indian policy had directed local commandants to give even the most belligerent adversaries peace "whenever they ask for it."[28] The Osages took full advantage of this directive, deflecting war by continually asking for peace. Every time the Spanish tried to cut off trade or organize a punitive expedition, the Osages sent a delegation to New Orleans, St. Louis, or Arkansas Post to explain and apologize for offenses and to promise that they would not happen again. In contrast to other Indians' portrayals of them, Osage chiefs described their people as a steadfast Spanish ally. They blamed the violent raids on a few restless young men who did not represent the chiefs or their people generally.

Developments along the Arkansas River were key to this explanation. Beginning in the mid-eighteenth century, as they displaced the Caddo and Wichita peoples, some Osages had begun living along the Arkansas River for much of the year in order to protect their hunting grounds and to trade along the river. Because they had only recently claimed this land, most of their attacks on rival hunters and traders occurred here. For decades the Osages had seen little reason to make excuses for such raids; they were the dominant power in the region, after all. But in response to threats of a coalition against them in the 1780s and 1790s, Osage negotiators developed a rhetorical dissociation between the "legitimate" Osage "nation" and a so-called outlaw band on the Arkansas. Their leaders responded to Spanish accusations of violence by bemoaning their lack of control over the Arkansas band. For example, in 1792 an Osage chief blamed "young men" in the Arkansas hunting grounds for recent raids, explaining to Trudeau that the chiefs would have more control over these "bad" warriors if trade resumed. After several horse thefts and murders along the Arkansas River in 1793, Osage ambassadors accused "bad men" over whom chiefs had no power. They described the Arkansas band as mixed-bloods and "allied to women of their enemies" who clearly "cannot be their brothers."[29]

Spanish acceptance of these explanations helped foil the sort of coalition that might have driven the Osages from the Arkansas River entirely. Repeatedly in the 1790s officials rescinded trade bans instituted at the request of Osage enemies after being importuned not only by merchants but by the Osages themselves. In 1792, for instance, Osage pressure, compounded by the constant lobbying from St. Louis merchants and his own financial losses, proved more than Trudeau could take. He decided that since illegal trade was continuing anyway, he would reinstate official Osage trade. To make up for giving in, the lieutenant governor vacuously warned that this would be the "last time" he would show the Indians leniency. The Spanish, of course, were in no position to ignore Osage overtures. Privately Trudeau advised the governor to accept Osage friendship and overlook their misdemeanors because the Spanish could not win a war.[30]

In reality the "Arkansas band" remained more connected to Osage society and policies than the chiefs admitted.[31] In March 1785 Benito Vasquez, an official trader to the Arkansas band, encountered in one of the towns along the Osage River two men whom the Spanish had recently officially recognized as the two "medal chiefs" of the Arkansas band.[32] Osages had always spent months on the hunt every fall and winter. Now, many men and women probably lived along the Arkansas for more than half the year, hunting and preparing hides, but returned to the Missouri valley in the spring.

Yet the chiefs' excuses were mostly true. Young Osage men really were committing violence on their own initiative. In decentralized Osage society, chiefs were respected elders, not authoritative rulers, and had little control over raiding. Perhaps they would have liked to have controlled their warriors as much as Spanish officials wanted to control Spanish subjects. More likely, the chiefs would have seen such authority as undermining the natural ways of running a society.

The Arkansas valley was attractive to many young Osages precisely because of its distance from the tribe's established leadership. Young warriors used their relative independence and the plentiful opportunities the region provided for hunting, trade, and raiding to increase their prestige within the nation.[33] While becoming an Osage chief normally required the correct clan membership and heredity, opportunities along the Arkansas and relations with Spanish authorities could open additional routes to leadership, as they did for one young party leader named Cuchechire in the 1780s. Although apparently not of the proper clan to be a chief, Cuchechire persuaded Arkansas commandant Du Breuil to give him a medal.[34] For young Osage men, new lands created new opportunities for commerce and honor, which could enhance social standing and political power. Osage women found new opportunities in preparing the abundant hides for market. Although set in different terms, Osage expansion brought the same benefits that young Anglo-American men and women would seek on these same lands after the Louisiana Purchase.

Ironically, Osage chiefs could enforce a consistent policy of violent expansion and compensatory diplomacy in part precisely because they had little power over their own warriors. Osage peace chief Clermont and other leaders could disavow the robberies and murders committed by young men they did not control at the same time that those violent acts worked to bolster their nation's hegemony.

The Osages found other ways to manipulate Spanish officials. On one occasion in 1781, the Arkansas Post commandant sent an interpreter up the Arkansas River to tell the Osages of a decision to end trade. Upon hearing the news, Osage representatives traveled to Arkansas Post, where they surrendered the Spanish symbols of alliance—a medal, flag, and commission—belonging to Brucaiguais, the man they said was guilty of recent attacks. They explained that he was dying and therefore could not come himself. But they offered several other "chiefs" as hostages in his place. The Arkansas commandant approved this peace measure and provided the representatives with abundant provisions and munitions for their return journey. The next morning he awoke to find that the Osage representatives had left, taking with them the goods as well as all of the "hostages." The supposedly "dying" Brucaiguais was still alive five years later.[35] On other occasions the Osages brought hostages to answer for past offenses or as insurance against new ones, but these people were not the "chiefs" the representatives claimed them to be. At times they were not even Osage.[36]

Spanish officers did not like being duped, and they tended to doubt the chiefs when they attributed all Osage violence to a few unruly young men. Still, accepting the explanation that most Osages opposed the violence had the advantage of disguising Spain's inability to organize a punitive alliance. As Osage chiefs incorporated warrior independence into their diplomatic strategies, local Spanish officials folded this independence into their construction of the Arkansas valley. They preferred to accept (and forward to their superiors) the Osage explanation of peaceful but powerless chiefs rather than acknowledge Osage dominance over Spanish "colonizers."

In 1794 a new Spanish plan to lure the Osages into subordination, or at least supervision, only exacerbated Spain's diplomatic problems with other Louisiana Indians. In consultation with Governor Carondelet, St. Louis traders Auguste and Pierre Chouteau built a fort near the Osage towns in the Missouri valley for the purpose of "subjecting" the Osages. In exchange for building and maintaining this shrewdly named Fort Carondelet, the Chouteaus received a monopoly on official Osage trade.[37] The Osages eagerly agreed to the plan. To them the fort by no means signified subjection. Rather, having their own fort guaranteed steady trade and publicly acknowledged their people's preeminence in the region. As an Osage man who traded at the new post put it, without the Spanish and French, "we have no nerves in our arms and we can scarcely move our bows." But "now that they will not abandon us any more," Osage arms had become "so large and so strong that we can break trees."[38] And because the fort was near their permanent towns in the north, it did not limit their expansion to the south, where they continued to raid French and Indian adversaries. While the Spanish declared that they were "subjecting" the Osages, the Osages believed that they had won a major concession from the Spanish.

Historians have generally claimed that the Chouteaus established "control" over the Osages in order to build their trading empire, which lasted from the 1760s well into the nineteenth century.[39] The Chouteaus certainly benefited, but Osage leaders' friendship with the family was a mutually profitable one. The Chouteaus did not rule the Osages despite their efforts to persuade Spanish officials that they did. When a member of a Natchitoches nation killed an Osage chief's father-in-law, a one-hundred-man vengeance party set out despite the Chouteaus' efforts.[40] Neither were the merchants able to stop illegal trading and occasional raids along the Arkansas River.[41] In 1797, Osages traded with the commandant at Arkansas Post, then killed a hunter of the post and took several horses from a neighboring settlement.[42] In response to the governor's reprimand, the Chouteaus protested that they could not possibly be expected to control this dangerous tribe completely and that the Spanish should be happy that the raids were less frequent than they had been before 1795.[43]

The compromise was good enough for the Spanish. Troublesome friends were better than resolute enemies. In response to the continuing raids on the Arkansas, Lieutenant Governor Trudeau concluded in 1798 that "without doubt the Osages have been harmful in the river of Arkansas, but I do not know whether it would be prudent to break with them" as long as they left the St. Louis area in peace. The Osages were powerful and profitable friends. The victims, unlicensed French traders, were, as Trudeau put it, "the scum of the posts."[44]

Louisiana's other native peoples were enraged by the fort's construction (and even more angry when the Osages rubbed it in by bragging about it).[45] Miami chief Pacane complained that the fort was designed to "sustain them in their rogueries." He accused the Spanish of applying a double standard to the Osages and other Indians: "We, if one of us steals a horse, or any other thing, are treated as thieves and as bad savages. In the same manner if anyone of us becomes intoxicated, and tries to commit any extravagance, one hears immediately: 'They are dogs; they must be killed. Results have proved it.' They spare us in nothing, and treat us with harshness. It is quite the contrary for the Osages where they steal, pillage, and kill. They get nothing but caresses, and are supplied with everything."[46] First the Spanish had failed to organize the war, and now they were giving the Osages special favors. Other Indians would remember this betrayal as threats from the east increased.

The would-be collaborators were in a bind. The Spanish had neither the forces nor the budget to enforce trade sanctions and provide troops and expensive supplies. Without these, their Indian allies would not fight the Osages. Without Indian warriors, the Spanish had to compromise with the Osages. But accommodation made the other Indians even angrier. The Spanish, French, and Indians could never develop the trust required for a successful military or economic effort against the Osages because none could surrender their own objectives to a common cause. Each group feared that the others would not commit fully to the joint effort, and most harbored doubts that their objectives would come first in a collaboration. Thus, each pursued its own interests, and Osage dominance continued. This failure to join in common cause would continue into the nineteenth century.

As fears of U.S. expansion grew in the mid-1790s, the people of Louisiana were ill prepared to respond. In November 1794 Governor Carondelet proposed defending Louisiana and driving Anglo-Americans out of the contested areas east of the Mississippi with the help of the Choctaws, Chickasaws, Creeks, Cherokees, Shawnees, Delawares,

Quapaws, and Osages. He surmised that, being "fearful of the usurpations of the Americans," these Indian nations would "be disposed to make the most destructive war on them."[47]

But a European-Indian coalition that included the Osages was hardly feasible after years of trying to make war on them. The Osages had long traded with the British, and they correctly believed that they could profit from trade with the United States.[48] And in the 1790s they had little reason to suspect that the Americans would prove a less malleable force than the Spanish. The Osages had dominated Louisiana by protecting their lands through violence, providing irresistible trade opportunities, and negotiating to win over the Spanish. Even though Tecumseh and others would spread word of settlers devouring eastern lands, the Osages' domination in Louisiana was too great to give them much cause for worry. With little affinity for the Europeans and Indians who had aspired to attack them and little fear of the United States, the Osages were not likely to join the Spanish-led coalition.

A coalition without the Osages might yet have been powerful enough to defend the west bank of the Mississippi against U.S. encroachment. But the earlier failure to organize against a common enemy had left a bitter taste in the mouths of everyone involved. When Louisiana officials began to look for allies against the United States in the mid-1790s, the nations they tried to recruit invoked the Spanish inability to organize retribution against the Osages in their explanations of why they felt no obligation to risk their lives in such an effort. In 1794, Shawnees living along the St. Francis River (in present-day northeastern Arkansas and southeastern Missouri) sent a messenger named Netomsica to chastise the Spanish for their hypocrisy. He reminded them that the Osage "war has been avoided by delays, or by other pretexts." It seemed to him that the Spanish had abandoned the Shawnees in that effort, but now the Spanish summoned the Shawnees "in their necessity." Netomsica pointedly asked how his people could leave their homes to fight for the Europeans, not knowing "where to place [our] families in order that they may be sheltered from the courses of the Osages and from those of the American enemy."[49] In the eighteenth century, Anglo-Americans had pushed Netomsica's band west of the Mississippi. Now facing two powerful enemies, the Shawnees needed first and foremost to provide for their own defense.

In their response to the same call for assistance, the Miamis charged that the Spanish had lied when they promised to ban Osage trade. They were doubly appalled when they discovered that the Spanish were at that very moment sending a new shipment of artillery to the Osage towns.[50]

Having failed to overcome their differences in previous instances, the Indians and Europeans could neither organize themselves to defend Louisiana nor recruit the powerful Osages to that effort.

It probably also had not escaped some Indians' attention that the Spanish themselves had undermined any anti-American project by welcoming U.S. settlers into Louisiana to build up the population in their borderlands. Few Anglo-Americans accepted the Spanish offer of small plots, monarchy, and Catholicism. Still, when the governor placed an ad in the *Kentucky Gazette* seeking American settlers for western lands, Indians living on those lands could hardly have gained confidence in Spain's faithfulness or resolve as an ally.[51]

Shawnees and other westward-migrating Indians knew the dangers that the new United States posed to their rights, but those from west of the Mississippi based their own calculations of the Anglo-American threat on their experiences along the weak fringes of the French and Spanish empires. Despite rumors, the Osages, Quapaws, and their native neighbors did not believe that these newcomers were different from the Europeans, whose presence for over a hundred years had seemed largely to benefit them. Certainly they remembered French atrocities against the Natchez and suspected that the diseases that struck frequently and disastrously had something to do with Europeans, but they generally believed that white people did not pose a significant threat.[52] They may have assumed that conflict east of the Mississippi resulted from diplomatic or military inadequacies on the Indians' part rather than Anglo-American power. With more than a century's experience learning and manipulating the differences among rival French, Spanish, and British traders, bureaucrats, soldiers, settlers, and priests, there seemed little reason to choose an exclusive Spanish alliance now. Initially the western Indians' experiences with Americans may have seemed to confirm their beliefs. Osage delegates returned from their official (and lavish) 1804 visit to Washington, where they had forged an alliance with Pres. Thomas Jefferson, "loaded with valuable presents & puffed up with ideas of their great superiority to other nations" because they were the first Louisianans to visit Washington. Fearing no retribution from their new ally, some of the Osages on their return trip plundered a group of white hunters.[53]

Spain's inability to build anti-Osage and anti–United States coalitions may well have entered into its decision to divest itself entirely of Louisiana. On October 1, 1800, Napoleon persuaded King Carlos IV to exchange Louisiana for lands north of Tuscany. The threat from the United States figured into the king's decision. He hoped that France would build up

Louisiana's military defense and thus provide a strong buffer between the United States and the American territory Spain valued more highly than Louisiana—Mexico.[54] Perhaps if Louisiana's local officials and Indian peoples had shown any capacity for constructing a strong barrier to Anglo-American encroachment, the king would not have given in to Napoleon. But, as little as Spain spent there, Louisiana was a drain on royal coffers, and the appealing thought of the French taking over these expenses made more palatable the fact that Napoleon was probably going to get whatever he wanted from Spain anyway.

Maybe French officials could have succeeded where Spanish ones had failed. Maybe they could have sent the troops and supplies that Spain could not afford and used them to organize French and Indian Louisianans to defend their land together. But war with Britain and a rebellion in St. Domingue drew Napoleon's attention away, and he cut his losses in Louisiana. Breaking his promise to King Carlos IV, Napoleon sold the entire region to the United States in 1803.[55] In the coming decades American settlers would overwhelm western native peoples, including the Osages. Having lost even the possibility of European support, Indians were no more able or disposed to unite against this incursion than they had been in the Spanish era. For instance, even as Anglo-American settlers and federal removal policy buffeted both the Osages and the Cherokees, they made bloody war upon one another in Arkansas Territory.[56]

Was an anti–United States coalition in Louisiana possible? Could the Trans-Mississippi West have become the Republic of Hispano-India? Probably not. For this kind of coordinated action, Louisiana's peoples would have had to have been entirely different from what they were. The prerequisites for a stable alliance did not exist in Louisiana, either between Europeans and Indians or within those broad groups. French Louisianans were not particularly loyal subjects of the Spanish crown; indeed, French residents of New Orleans had rebelled against Spanish rule in 1768. Caddos did not necessarily get along with Pawnees or Miamis, much less with Osages. The anti-Osage maneuvering had itself illustrated how Louisiana Indian groups had continued to regard one another—rather than European or American intruders—as the chief threat. In the best of times, Louisiana saw only a tenuous stalemate. This was not a foundation on which to build a force to fend off the United States.

PART TWO

Transforming
THE
Territory

4

A Shifting Middle Ground

*Arkansas's Frontier Exchange Economy
and the Louisiana Purchase*

JEANNIE M. WHAYNE

For U.S. citizens, the Louisiana territory in 1803 stood as a mysterious and unexplored wilderness full of unrealized potential. Few understood the complex political economy that existed within the region. That it was sparsely populated by contemporary standards goes without saying, yet those who hunted and traded there created an economic and social order that had both an internal logic and an external focus. Indian and white hunters had an established system of trade that fit the realities of life in this thinly settled region. Historian Richard White labeled such settings the "middle ground," places where whites and Indians, thrown together by happenstance and necessity, borrowed from each other culturally, intermarrying and adapting each other's dress and customs, and pursued their mutual interests in terms of both livelihood and defense. Whites, too few in number to sustain themselves, established both personal and professional relationships with Indians. Indians received the newcomers, seeking opportunities to trade and to secure allies against their enemies. Over time more intimate bonds formed.[1] In the lower Mississippi valley, such alliances were sealed in what Daniel Usner has called a "frontier exchange economy."[2] Arkansas offers a case study of such economic and cultural arrangements and the effect of the Louisiana Purchase upon them.

As whites and Indians encountered each other in colonial Arkansas, they had carved out economic relationships that made the most of the limited possibilities open to them. Those of European extraction hunted and traded for buffalo tallow, bear oil, and other animal products, but this commerce in the lower Mississippi valley differed substantially from that of British Canada, where a thriving international trade in furs made some men wealthy. The realities of the southern environment limited the trade in fur and skins, as the higher temperatures rendered it difficult to preserve them adequately for the European market.[3] Still, there was money to be made in exporting products to the North American colonies and the Caribbean.[4] White traders bent on profit and Indian hunters seeking to make the most of the situation formed alliances that were often deepened by intermarriage and cultural blending.

Indians slowly altered their lifeways to accommodate—and benefit from—the arrival of the newcomers. The process of cultural blending, though, had serious consequences for Arkansas Indians, such as the Quapaws concentrated around Arkansas Post. Archeological evidence suggests that Arkansas Indians had engaged in trade with other Indian groups across great distances long before whites appeared, but the demands of the international trade that the French had introduced early in the eighteenth century put greater pressure on native society and transformed it in unprecedented ways. Growing dependence upon European goods—steel axes, brass kettles, and so on—forced an adaptation that fundamentally altered the social organization of work. Quapaw men began to hunt buffalo with much greater frequency, and Quapaw women began to spend far more time processing buffalo products, all in order to participate more vigorously in the frontier exchange economy. As these changes became more ingrained within their social structure, the Quapaws became ever more dependent. Through the system of advances that tied them to trade with the Europeans, the Indians fell into debt. They also became more dependent on the annuities they received from French and Spanish officials in exchange for their support of tiny and vulnerable Arkansas Post.[5]

If the establishment of a middle ground in Arkansas made for considerable change in the lifeways of Indians like the Quapaws, the Louisiana
Purchase altered the terrain far more radically. After the United States
acquired the territory, the middle ground eroded and the frontier exchange
economy gave way. Eventually white Americans came to vastly outnumber Indian, French, and métis hunters, and because they were chiefly
intent on farming, these American settlers had little need for Indians as
trading partners or allies. The interregional trade networks that Arkansas
participated in would no longer be based on animal products but exploitation of the international demand for cotton. This demand encouraged the
development of a plantation system in this portion of the Louisiana territory where it had not existed before 1803.

The diaries kept by two men who led an expedition up the Ouachita
River in the winter of 1804–5 provide one window on the Arkansas middle
ground in the immediate aftermath of the purchase, while the letters of a
government trader dispatched to a remote post shortly afterward provide
a second. What William Dunbar and George Hunter describe on the
Ouachita River and what John Treat reveals about life at Arkansas Post
illustrate the symbiotic—but sometimes fractious—relationship that pre-
vailed between the Indians and whites who resided in the Arkansas portion
of Louisiana. They also reveal a world in the midst of transformation.
New actors, not only white but also Indian, presented unprecedented
challenges to the Arkansas middle grounders.

The transition from a predominantly Indian population with a scat-
tering of whites to one composed largely of white and enslaved black
people—and from a hunting-and-trading to a predominantly agricultural
economy—was neither sudden nor smooth, in part because the U.S. government was curiously conflicted in its designs for the region. Thomas
Jefferson had a vision of Louisiana not only as a sanctuary for Indians
but also as a place in which Indians would be acculturated or eventually
(again) removed. The president proposed moving Indians then living east
of the Mississippi River to the territory, but he did not necessarily foresee
the territory becoming a permanent reserve for them. White Americans,
he thought, would advance into the region, and Indians who would not
submit to white civilization would have to move still farther west. His
hope was that Indians in the Arkansas area would have time to adapt to
white culture and become agriculturalists. He believed that with the
proper encouragement many natives would abandon the hunt and
assume the trappings of civilization. The Indian reliance on the hunt,

then, was a problem, one that could be overcome if only they would turn to farming.

In the meantime, however, Jefferson continued a policy launched under Washington's administration of sending government "factors" to trade with the Indians. The plan was designed to eliminate the disreputable traders who cheated the natives and plied them with liquor, sowing discord and unrest among the tribes. Although the creation of the factorage system was in part to "protect" Indians from unscrupulous traders, there was also a more sinister motive. Even before the Louisiana Purchase, Jefferson understood such trade could be a mechanism for acquiring land from the Indians. Writing to the secretary of war in 1802, he said there was "no method more irresistable [sic] of obtaining lands . . . than by letting them [the Native Americans] get in debt which when too heavy to be paid, they are always willing to lop off by a cession of land."[6] He believed, perhaps sincerely, that they would have no need for all the lands they claimed if only they would become farmers. Whites, who needed the excess land and would put it to good use (agriculture, in other words), could then have it without materially disadvantaging the Indians.[7] Both of Jefferson's goals—establishing Arkansas as an Indian sanctuary and ultimately dispossessing them of that sanctuary—were served, then, by the maintenance of the Indian-white trade relationship.

Arkansas would prove to be a more temporary way station than Jefferson imagined, however. As historian S. Charles Bolton suggests, "Americans crossed the Mississippi River faster than the president thought they would, traveling pell-mell rather than, as he had hoped, 'advancing compactly as we multiply.'"[8] In the end nothing could prevent the middle ground from collapsing or the international market in cotton from overcoming the frontier exchange economy. But in the years immediately following the purchase, there would be a sort of twilight period in which immigrant Indians reconstituted Arkansas's middle ground, sometimes to the detriment of native peoples like the Quapaws, and existing trade relationships remained strong enough to sometimes frustrate—or at least complicate—the efforts of government agents to get their own trade system up and running.

The first detailed look white Americans got at this Arkansas middle ground came in the reports of William Dunbar and George Hunter. Their expedition up the Ouachita River in 1804–5 was, like Lewis and Clark's Corps of Discovery, a federally sponsored venture into the newly acquired Louisiana territory.[9] Yet it would also prove merely a consolation prize for those who had been planning a much grander exploration of the Red and Arkansas Rivers. Spanish hostility to an American incursion up the Red and the existence of a splinter group of fierce Osage Indians operating along the Arkansas caused Jefferson to delay what he called his Grand Expedition. The expectation that the Spanish would resist exploration on the Red would, as Dan Flores describes, be confirmed when their troops turned back Thomas Freeman and Peter Custis in 1806.[10] For their part Dunbar and Hunter, by avoiding the Arkansas River region, encountered no trouble with the Osages, but the tribe would continue to be a formidable obstacle to both Native American and white immigration into Arkansas.[11]

While initially wishing the Grand Expedition to be led by an explorer of the Meriwether Lewis sort, Jefferson, thwarted by the Spanish and the Osages, had settled on the two scientists, who by themselves would have been ill equipped for a grander exploration along the Red and Arkansas Rivers. William Dunbar, a Scotsman of aristocratic birth who had immigrated to the American colonies in 1771, owned a substantial plantation —the Forest—near Natchez, Mississippi. Dunbar's principal crop was cotton, which fetched a handsome price on the world market, rendering him secure in his fortune.[12] But Jefferson had become acquainted with Dunbar through the American Philosophical Society, knew him as a scientist, and had engaged in a long correspondence with him. George Hunter, another Scotsman, had immigrated to the colonies in 1774, settling in Pennsylvania, and was an apothecary and chemist; Jefferson said of his knowledge of chemistry, "in the practical branch of that science [he] has probably no equal in the U.S." Although Hunter owned a wholesale drug house in Philadelphia, he began his life in the New World as an apprentice and had acquired his moderate wealth through hard work and perseverance. He was still a man-on-the-make, and his journal reveals a preoccupation with finding anything—gold, silver, coal, iron, salt—that might turn the expedition to profit.[13]

George Hunter left Philadelphia in May 1804, when an expedition along the Red and Arkansas Rivers was still the objective. He supervised the construction of a fifty-foot flat-bottomed boat of the "Chinese style" in Pittsburgh, having found that he could not secure passage to Natchez in any other vessel. He arrived in Mississippi in July and visited Dunbar at his plantation. Dunbar viewed the boat Hunter had designed with justifiable skepticism—it lay much too low in the water to traverse the shallow interior waterways—and suggested that Hunter take the boat to New Orleans to have it repaired and refitted. Dunbar privately hoped that Lt. Col. Constant Freeman, who was in command at New Orleans, had already secured a more suitable vessel, but this was not the case. Hunter made the necessary repairs and improvements to his boat and was still in New Orleans when he received word from Dunbar that the proposed Grand Expedition had been cancelled. But Dunbar had persuaded Jefferson that a trip up the Ouachita River to the legendary hot springs might be an appropriate alternative. The scientist reasoned that at the least they could test their equipment on the trip and then experiment on the springs to determine if there was anything to the rumors of some special healing powers in the waters there.[14]

On October 16, 1804, Dunbar and Hunter departed St. Catherine's Landing on the Mississippi River, near the former's plantation, and began their not-so-grand expedition. Dunbar boarded the scow accompanied by a servant and two slaves. Already aboard were Hunter, his teenage son, twelve soldiers, and a sergeant. They descended the Mississippi, passed Fort Adams the next day, and camped at the mouth of the Red River.[15] On the eighteenth they began the ascent of the Red, took the mandated detour up the Ouachita River when they reached it five days later, and arrived at the Post of Ouachita on November 6. At the post, which was also known as Fort Miró and would later become the city of Monroe, Louisiana, Dunbar and Hunter rented a flat-bottomed barge to replace the inadequate scow and hired a pilot-guide who was familiar with conditions upriver.[16]

They resumed their journey on November 11, and four days later they crossed thirty-three degrees north latitude, which recently had been designated by Congress as the dividing line between the territories of Orleans and Louisiana; it would eventually become the border between the states of Louisiana and Arkansas.[17] While the trip thus far had been difficult, it was to become even more so as the weather worsened and the rapids grew more fierce. The barge they secured at the post, however, negotiated the shoals and rapids much better than Hunter's scow had, a fact not lost on Dunbar, who carefully recorded his observations about the kind of craft necessary for exploring rivers in the newly acquired territory.[18] Excluding the five days they spent at the Post of Ouachita, it took them almost twenty-four days to reach the Arkansas line from St. Catherine's Landing, a distance of roughly 240 miles. It took another twenty-two days for them to travel the nearly 248 miles to their destination, which, considering the rougher rapids upriver, was a significant improvement in pace.

Still, it was rough going. Although Dunbar sometimes praised the soldiers for the work they performed, Hunter complained in his diary of their surliness and the inability, or unwillingness, of the sergeant to enforce discipline. It was the soldiers' task to perform the hard labor necessary to overcome the many obstacles they encountered, and they sometimes complained bitterly or, as Dunbar put it, were "slow in their movements."[19] Hunter put it more bluntly. Some of the men were "often grumbling & uttering execrations against me in particular for urging them on, in which they had the example of the sergeant who on many occasions of triffling difficulties frequently gave me very rude answers."[20] But perhaps the sergeant's complaints were warranted. Traveling during the season when the river was at its lowest, the soldiers routinely waded into the water, which plunged in temperature from seventy-four to forty-seven degrees on the trip upriver, and dragged the boat through the rapids. At times the obstacles were so severe the men had to twine ropes around trees and, using a process known as cordelling, winch the vessel over shoals and sandbars. In the worst of situations, they offloaded some of their supplies to lighten the boat. On a good day they could make eighteen miles; on a bad day they were lucky to do more than two.[21]

Sickness accompanied the travelers, but the only injury sustained occurred when George Hunter accidentally shot himself in the hand while loading his gun, causing him some discomfort and inconvenience.[22] He was unable to use his gun for several days afterward but hardly had need of it. Neither he nor Dunbar made mention of attacks by wild animals, though both reported sighting alligators as far upriver as Chemin Couvert, a creek now called Smackover Creek and located in present-day Union County, Arkansas. In addition to briars, thorns, and thick growths of cane, the explorers remarked on the larger and greater variety of trees, including longleaf pine, holly, birch, maple, dogwood, ironwood, ash, sweetgum, and oak, along the shore as they penetrated the Arkansas region. They also took note of the soil on the banks of the river and speculated about its fertility.[23]

Although Dunbar was frequently indisposed, much more so than the other members of the expedition, he concentrated considerable attention on securing precise readings of their exact position whenever possible. He had devised a unique method of determining longitude, which he hoped explorers without possession of a chronometer nor the assistance of a second person would find useful. It required a view of the sun, so when the sky cleared, he often called upon the men to put the boat ashore hastily so that he could make his calculations. They endured many cloudy days when no calculations could be made at all. While Dunbar was generally pleased with his field measurements, which he later reported in detail to President Jefferson, Hunter confided in his diary that his own measurements, made the traditional way, were more accurate.[24]

Hunter, however, seemed to devote a greater portion of his time to various other activities. Although a relatively prosperous businessman and entrepreneur, he had suffered serious business reverses earlier in his career and likely never rested comfortably in the success that later came his way. Even the president, who had instructed him to note any deposits of minerals seen during the expedition, worried that the entrepreneur might become too preoccupied with searching for gold or silver.[25] If Hunter had that in mind, he was disappointed on his trek up the Ouachita. Although he found traces of ore and reported hunters' tales of silver up the Arkansas River, he located no precious metals. On at least two occasions, while the rest of the company camped on the banks of the river, Hunter took excursions to view deposits of salt, a valuable commodity in the early nineteenth century, but he apparently found nothing of commercial quantity or value.[26]

As Dunbar and Hunter made their observations, it was the soldiers' job to hunt, a duty they seemed to enjoy. They kept the expedition furnished with deer, bear, turkey, raccoon, and waterfowl. Once they left the last settlement along the river and crossed into Arkansas, they encountered game in somewhat greater abundance, particularly ducks, which the men shot when they could from where they sat in a canoe that rode ahead of the barge.[27]

Of all aspects of the expedition, the party's fortunes in hunting and their encounters with hunters as they traveled the Ouachita probably tell us most about the middle ground and the frontier exchange economy in Arkansas. The trade in animal products made the expedition's own foraging for provisions more difficult. They were traveling just in the season when white and Indian hunters were abroad and discovered that, even in this seeming wilderness, game was particularly shy of the river. Thus whenever they stopped for meals or to camp for the night, some men had to take to the woods to secure fresh provisions.[28] The hunters—white and Indian—the expedition met up with or saw evidence of highlighted Arkansas's complicated and fluid geopolitical situation.[29] French hunters had long been in the area, but their numbers had increased substantially during the late eighteenth century. French and other European settlers began to move west of the Mississippi as the United States secured its authority in the lands east of the river. The U.S. military presence was irksome to those settled in what had been French Illinois, for the government demanded provisions and required the quartering of troops in private residences. The Northwest Ordinance of 1787 acted as an additional impetus for migration since it banned slavery north of the Ohio River, stimulating an exodus from Illinois Territory into what was then Spanish Louisiana. While these émigrés established settlements principally above what would become the Missouri-Arkansas state line, some secured Spanish land grants and gathered in small villages below the line along the Black, White, and St. Francis Rivers in northeastern Arkansas. Their inhabitants may have hunted as far south as the Ouachita.[30]

On November 29, 1804, Dunbar and Hunter encountered a colorful example of Arkansas's varied immigrant population, an "old Dutch hunter" named Paltz who had lived along the Ouachita for forty years and had been traveling the Arkansas, White, and St. Francis Rivers for an even longer time.[31] Later they met a Mr. Le Fevre, one of the Illinois Territory immigrants to Arkansas. He had amassed a substantial number of skins with the help of several Delawares and other Indians and apparently had an arrangement to supply them in return for peltry.[32]

Perhaps the most interesting encounter reveals more about the white and Indian actors in this trade, suggesting an ethic that both groups honored and that allowed commerce in this thinly but variously populated district. On November 18 Dunbar noted the hunters' custom of depositing their skins over two forked posts in sight of the river. Such deposits were sacrosanct, and no other hunter would violate them. Rather than being an uncivilized wilderness without rules, the territory had its unwritten laws that men typically abided by.[33] On the twenty-first, just a few days after Dunbar remarked upon the custom, the explorers noticed a pictograph—Hunter called it a hieroglyphic—on a tree near their breakfast encampment. The pictographer had removed some bark from the tree and painted a scene depicting a man on horseback with one hand pointing toward the river and the other pointing toward the woods. Two other figures, one of them wearing a round hat, a typical Indian symbol for a European, were apparently shaking hands. This clearly represented an expression of friendship. When Hunter took a party into the woods in the direction the horseman pointed, they found a hunter's camp and fourteen deerskins tied in a bundle on a pole. Just as the explorers arrived, a white man by the name of Campbell also appeared. Campbell, a carpenter by trade who was taking a consumptive man to the hot springs, had been encountered the day before encamped near the expedition and had apparently left his boat to hunt in the woods. He claimed that he had placed the skins there a year before for an Indian chief by the name of

Habitant, but Hunter doubted his story, concluded that the skins belonged to a Choctaw Indian, and took possession of them, determined to locate the rightful owner or deposit the skins for safekeeping at the Post of Ouachita on the way back downriver.[34] Hunter believed that if he left the skins in place, Campbell would take them and the expedition might be blamed and suffer retaliation for violating the custom.[35] Whether or not Campbell was telling the truth, his claim that he had such an arrangement with an Indian, as well as Hunter's fears of the consequences of the custom being violated, suggests how well established the tradition had become.

Another encounter shows that in Arkansas, as elsewhere in the American middle ground, Indian-white bonds could be more intimate and complex than a simple shared interest in trade. A Delaware Indian whom Dunbar and Hunter met in November personifies a borderlands accommodation process. He introduced himself as Captain Jacobs, and though he had an English name, he had painted vermilion around his eyes. While Hunter failed to describe him in more detail, and Dunbar did not mention him at all, Jacobs clearly inhabited two worlds, Indian and white.[36]

Further illustration of the existence of the middle ground awaited Dunbar and Hunter at the hot springs. On December 6, after enduring some of the most treacherous rapids they encountered—including the infamous Great Chute near present-day Malvern, Arkansas—the explorers reached their destination. They established a camp at Ellis Landing, which the pilot identified as the ideal place to disembark for the nine-mile hike to the hot springs.[37] The men were put to the task of transporting supplies, and though this work was met with the customary grumbling, they ended up not having to bear the tents, for they discovered a cabin and several rough huts for use by convalescents located adjacent to the springs.[38] Believing that the waters had curative powers, both Indians and whites bathed in and drank from them, showing that as sparsely populated as the territory was, a wide variety of people utilized this resource. Ellis Landing had been named after a Major Ellis from Natchez, who, along with two companions, was purportedly cured of his ailments there. The pilot reported that he himself had been restored to health by bathing in the springs the previous year and that an Indian had been brought in and after two weeks was "perfectly recovered."[39] Hunter apparently preferred exploring the region around the springs, presumably looking for ore or salt deposits.[40] But the two scientists did conduct experiments on the waters, looking for any evidence of its medicinal properties. Even on Christmas Day the two men amused themselves with such experiments, while the soldiers, who had hoarded their liquor rations for the occasion, celebrated loudly. In the end Dunbar and Hunter found no evidence of any unusual ingredients.[41]

On December 28 the party began to load the boat for the return trip, but the Ouachita River was at its lowest stage of the year, so for nine days they watched the sky for rain. It finally came on January 7, 1805, and the river rose quickly. They embarked the next day, and though they had to stop at various times to reconnoiter treacherous rapids, they cut their travel time by more than two-thirds. It had taken them twenty-two days from the future Arkansas state line to the springs on the way up the river; it took only six and a half days on the return trip. They reached the Post of Ouachita on January 16. It was here that Dunbar and Hunter parted company. On the nineteenth Dunbar hired a canoe with a view to hastening his return to the Forest. Hunter caught up with him there on the thirty-first and deposited their remaining "public property to be placed with the bulk of the Indian presents I had left there before to be ready for the expeditions up the Red & Arkansa [sic] rivers."[42] As it happened, neither Dunbar nor Hunter made such an expedition. Dunbar's health was too fragile, and Hunter returned to Philadelphia, presumably to attend to his business interests there.[43]

While their reports show the economic and cultural characteristics of a middle ground to have existed in Arkansas in 1804, they also hint at the changes in store. Paltz, the old Dutch hunter Dunbar and Hunter encountered, told them of hostilities between the Osages and the Chickasaws, Choctaws, and certain other "Indian nations" more recently arrived in the Arkansas area.[44] In fact pressure from encroaching white settlements east of the Mississippi River had led to clashes that caused some Indians to move westward. In the 1790s a group of Cherokees, refugees from Indians wars in East Tennessee that caused serious divisions within the tribe, settled in eastern Arkansas, due west of the Chickasaw Bluffs. Not only conflict but also a sharp decline in the number of deer, the animal most frequently hunted in the Southeast, encouraged eastern Indians such as the Illinois, Delawares, Shawnees, Chickasaws, and Choctaws to hunt in increasing numbers in the region. By the end of the eighteenth century, some had established villages, particularly in northeastern Arkansas.[45] Because they feared the American push westward, the Spanish tolerated such migration, and some officials secretly encouraged these disaffected Indians to wage guerrilla war against Americans. At the same time, they hoped that the Indian newcomers might serve as a buffer between the Osages and the Spanish-allied Caddos.[46]

The Indians already residing west of the Mississippi had less reason to welcome the immigrants—as various items in Dunbar's and Hunter's journals suggest. The Quapaws, for example, had traditionally hunted bison, but the explorers sighted only a few buffalo during their expedition. The skins the party saw deposited along the river were instead those of deer. Deer-hunting Indian immigrants, it seems, were scaring off bison. The growing scarcity of buffalo would ultimately make the Quapaws less important players in the frontier exchange economy.[47] Arkansas Indians would find, then, that their middle ground would need defending against the intrusion not only of white Americans but also of eastern Indians.

John B. Treat's letters from Arkansas Post, written in the years immediately following the Dunbar-Hunter expedition, illustrate in other ways both the strength of the exchange relationships between Indians and whites and how they stood to be disrupted by Indian newcomers and the new governing power. Treat, an agent dispatched by the U.S. government to open a "factory," or trading house, with the Indians, arrived at Arkansas Post on September 4, 1805.[48] The United States had created the factory system in 1795 in order to insinuate government traders into the frontier exchange economy; to eliminate "foreigners, whiskey runners, and corrupt entrepreneurs"; and, as noted, to make the Indians dependent upon the American government for supplies, a reliance that might eventually force them to cede their lands.[49] Thirty-one such factories opened between 1795 and 1822, most of them along the Mississippi or its southern tributaries, and they all struggled against a number of obstacles. Treat's operation at Arkansas Post serves as an example of the difficulties the government faced in intruding on an existing frontier exchange economy. Not the least of these challenges was the unwillingness of Indian and white hunters to abandon a system that served their interests in favor of one that seemed to offer them less. Initially at least, even many of the items Treat carried at the trading house were of no value to the Indians.[50]

Treat found it difficult to comfortably or profitably fit himself into Arkansas trade networks. First, he faced significant competition, being only one of several traders at the Post, and some of the others—including men who worked for firms headquartered as far away as Detroit and Philadelphia—had longstanding relationships with particular groups of hunters. The other merchants at the Post actively opposed the government factory and attempted to form an alliance with one another to undermine the enterprise. And while private traders were supposed to be licensed, Treat complained of "Illicit Traders, which for the want of Troops, there being but sixteen or seventeen station'd with us we could not prevent." A second obstacle was that, apparently, government officials did not really understand how the trade system operated in Arkansas. When Treat first arrived at Arkansas Post, he found that a number of merchants competed with one another to advance supplies to "honest and active" persons who then assembled parties, some as small as ten but others much larger. Chickasaws, Choctaws, and Quapaws had been fitted out on this basis. Their hunting parties worked an area between the Arkansas and St. Francis Rivers and as far northwest as the Osages would allow. Treat had been ordered to commission hunts directly with the chiefs of the respective Indian groups rather than individuals, but that would prove impractical because it ran against the existing practice.[51]

Wavering government policy prevented Treat from eliminating his competition. Although the idea behind establishing official factories was explicitly to displace private traders, the government provided a Philadelphia firm, Morgan and Bright, with a license to trade with the Osage in 1806. That April, Secretary of War Henry Dearborn, while correcting Treat's impression that Morgan and Bright had been granted a monopoly on trade with the Osages, informed him that the government had never intended to restrict licensed hunters from trading. Although it contradicted the avowed purpose of the factory—to displace private traders—Dearborn also indicated that Treat was himself free to issue licenses.[52]

Government policy also complicated Treat's effort to secure his place in Arkansas trade by preventing him from practicing the sort of diplomacy that Richard White suggests facilitated middle-ground relationships.[53] The United States failed to continue the French and Spanish system of Indian diplomacy and was slow to establish formal relations with the resident Indians (though American representatives presented the Quapaws with "two hogsheads of tobacco and four barrels of whiskey" in May 1804).[54] Although Treat was clearly expected not only to make a profit through the trade at Arkansas Post but also ensure good relations with the Indians, he was not formally made an Indian agent until 1807. Just as Dunbar and Hunter had been instructed to deal with Indians but had been provided little beyond trinkets and beads with which to do so, Treat had few resources and little authority to secure his relationship with the Quapaws.

Treat complained in March 1806 that the Quapaws had repeatedly entreated him for an exchange of medals with the United States, in keeping with French and Spanish practices. Having no authority at that time to establish a formal relationship with the Quapaws, Treat initially refused to meet with them. After finally running out of excuses, he reported,

"They say that their Grand Father the French, also their Father the Spanish, with whom they lived in the greatest harmony, frequently gave them talks and Annual Presents, but since the privation of those friends, they have not receiv'd either talks or presents from their present Father."[55] Two months later Treat wrote another letter, stating that the Quapaw chiefs "wait anxiously your reply to their wishes as mention'd in my [March] letter."[56] By November of that year, Treat reported that the Quapaws had reacted with joy when they heard a rumor that the Spanish were returning. When asked why, the reply was "they were long our friends, who presented the Chiefs with medals and annually bestow'd presents to all in our Villages." Such had not been forthcoming from their "Present Father, the President," thus they rejoiced at the prospect of a Spanish return.[57] Treat's inability to negotiate special privileges for the Quapaws not only undermined his relations with them but also likely suggested to other hunters that trading with the U.S. government factor offered no particular advantages.

Federal actions undermined their factory in still other ways. By the time Treat reached Arkansas Post, one group of Osages had broken off from the main tribe located in southwestern Missouri and established quasi-permanent villages along the Arkansas River in western Arkansas. They jealously guarded the area in northwestern Arkansas they regarded as their hunting preserve and murdered and plundered Indians and whites alike who trespassed into their territory. In an attempt to quell the violence, Gen. James Wilkinson, the newly appointed governor of the Louisiana Territory, temporarily suspended trade up the Arkansas, White, and St. Francis Rivers in 1805, seemingly to the detriment of the Arkansas factory. The prohibition did not last long, however. The Arkansas Osages appealed, and the embargo was soon rescinded.[58]

Part of Treat's problem with the federal government lay in his difficulties in simply keeping abreast of Indian policy. Communications between Arkansas Post and Washington proved sporadic and unreliable. Correspondence to and from the Post was routed through Chickasaw Bluffs or New Madrid. Treat reported that letters from the East arrived at New Madrid nearly a month after being sent and then had to travel "from thence here a distance of nearly two hundred miles."[59] They were forwarded by whatever boat happened to be going to or from the Post, and Treat noted "the many accidents to which letters are liable."[60] The difficulties this created for him when it came to Indian diplomacy could border on the ridiculous. In early 1807 Treat wrote that he had received "your several favours of Sept. 30th, Oct. 3rd & 6th" but that "the Act of

Congress to which you allude is not in any of the Gazettes rec'd at Arkansas, during the past year in Sept last a gentleman handed me part of a law relative to Indian Trade which came as a wrapper from New Orleans, but it being torn, without date, & the remainder most mutilated we could not make any thing of it as a data, therefore probably we must wait being favore'd with it, 'till receiving it through your office."[61]

Treat's correspondence also demonstrates how, at least as far as the Quapaws were concerned, middle-ground relationships were threatened not only by U.S. inattention but also by the Jefferson administration's interest in increasing the flow of eastern Indians into Arkansas. The Quapaws had felt the presence of these new groups almost immediately. As noted, Dunbar and Hunter had observed the scarcity of bison in southern Arkansas. But the situation of the buffalo-hunting Quapaws grew even more tenuous as immigrant Indians insinuated themselves into existing trade networks. Treat suggested that the increase in the peltry trade at the Post in 1806 was not "from the old sources, but almost entirely from a New One, that of the different Tribes coming from over the Mississippi to hunt upon this place."[62]

The Quapaws' problem at this point was less that the middle ground was being destroyed than that it was being refashioned by immigrant Indians so as to increasingly marginalize the Quapaws. Cherokees recently arrived in Arkansas, for instance, established their own profitable relationships with traders. Métis leaders like Connetoo and William Webber served as middlemen, supplying trade goods to Indians and collecting skins in payment. The Arkansas Cherokees also carried cultural accommodation further than the Quapaws, engaging in staple agriculture and stock raising, enslaving African Americans, adopting certain European architectural forms, and operating stores.[63]

Before the purchase, the Quapaws had attempted to preserve their central role in Arkansas's middle ground by absorbing such newcomers. Beginning "in the late eighteenth century," historian Joseph Key writes, "the Quapaws strengthened ties with the Chickasaws, Choctaws, and Cherokees through intermarriage. The Quapaws sought to incorporate these Indian newcomers as they had the French rather than having independent villages established in competition on the Arkansas."[64]

But as federal policy threatened to increase the volume of Indian migration into Arkansas, the Quapaws began to maneuver. In May 1806 Treat reported that the Quapaw chiefs might attend a grand council near New Madrid and join with "the Delawares, Cherokees, Choctaws, and Chickasaws" in an alliance against the Osages. According to historian

W. David Baird, the Quapaws were less interested in subduing the Osages than "to exacerbate the turmoil and endanger American efforts to curtail the fighting." The object of this proposed alliance with immigrant Indians, then, was to discourage the further resettlement of eastern Indian groups in Arkansas.[65]

The middle ground of both the Quapaws and the Indian newcomers, as well as Treat's factory, would also be undermined by events beyond the control of the U.S. government. The international market for furs declined as a result of the Napoleonic wars. Although the trade to Europe from the lower Mississippi valley had never been as extensive as that from Canada, restrictions on American shipping imposed by Britain and France shortly before Treat set up his operation worked an additional hardship on him. Southern furs had never been as marketable as northern ones because they were usually of much poorer quality. Thus those attempting to sell them in a glutted market found themselves at a special disadvantage. In late 1807 Congress further complicated matters by passing the Embargo Act, forbidding U.S. ships from trading with any foreign port. Even before Congress passed the embargo, it was discouraging the shipment of furs to Europe. In the summer of 1807, Treat received a communication from the principal agent for Indian factories, John Shee, stating: "I am sensible that it was the intention of government to barter our goods with the Indians for the produce of their toils but avoid as much as possible the taking of deer skins and dispose of them when taken if possible on the spot. You know not how much I am embarrass'd with them and rather than see them eat up by the worms I am necessitated tho in defiance of law to scatter them through different parts of Europe."[66] Treat was undoubtedly accepting the skins despite orders to the contrary in order to insinuate himself into the trade. But that commerce in animal products—and the frontier exchange economy—was to have only a limited future in this portion of the Louisiana Purchase territory.

An apt symbol both of Treat's failure to integrate himself into existing trade relationships and of the dimming prospects of that trade may be his abortive construction of a factory building in which he could, among other things, store skins he received. Clearly Treat envisioned a volume of trade that would warrant the expenditure of funds. The growing numbers of immigrant hunters in the area certainly seemed to portend opportunity. The building he hoped to construct could provide them temporary shelter and encourage their trade with him, thus augmenting his profits. He began plans for the construction of the building upon his arrival in 1805 and asked the government to supply a carpenter since none was to be had at the Post. Authorities refused, but Treat pressed on, reporting periodically on his progress. Yet when he left Arkansas Post in early 1809 on an extended leave—he was suffering from ill health—the building was still incomplete. His assistant agent, James Waterman, who was put in charge upon Treat's departure, apparently made no effort to continue construction. Treat was finally well enough to resume his duties, but by 1810 the factorage was all but defunct. Rather than send him back to Arkansas Post, which had proved to be both an unprofitable and unhealthy environment, the government moved operations to Chickasaw Bluffs. The factory building stood unfinished and abandoned, The closure of the factory at Arkansas Post must have signaled to the Indians there that the American government had limited use for their trade.[67]

Treat's letters show how the Quapaw middle ground was refashioned as the United States encouraged the introduction of eastern Indian groups to Arkansas. But the newer middle-ground relationships established by immigrant Indians would also be quickly overwhelmed by white settlers. The French and Spanish had been unable to secure substantial migration of their own people to the area, leaving those who did settle little alternative but to come to terms with local peoples. By contrast, the U.S. government at first could not, and finally would not, contain the American settlers who flooded into the region. The kind of trade network that thrived when white traders were few in number was to be forever transformed by the arrival of growing numbers of white settlers intent upon establishing plantation agriculture and making their fortunes in the international cotton market. Richard White tells us that whites participated in the creation of middle grounds when they needed Indians "as allies, as partners in exchange, as sexual partners, as friendly neighbors."[68] But by the second decade of the nineteenth century, all that white settlers in Arkansas needed was for Indians to vacate their land. Resistance was futile, and even those who most successfully adapted to white culture and customs, such as the Cherokees, would find that accommodation was no refuge from the onslaught of land-hungry whites.

5

Jeffersonian Indian Removal and the Emergence of Arkansas Territory

S. CHARLES BOLTON

The phrase "Indian removal" is often associated with the Trail of Tears, the forced migration in the 1830s of the so-called Five Civilized Tribes—the Cherokees, Chickasaws, Choctaws, Creeks, and Seminoles—initiated under Pres. Andrew Jackson. Arkansas was an important part of the trail, traversed by all five of the tribes on their way into exile in what is now Oklahoma, but it played a larger role in the less well-known removal program that was initiated by Pres. Thomas Jefferson and continued to be national policy through the 1820s.[1] Jeffersonian Indian removal had its origins in the president's long-held view that the migration of eastern tribes across the Mississippi River would be good for both whites and Native Americans, providing economic opportunity for the former and giving the latter time and space in which to develop their potential for what he thought of as civilization, the critical element of which was farming individually owned plots of land rather than hunting on vast amounts of communal acreage. The Louisiana Purchase provided

Jefferson with an opportunity to test this concept, and for twenty years, beginning in 1808, Arkansas was the federal government's destination of choice for removed tribes. As a result, it became home to the western Cherokee nation, a group of settlers who represented at least 20 percent of the total population of Arkansas by the time it became a separate territory in 1819.[2]

While historians have analyzed Jefferson's ideas and policies with respect to Indian removal, they have paid less attention to their influence on the settlement and development of the Louisiana Purchase and have generally ignored the role of Arkansas as the focus of migration.[3] Similarly, recent studies that have added greatly to our knowledge of Indian newcomers to Arkansas have paid relatively little attention to the Jeffersonian policies that helped bring about this immigration.[4] There is good reason for emphasizing, as they do, that Native Americans exercised a large degree of control over their own affairs, but it is also true, in this case at least, that federal policy shaped Indian fates.[5] In addition to these factors, geography affected the development of upper Louisiana and made the Arkansas portion of it a potential home for eastern Indians. The movement of the Cherokee nation, in particular, was a product of both Indian initiative and Jeffersonian persuasion.

Geography had long been a factor in the political development of the Mississippi River valley. Under the Spanish colonial regime, the Mississippi River basin was divided into two districts, with the lower portion administered by the colonial governor in New Orleans and upper Louisiana, or the Illinois Country as it was called, under the control of a deputy governor stationed at St. Louis. The imprecise but recognized boundary between the two regions extended west from the mouth of the Ohio River, though the village of New Madrid, located thirty miles below that line, was also included in upper Louisiana.[6] The substantial trading center at Arkansas Post, near the mouth of the Arkansas River, and the tiny garrison at Chickasaw Bluffs (at the site of present-day Memphis, Tennessee) were the northernmost outposts of lower Louisiana. Distance was the critical factor in creating this division. An upstream barge trip from New Orleans to St. Louis required at least two months, and the overland journey, which followed a circuitous route through Natchitoches on the Red River, Fort Miró on the Ouachita River (at present-day Monroe, Louisiana), and Arkansas Post, took over a month. Arkansas Post was somewhat less than halfway from New Orleans to St. Louis by water.[7]

Of critical importance to the growth of upper Louisiana was the natural population basin formed by the Mississippi River between the mouths of the Missouri and Ohio Rivers.[8] That geographical feature, which had made Cahokia a Native American population center in the thirteenth century, created a nexus of European settlement on both sides of the Mississippi by the middle of the eighteenth century. After the French and Indian War (1754–63), as the eastern side of the river became part of British North America and then the United States, a significant number of French settlers moved to the west bank. In the 1790s Americans began to move down the Ohio valley and settle on fertile land across the Mississippi made available to them by the Spanish regime. New Madrid, blessed with an excellent harbor and dry land immediately behind it, was the southernmost town of any size in upper Louisiana, though the small community of Little Prairie, near present-day Caruthersville, was thirty miles below it.[9]

Below New Madrid, population dwindled because of the low-lying swampy lands that dominated the region between the Mississippi and the St. Francis Rivers as far south as the mouth of the St. Francis above present-day Helena, Arkansas. Evidence from a later period makes the situation clear. Capt. Amos Stoddard, the first American commander at St. Louis, noted that "Nearly half of the lands between these two rivers are covered with swamps and ponds, and periodically inundated." Stoddard thought that river bottoms and small prairies in the area would make excellent farmland, but he also noted that it was "more insalubrious" than any other part of what would become the Missouri Territory, a damning indictment as far as Americans moving west were concerned.[10] When Fortescue Cuming floated down the Mississippi in 1808, he found no settlements between Little Prairie and Chickasaw Bluffs, one hundred miles due south. Overland travelers from Arkansas Post to St. Louis avoided the area between the St. Francis and the Mississippi by following the White River northwest for a hundred miles and then heading northeast toward New Madrid. The earthquakes of 1811 and 1812 made the swampy area still more difficult to settle or even to penetrate.[11]

Growing season was another geographical phenomenon that distinguished upper Louisiana from lower Louisiana. Edward F. Bond, an American immigrant living in the Cape Girardeau area just above New Madrid, aptly described the situation in 1805: "We are in the worst climate for Product of any in Louisiana[,] situated too much to the south for wheat and too Much North for Cotton[,] in as much that neither of these Staples of America are certain crops in our District."[12] The distinction between lands best suited for one staple crop or the other had not been very important to the colonial economy. Native American and white hunters from as far south as New Orleans came upriver to take advantage of the lush hunting grounds in the lower St. Francis River valley, and beginning in 1764 Auguste Chouteau and his partners shipped vast amounts of hides and furs from St. Louis to both New Orleans and Canada. The economy of Arkansas Post was based on the deer, buffalo, and bear killed by local white hunters, the nearby Quapaw Indians, and the Osages to the northwest, who traded both there and at St. Louis. The small French population did produce wheat along with equal amounts of corn, but they often imported flour so they could concentrate on hunting and trading. The one significant source of wheat production along the colonial Mississippi River was Ste. Genevieve, located above Cape Girardeau, which sent enough flour downriver to bring Louisiana close to self-sufficiency in food production.[13]

After the Louisiana Purchase, however, growing season would become critical to economic development. Cotton did not grow well in Missouri, but southeastern Arkansas was an ideal environment. What would become Arkansas Territory grew slowly during the first two decades of the nineteenth century as hunters and small farmers from Missouri entered from the northeast, some of them settling in the White River region and others moving on toward the Red River in the southwest. Beginning in the 1820s, however, as the cotton kingdom expanded, an increasing number of settlers came from southern states. What had earlier seemed like an ideal place to relocate southeastern Indians became after 1820 an economic environment similar to the one from which they were being expelled.[14]

The expansion of cotton culture into the middle Mississippi valley was still in the future, however, in 1803 as the United States faced the problem of how to govern and develop the vast territory it had purchased from France. The first and best known attempt to do that was contained in President Jefferson's proposal to amend the Constitution in order to provide specific authority for the acquisition. Jefferson's initial draft called for a division of Louisiana at thirty-one degrees of north latitude. The southern portion, containing only New Orleans and its hinterland, would be given a territorial government with the prospect of advancing toward statehood, while the area to the north, despite its existing French population, would become Indian country. Jefferson proposed to confirm the hunting-ground claims of resident tribes and authorize Congress to exchange other areas with eastern Indians who would agree to give up their current holdings. Writing to friends, the president explained that the Native Americans would prevent settlers from the United States from crossing the Mississippi River until the eastern portion was settled. Then, as the American population filled the empty space in the East, "we may lay off a range of States on the western bank from the head to the mouth, and so range after range, advancing compactly as we multiply."[15] Even at this point Jefferson was not proposing that the purchase territory be Indian country in perpetuity.

As the president refined his proposal, defining a boundary between lower and upper Louisiana to replace the Spanish divisions proved to be a problem. Jefferson's initial choice at thirty-one degrees was probably based on the fact that this latitude was the current border between the United States and West Florida, which he believed was included in the purchase.[16] Later, however, he moved the line northward to the mouth of the Arkansas River, about thirty-four degrees, probably on the erroneous notion that it was the Spanish boundary between lower and upper Louisiana.[17] Meanwhile, Robert Smith, secretary of the navy, offered Jefferson a version of the amendment that called for a boundary at thirty-two degrees, perhaps thinking of the Red River settlement at Natchitoches as a reasonable extension of the New Orleans penumbra.[18] Finally, in March 1804, Congress settled the issue, dividing the purchase at thirty-three degrees, which added a large segment of the Ouachita River basin to the southern portion; this was destined to become the boundary between the states of Louisiana and Arkansas.[19] The division also meant that Arkansas Post was within the political sphere of St. Louis rather than that of New Orleans.

Providing for the government of these areas, Congress first created a Territory of Orleans in the southern portion, which had a complex economy and a substantial population, including fifteen thousand whites, eleven thousand slaves, and fifteen hundred free blacks. In addition to providing for an appointed governor, territory secretary, and legislative council, the act created a system of federal courts and required adherence to basic American civil liberties, such as trial by jury and habeas corpus, but left most of the French- and Spanish-based civil law intact.

With that out of the way, the young republic's leaders in Washington turned to upper Louisiana, what it called "the residue" of the purchase, probably unaware that there were more than nine thousand non-Indian persons living between the Missouri River and New Madrid. Congress created a separate political entity called the District of Louisiana but placed it under the control of Indiana Territory, which was still in the first stage of territorial government under Gov. William Henry Harrison. In a telling departure from previous practice, the legislation provided for a degree of military rule, creating districts (subdistricts actually) under the control of army officers who were appointed by the president and would command any regular troops stationed within their civil jurisdiction. It also declared that existing laws would remain in effect, unless modified by the government of Indiana Territory, and confirmed all valid land claims made by Spain prior to the cession of Louisiana to France in the Treaty of San Ildefonso (October 1, 1800), leaving open for the moment how the question of validity would be determined.

With respect to new settlement, Congress made provisions to implement Jefferson's concept of Indian removal. Despite an earlier warning by a senator that if the government tried to keep white settlers east of the Mississippi, "you had just as well pretend to inhibit the fish from swimming in the sea," Congress authorized the president to use U.S. military forces to prevent the settlement of American citizens in the new district, providing for a penalty of up to $1,000 or imprisonment for up to twelve months. It gave Jefferson the right to exchange land in the District of Louisiana with any Indian tribe who would give up their holdings in the East and place themselves under federal protection. The measure also extended to Louisiana the Acts of Trade and Intercourse that regulated relations between the U.S. government and the Native American tribes.[20]

Creole French leaders in St. Louis were not at all happy with the creation of the District of Louisiana. They had accepted the American takeover and befriended army captain Amos Stoddard, the U.S. commandant, but now felt a real threat to their political and economic interests. Under the leadership of Auguste Chouteau and Charles Gratiot, representatives from the area met in December 1804 and drew up a lengthy petition to Congress. Their chief concern was being placed under the control of Indiana Territory, a denial of self-government they believed violated their rights as American citizens as well as the provisions of the treaty between France and the United States. Indian removal was the next-most-important grievance. It would result, in their words, in "an incalculable accession of savage hords to be vomited on our borders." A House of Representatives committee responded, somewhat defensively, that upper Louisiana had not been treated unfairly but concluded by recommending that it be made into a separate territory. In part, this new respect may have been owing to a detailed report sent to President Jefferson by Moses Austin, the future promoter of Texas settlement, lauding the potential of the lead mines in the Cape Girardeau area, to which Jefferson called attention in his message to Congress in November 1804.[21]

In March 1805 Congress passed three laws intended to provide a more permanent solution for the government of the Louisiana Purchase. The first moved the Territory of Orleans into the second stage of territorial government, allowing the citizens to elect a legislature and a nonvoting delegate to Congress. The second created a board of commissioners to hear evidence and adjudicate individual land claims dating from the periods of French and Spanish control. The third turned the District of Louisiana into Louisiana Territory and made St. Louis its capital, giving the people of upper Louisiana their own government, even if at the hands of appointed officials. In a significant shift Congress said nothing about prohibiting white settlement or encouraging the immigration of Indians.[22]

While the legislation demonstrated a new appreciation of the white population in upper Louisiana, it did not cause Jefferson to give up on the idea of resettling eastern Indians there. He began to narrow his focus from the Louisiana territory in general to its southern portion alone and to consider the possibility of relocating the small number of white occupants there in order to make room for Native Americans. Still acting as if the newly renamed Louisiana Territory were a military district, he appointed Gen. James Wilkinson as its governor while allowing him to remain as commander of U.S. Army forces west of the Appalachian Mountains, combining military and civil authority in a manner that he had recently refused to do with respect to Mississippi Territory.[23] He also gave Wilkinson private instructions to accomplish, as the general put it, "the depopulation of our loose settlements below this on the Mississippi & its branches—and the transfer of the Southern Indians to this Territory."[24]

Wilkinson's letters make clear that the "loose settlements below" referred to the District of New Madrid, which stretched south to the border with the Territory of Orleans and included all of Arkansas. "In fact," wrote the governor, "the settlements below Cape Girardeau are composed very generally, of a medley of our loose erratic Country men, whose local attachments are as fluctuating, as their principles are unsteady."

Wilkinson warned Secretary of State James Madison, however, that pushing these people off their land would injure their "Amour Propre" and "probably excite some seditious emotions," by which presumably he meant a disposition to return to Spanish government. He concluded, "my course . . . must be rather indirect." Wilkinson claimed to have discussed the plan with the territorial judges, who were not enthusiastic about its success, and suggested they needed some private encouragement from the secretary of state.[25] To the president he wrote that convincing the present settlers to go would require "discouragements to the present Establishments, & allurements to a change of position." Wilkinson stressed the negative incentives, which he thought might include squelching any idea of future statehood and refusing to provide for the sale of public lands, for, asserted the governor, "it is not by preparing Beds of down, that we are to get rid of unwelcome Guests."[26]

The Jefferson-Wilkinson machinations came to naught, however, and one wonders if the slippery governor had simply been humoring the president. On January 1, 1806, shortly after urging Jefferson to be stern with whites living in the southern part of the territory, Wilkinson divided New Madrid District and created a separate District of Arkansas. Giving the settlers in and around Arkansas Post an element of self-government provided them a softer bed, as it were, and would seem to run counter to the idea of depopulating the area. By that time the governor was also at the center of intense political controversy involving the territorial judges and other elites in the St. Louis area and in no position to carry out a sustained program of any sort. Then in the spring of 1806, as a result of rumors that former Vice Pres. Aaron Burr was leading a force to detach part of the Southwest from the United States, Jefferson reassigned Wilkinson to New Orleans, apparently unaware that the general was Burr's co-conspirator. As late as October 1808, however, the resettlement plan was still a live issue to Cape Girardeau resident Edward F. Bond, who wrote the president that settlers there could be induced to move if they were offered two acres elsewhere for every one they gave up.[27]

If less was heard about discouraging white settlement, the president was nevertheless insisting to eastern tribes that resettlement represented their best hope for the future and directing them to Arkansas. His chances of success were improved by the fact that a significant number of Native Americans had already come to the same conclusion. In September 1803 Daniel Clark, a resident of New Orleans knowledgeable about Louisiana, had sent the president a report concerning the Indians along the middle Mississippi River. In the area around Cape Girardeau and New Madrid, he indicated, were "emigrants from the Delawares, Shawnese, Miamis, Chicasaws, Cherokees, [and] Piorias," perhaps five hundred families in all. Along the Arkansas River there were frequently Cherokees, Choctaws, and Chickasaws who came to hunt, and some members of those tribes had settled among the Quapaws, who were permanent residents. Farther south he estimated that there were four hundred or five hundred Choctaws living along the Ouachita and Red Rivers.[28] Although Clark did not make it clear, most of these immigrants were refugees who had chosen to settle on what was then Spanish territory in order to avoid further conflict with the United States and its advancing population.[29]

The most significant group of Native American immigrants in Arkansas may have been unknown to Clark. They were a group of Cherokees who lived along the St. Francis River more than a hundred miles south of New Madrid. Unlike those Indians farther upriver, these Cherokees had not crossed the Mississippi near the mouth of the Ohio but rather ascended the St. Francis from its mouth far to the south. The origins of this settlement lay in a Cherokee attack on a group of Americans traveling on the Tennessee River in 1794, which led to massive retaliation by U.S. military forces that pressured Cherokee leaders into sending the perpetrators into exile. A mixed-blood chief named Connetoo, also known as John Hill, arrived at the St. Francis in 1796 with a small group, augmented by later arrivals, and formed a settlement some fifty miles upriver.[30] At the end of 1806, Connetoo told John B. Treat, who was in charge at the newly established U.S. trading house, or factory, at Arkansas Post, that there were six hundred Cherokees with him and that more were expected.[31]

Jefferson first spoke to the Cherokees about removal in January 1806. Addressing a delegation from the tribe in Washington, he took the opportunity to praise their progress toward the white man's version of civilization and to offer advice for the future: "You are becoming farmers, learning the use of the plough & the hoe, enclosing your grounds, and employing that labor in their cultivation which you formerly employed in hunting & war." A next step, he thought, would be building "mills to grind your Corn, which by relieving your Women from the loss of time in beating it into meal, will enable them to spin and weave more." Having created a farm and stocked it with animals, the president opined, a man would come to believe that "when he dies that those things should go to his wife and children," and laws of inheritance would become necessary. And property rights in general would become more important, meaning the Cherokees would want to pass appropriate laws and select capable judges to protect individual rights.

Jefferson did not encourage the acculturating Cherokees to move across the Mississippi, but he made it clear that those who wanted to follow the old lifestyle of the tribe were free to go there. He began by expressing his concern that young Cherokee men were crossing the Mississippi River to participate in fighting there, presumably in the Indian coalitions against the Osages, and that it could lead to attacks on American commerce on the river. He wanted the assembled chiefs to put a stop to that, but these eastern Cherokees were welcome to "visit or to live with the Cherokees on the other side of the River. . . . That Country is ours—We will permit them to live in it."[32]

Immigration did continue, increasing in scale. Based in part on Jefferson's support, it was also related to a major conflict between the Upper Towns of the Cherokee nation, in northern Georgia, eastern Tennessee, and the western parts of North and South Carolina, and the Lower Towns along the Tennessee River in northern Alabama, where militant members had moved to continue fighting the Americans after the main body of Cherokees had made peace in 1777. A critical figure in the internal feuding was a chief from the Lower Towns named Doublehead, who had played a leading role in warfare into the 1790s but became an advocate of accommodation with whites and adaptation to their modes of economic activity. Acting with the support of Cherokee agent Return J. Meigs, Doublehead engineered the sale in 1805 and 1806 of Cherokee claims to perhaps a third of Tennessee and small portions of both Kentucky and Alabama. The payment included not only annuities and economic assistance for the Cherokee nation but also a large private grant of land to Doublehead and cash payments to him and a number of other chiefs, including his close associate Tahlonteskee and their white ally and advisor John D. Chisholm.[33]

In the latter part of 1806, young chiefs of the Upper Towns in Georgia, among them James Vann, who had played a role in the land sales, and emerging leaders, such as Charles Hicks and The Ridge, rose in opposition to Doublehead. Motivated by a new Cherokee nationalism that accepted economic development as necessary but wanted it to occur within the context of a united tribe maintaining control over its land, these leaders engineered the assassination of Doublehead in 1807. They also won a significant victory at the September 1808 national council in Broomstown, where they removed Doublehead's supporters from power, created a national police force, and began discussions that would lead to the creation of a constitution similar to that of the United States.[34]

While the Upper Towns faction attempted to strengthen tribal government, Lower Towns leaders like Tahlonteskee began to work with Meigs on a plan to cede eastern land in exchange for acreage across the Mississippi. Doublehead's concept of accommodation with the United States had always included the possibility of removal, and Agent Meigs had promoted the idea ever since the acquisition of Louisiana. Jefferson's offer to let Cherokees settle in the Trans-Mississippi made it a clear possibility. Removal became particularly appealing to Lower Towns chiefs after their loss of power in the national conference, and it quickly became a major issue in the dispute between the two factions.[35]

Early in 1809, leaders from both the Upper and Lower Towns visited Washington, each group seeking support for its vision for the Cherokee future from Jefferson, now nearing the end of his second term. The president's response ignored the concept of Cherokee nationalism and tacitly accepted a permanent division of the tribe. Jefferson dealt with the conflict solely in terms of his own dichotomy between acculturation and removal. On the one hand, in his formulation, was a group (the Upper Towns) "desiring to remain on their lands; to betake themselves to agriculture and the industrious activities, of civilized life"; on the other was one (the Lower Towns), who, "retaining their attachments to the hunter's life, and having little game on their present lands, are desirous to move across the Mississippi." Jefferson made clear his approval of the goals of the first group and, implicitly at least, their right to remain where they were. He also claimed to appreciate the wishes of the would-be hunters and told them they were free to settle in the Louisiana Purchase, where the United States would give them land in exchange for a part of the existing Cherokee lands "proportioned to the numbers."

Jefferson explicitly directed the westering Cherokees to Arkansas. Declaring that the "regular districts of the government of St. Louis are already laid off to the St. Francis River," he suggested that they "reconnoiter the country on the waters of the Arkansas and White rivers" and settle as far up the rivers as possible, "as they will be the longer unapproached by our Settlements, which will begin at the mouths of those rivers." There is no evidence as to whether the Cherokees recognized this last phrase for what it was: a tacit but ominous admission that the new homeland would probably not be permanent but instead would simply be a place where acculturation could proceed at a more leisurely pace.[36]

Acting on Jefferson's advice and with assistance from Agent Meigs, Lower Towns leaders began to make preparations to leave. They felt no need for more information about the destination, but Meigs sent John Ross, the future Cherokee nationalist leader, and three other young men to explore the Arkansas River valley, perhaps concerned the emigrants would settle elsewhere. In December 1809 Meigs believed there were about 1,000 Cherokees in Arkansas, "some of them very wealthy," and that they were settled along the White and Arkansas Rivers. In June 1810 Tahlonteskee gave Meigs a list of 1,023 Cherokees who were planning to emigrate, slightly more than 8 percent of the entire nation, according to a detailed population estimate made in 1809. Several other small groups stated the same intention. How many actually left is not clear, though Tahlonteskee's party took with them about 6 percent of the horses and cattle owned by the tribe. A reasonable assumption is that about 1,000 Cherokees emigrated from their ancestral lands in 1810.[37]

Tahlonteskee led his group to the St. Francis and White River region and joined with Connetoo rather than settle along the Arkansas. By the summer of 1811, however, he was ready to move, and most of the St. Francis Cherokees left the area after the New Madrid earthquakes in late 1811 and early 1812. That March the editor of the *Louisiana Gazette* in St. Louis thought that "the Cherokees who were exploring that tract of country between the Arkansas and White rivers have returned home, terrified by the repeated and violent shocks." By the end of the year, however, the Indians were settled along both sides of the Arkansas River from Dardanelle westward. Arguing for a separate agency to serve the western Cherokees in early 1816, Return J. Meigs said that he had a report that they numbered twenty-six hundred but thought the figure was probably closer to two thousand.[38]

The status of the Arkansas Cherokees was formalized in a treaty between the Cherokee nation and the United States negotiated in July 1817. According to its preamble, the new compact was a response to those who had immigrated as a result of Jefferson's offer of January 1809 and now wished a "full and complete ratification of his promise." Under its provisions the Cherokees ceded land in the East in exchange for an equal amount, "acre for acre," in a tract lying west of a line running northeast from the Arkansas River near present-day Morrilton to the White River near present-day Batesville. The size of the Arkansas grant would be proportional to the percentage of all Cherokees who had or would remove to the West, the numbers to be determined by a census to be taken in 1818. The western Cherokees would also get a proportional share of the annuities of the tribe. To encourage emigration the United States agreed to provide each adult male with a rifle, ammunition, a blanket, and either a brass kettle or a beaver trap as well as assistance with the move. In addition, those with substantial improvements on eastern land would be reimbursed for their value. Indians who wished to stay on eastern land that was ceded to the United States could become citizens and receive 640 acres of land surrounding their present homesteads.[39]

Despite its claim to validate what had been a voluntary decision on the part of some Cherokees to accept Jefferson's offer, the Treaty of 1817 was actually the beginning of a transition to the more compulsory removal program of the 1830s. Gen. Andrew Jackson and Gov. Joseph

McMinn of Tennessee were the chief American negotiators of the 1817 document, and their goal was to force the Cherokees into leaving the East or accepting an offer of private individual landholdings and U.S. citizenship, the latter a status that McMinn envisioned as similar to that held by free blacks in the South. Cherokee nationalists, who were not well served by their representatives in the treaty-making process, argued that members of the tribe had a third alternative, unmentioned in the treaty, of remaining where they were and holding land in their traditional manner. Pressure from northern missionary friends of the Cherokees and the high cost of administering the removal provisions of the treaty convinced Secretary of War John C. Calhoun to accept a compromise that left the eastern Cherokee nation intact. Under the terms of a second treaty signed on February 12, 1819, the Cherokees who remained had to give up only four million of the fourteen million acres they owned and one-third of their annual annuity. The census called for in the earlier agreement was never carried out, and the 1819 document was based on Calhoun's estimate that there were 5,000 Cherokees in Arkansas and 10,000 in the East, rather than the Cherokee claim that the numbers were 3,500 and 12,500.[40]

Even at 3,500, the Arkansas Cherokees were a significant percentage of all people living in Arkansas Territory at its creation in 1819, which the census a year later enumerated as 14,273 non-Indians, 1,617 of them slaves.[41] Moreover, the Cherokees accounted for only a part of the Native American presence. In 1818 the Quapaws, who probably numbered less than five hundred persons by then, had given up their claim to a vast area between the Arkansas and Red Rivers but retained title to about two million acres in the southeast portion of the territory. In 1820 Andrew Jackson negotiated the Treaty of Doak's Stand with the Choctaws, an agreement that involved their removal to an area south of the Arkansas River similar in extent to that of the Cherokees in the north. A year after its creation, much of Arkansas Territory was either settled by Native Americans or promised to them.[42]

The conditions that had made the Arkansas portion of Missouri Territory a promising home for eastern Indians were rapidly fading, though. In the first decade after the Louisiana Purchase, the white population south of New Madrid remained centered in the Arkansas Post vicinity and tied to its colonial economy. Frederick Bates, a member of the St. Louis–based board of commissioners dealing with Spanish claims, visited the Post in July 1808 and found the French and American population preoccupied with hunting and was not surprised that "affairs requiring method, order and an observance of legal forms, should be totally unintelligible to them." So limited was local expertise that he wound up helping some residents prepare the land claims that he was suppose to evaluate.[43]

As people from southeastern Missouri moved into central Arkansas, however, the territorial government of Missouri began to take its southern region more seriously, creating Arkansas County out of New Madrid County in 1813 and then Lawrence County out of the northern portion of Arkansas County in 1815. Isolation remained a problem, though. Gov. William Clark of Missouri Territory declared Rufus Easton as the winner of the September 1814 election for territorial delegate despite the fact that no returns had arrived from Arkansas County, presumably because a forty-five-day deadline for reporting the votes had expired.[44] Significantly, in terms of the future, the St. Louis legislature also began to include Arkansas in requests related to Indian removal. It called for a reduction in the size of Quapaw holdings in January 1817 and, two years later, for the compensation of white settlers who had been living on land granted to the Cherokees. Congress approved both requests.[45]

Once Arkansas achieved territorial status, the growing white population began to do its own lobbying in Washington, and they were no more interested in sharing land with Indians than were their relatives in the East. The cultivation of cotton, to which the southern portion of the Louisiana Purchase was particularly suited, put Arkansas land at a premium in the eyes of white settlers. Within a decade a new series of treaties had dispossessed the Quapaws, moved the Choctaw line west to its current position as the southwestern border of Arkansas, and forced the Cherokees beyond the present northwestern boundary of the state. Oklahoma, not Arkansas, became Indian Territory.[46]

As for President Jefferson, most of his goals for the Louisiana Purchase were fulfilled. He wanted to move the Indians west, and they went, some on their own initiative, more because of his own efforts, and most after Jeffersonian persuasion gave way to Jacksonian coercion. Soon realizing that the St. Louis area was too well developed to suit his needs, he decided that Arkansas would be the new homeland, and for several decades it functioned that way; in fact the eventual Indian Territory was simply created out of the western portion of what had been the Arkansas Territory in 1819. Americans crossed the Mississippi River faster than the president thought they would, traveling pell-mell rather than, as he had hoped, "advancing compactly as we multiply." But it was the Cherokees who had to adapt, and Jefferson could live with that.

6

"Outcasts upon the World"

The Louisiana Purchase and the Quapaws

JOSEPH PATRICK KEY

The Louisiana Purchase set in motion one of the greatest demographic transitions in the history of the Trans-Mississippi West. Within a few short years of 1803, for instance, white American settlers vastly outnumbered Indians and colonists of French and Spanish descent in that portion of Louisiana that would become Arkansas. Explosive population growth had propelled these settlers west. Between 1700 and 1803 the population of the English-speaking settlements in the East had increased from 250,000 to 5.5 million. White Americans forcefully reworked the demography of the Mississippi valley not only by their own migration but also through the introduction of thousands of enslaved African Americans and the expulsion of Indians. Like so many places subject to America's westward expansion, Arkansas faced what historian Walter Nugent calls "a demographic inundation leading to complete political and cultural change."[1]

The Quapaws would feel the force of this flood as much as any Indian people. The wave of American immigration to Arkansas, while smaller than that hitting Missouri and Louisiana, overwhelmed them. At the time of the Louisiana Purchase, the Quapaw population stood at 555 in three villages located on the south bank of the Arkansas River. The first village (Kappa), under the tribe's principal chief Wah-pah-tee-see, had a population of 160; the second (Tourima), under Etah-sah, had a population of 166; the third (Osotouy), under Wah-to-nee-kah, was the largest with 229. By 1811, when the first census was taken, whites, 1,062 of them, outnumbered the Quapaws two to one. During the next decade the growth of the white population also outpaced that of other Indians immigrating into Arkansas from the East. Whites numbered 14,273 in 1820 and an estimated 30,000 in 1830.[2] By the 1820s, enslaved African Americans—not counting those among the Cherokees—also outnumbered Indians. The shift in political and economic relationships wrought by these demographic changes would ultimately cast the Quapaws out of Arkansas entirely.

Although white settlers began arriving on the west bank of the Mississippi well ahead of the Louisiana Purchase, the presence of the U.S. government would prove decisive for the Quapaws and other Arkansas Indians. Within two years after the purchase, the federal government established a trading factory at Arkansas Post. Two more would be established within the boundaries of the territory before 1822. The mission of these factories was to establish a fair trade with Indians in the region and impose a new set of commercial regulations on that commerce, including the prohibition of alcohol. The trading posts were followed by an increasing military presence on Arkansas's western frontier, intended to support the policy of Indian removal.

This policy had two components that affected Arkansas: the removal of Indians from the East into the less populated Arkansas River region, and the land cessions demanded of Indians already in Arkansas. The first component bred conflict as immigrants such as the Cherokees clashed with the Osages, one of the region's dominant tribes. More important in the long term for the Quapaws were the government's demands for land cessions, something they had not faced in their dealings with the French or Spanish. The American attitude toward land imposed boundaries and lines in areas of Arkansas that had only been recognized as hunting territory shared or fought over by Indians and a small number of Frenchmen. The federal government began a series of negotiations to acquire land from the Quapaws and the Osages. In 1816 the Osages agreed to cede claims in western Arkansas. Two years later the government turned its diplomatic attention to the Quapaws in order to open lands south of the Arkansas. Before these negotiations began, U.S. officials had demonstrated little interest in the Quapaws, which was in itself an entirely new experience for these Indians when it came to dealing with white settlers and their governments.

During the colonial period the Quapaws had developed a close and reciprocal relationship with French and Spanish officials, soldiers, traders, and hunters. Beginning with the first encounter in 1673, the Quapaws employed ritual to draw the French into their world. The progression of ceremony, culminating in the calumet dance, moved the French spatially and spiritually from stranger to kin. Through the eighteenth century, the Quapaws performed the calumet dance for each new commandant, whether representing the French or the Spanish, thereby expressing their economic and military alliance with the government of Louisiana in terms of fictive kinship. Just as important to them were the kin relations established with French Creoles through intermarriage. For nearly a century the Quapaws had intermarried with the French to such an extent that some observers could not tell the difference between the two groups.[3] At the time of the Louisiana Purchase, the Quapaws still performed their traditional rituals of incorporating newcomers, which were extended most conspicuously to immigrating southeastern Indians. Cherokee, Choctaw, and Chickasaw men married Quapaw women often enough to catch the eye of American officials. But Quapaw intermarriage with Anglo-American newcomers never occurred.[4]

In contrast to the literally intimate relations the French and Indians constructed, the United States failed even to regularly appoint an agent to the Quapaws, whose numbers admittedly had declined sharply since the French had first arrived. The Quapaws felt this American indifference so keenly that they were overjoyed when rumors circulated in 1806 that the Spanish had returned. "A majority of them left their homes" to greet the Spanish, John Treat, the government trading factor at Arkansas Post, reported. The Quapaws were almost to the Post before learning that the rumor was false. Perplexed, Treat asked the chiefs for an explanation. They replied, he wrote, that the Spanish "were long our friends, who presented the Chiefs with medals and annually bestow'd presents to all in our Villages which as yet neither the one or the other has been experienced from our Present Father the President." The chiefs continued to wear medals given them by the Spanish to make the point that they had not "received any such token of friendship" from the United States.[5] Treat himself had only made the situation worse from the Quapaws' perspective. He was slow to visit their villages after arriving and traded for provisions with local farmers rather than the Quapaws, therefore establishing no basis for the gift exchange or reciprocity that the Quapaws had come to expect from newcomers and friends.[6] The government's indifference reflected a more general posture on the part of American settlers. With the two banks of the Mississippi united by the Louisiana Purchase, the Quapaws did not seem particularly significant.

Before the purchase, by contrast, the Quapaws held a significant place in the local and regional economy and the defense of the French and Spanish colony. Arkansas's economy had been oriented toward the west, from which furs, deerskins, and even some captives flowed down the Arkansas River to Arkansas Post. The Quapaws participated in this trade as provisioners and laborers. They provided corn and horses to the traders at the Post and horses to eastern Indians coming west to hunt. As hunters they harvested buffalo meat, tallow, and bear oil. The Quapaws also had protected Louisiana's trade for decades from the raids of enemy Chickasaws of the eastern bank. Located at a strategic spot in the Mississippi valley between the settlements of the lower valley and the Illinois Country—and after 1763 perched on the border of the Spanish and British North American empires—the Quapaws were crucial to the colony's security and were lavished with gifts and supplies for their efforts.[7]

This economic and military influence eroded after the Louisiana Purchase. The Quapaws were marginalized economically, socially, and politically. The Arkansas economy reoriented itself eastward, to the detriment of hunting and trading, as the number of white farmers (and livestock) increased. By the 1820s, cotton bound Arkansas to the economy and labor systems of the Southeast. The advent of cotton cultivation increased the Quapaws' significance for white American settlers and their government—but that significance lay in their being obstacles to settlement rather than potential partners. Cotton growers demanded a certain kind of land, and the Quapaws had it. This set the stage for their removal.

Concurrent with changes in the Quapaws' economic standing was their cultural marginalization. Cultural differences between them and Americans were most stark in the failure to develop either fictive or real kinship ties, a means by which the Quapaws had expanded their population as well as their resource base. After the Louisiana Purchase, kinship would hold a very different meaning in Arkansas than it had during the French and Spanish eras. Unlike French Creoles, white Americans and their government viewed Indians as strangers or, at most, possible trading partners, not potential kin. The settlers who came to Arkansas thought of family almost entirely in terms of connections to kinship networks east of the Mississippi. They came in family groups or found their marriage partners among white American families. Some business-minded men did marry the daughters of French creole merchants. The Scull brothers, for example, married into two of the most prominent Arkansas colonial families. Hewes Scull married Athanasia Bogy, the daughter of merchant Joseph Bogy, and James Scull married Mary Felicite de Vaugine, the daughter of a former Arkansas Post military officer and granddaughter of a former Post commandant.[8] Such marriages allowed Americans entrée into established Arkansas families and allowed Creoles a means to strengthen ties to the new regime. But what was good for both of these groups was not necessarily good for the Quapaws, who soon found themselves outside marital alliances of power.

By 1819 the eastward-bearing kin networks among Americans had taken on political importance. The creation of Arkansas Territory that year brought a new influx of men and their families to the region. Through them, Arkansas became more closely attached to the American political elite. The first territorial secretary, who frequently acted as governor, was Robert Crittenden, the ambitious younger brother of Kentucky senator John J. Crittenden. Crittenden would be surpassed in importance in the 1820s by a network of extended kin known as the "Family." Like him, members of the Family had relatives with considerable influence in national politics, including Kentucky senator Richard M. Johnson, the reputed killer of Tecumseh and future vice president; and William Rector, the surveyor general for Illinois, Missouri, and Arkansas.[9] The culture they carried with them was not just American but also southern upper class. In Arkansas they hoped to replicate that culture, one increasingly tied to a new ecology—cotton agriculture. They apparently used their political influence to reshape federal Indian policy to that end.

Many new settlers, like the political elites, maintained connections with their eastern relatives, some of whom they encouraged to immigrate, and retained their emotional link to the eastern United States. For them Arkansas was a land of opportunity. In 1819 Robert Henry wrote to his brother that the territory was a land of "unspoiled forests and uninhabited prairies . . . [w]here government was in its first grade, where offices were not filled; in short, where all teeming possibilities of a new country were yet to be unravelled."[10] Whenever it became clear that Arkansas was not "uninhabited" territory, white Americans endeavored to make it so—at least as far as Indians were concerned.

American newcomers began to form their own ties to the land, exclusive of Indians. In contrast to the French, American settlers built communities in part to insulate themselves from the possibility of becoming Indian. Many immigrants—and their eastern families—feared that the Arkansas frontier could make them more like Indians in appearance and attitude. The expulsion of the tribes for them was part of the process of civilizing the frontier and preventing the acculturation of whites into Indian and wilderness life.[11]

For both the emerging elite in Arkansas and humble white settlers, then, the case for removal was not complicated. The Quapaws were impediments economically and threats to white Americans' cultural integrity. They were strangers rather than allies or kin. They had to go. Yet this ambition initially ran counter to federal intentions. The government hoped to civilize and acculturate the Indians so they could live in peace with their white neighbors. But Americans living on the frontier, competing with the Indians for land, did not see it that way.[12]

As white settlers expected the federal government to help expel Indians, the Quapaws tried to build bonds with that same authority once it finally got around to treating with them. U.S. officials sought the opening of Quapaw claims in western Arkansas to settlement by southeastern Indians, in this case the Choctaws. The Quapaws believed this signaled an American attempt to establish better relations. They had referred to the president as "Father" and other officials as "Brother" since the Americans' arrival, and they viewed the 1818 negotiations over a land cession as another opportunity to shape the relationship in the traditional manner—on kinship terms.[13]

The federal government did not establish the sort of relationship the Quapaws desired, but neither in its early dealings with the tribe did it pursue the complete displacement white settlers apparently demanded. U.S. officials had another objective—to negotiate a treaty that acquired land with the least conflict, controversy, and cost. Since the 1790s, the federal government had attempted to find a way to acquire land for the growing white population while respecting Indian wishes to remain on their homelands. By such treaties officials hoped to reduce tensions on the frontier.[14]

By 1816, negotiators were concerned about the rising disturbances between the Quapaws and their white neighbors and saw this as a chance to bring the Indians under the authority of American law. The Quapaws complained that whites intruded on their lands; whites claimed that Quapaws as well as Choctaws were killing their cattle and hogs and stealing their horses (with white settlers moving onto Quapaw lands, the livestock of each group might intermingle). The Grand Jury of Arkansas County went so far as to suggest that, "unless the growing evil can soon be checked, the situation of stockholders in the county will be deplorable, as well as the safety of the inhabitants." The hope on both sides was for the appointment of an Indian agent. Instead, the remedy offered by the 1818 treaty was to place offenses committed by or against the Quapaws under the jurisdiction of the laws of the United States or the Territory of Missouri (later, Arkansas). If it was proven that a Quapaw stole any property, especially horses, money could be deducted from the Indians' government annuity as compensation.[15]

Both objectives of negotiators, gaining land cessions and establishing legal jurisdiction, drew the Quapaws into American political relations but did not create the reciprocal, coequal relationship the Quapaws had established with European officials. Power had shifted. The Quapaws, who had once incorporated others who came to Arkansas, were now placed within a larger governing system unlike the colonial structures of either the French or the Spanish.[16] Gradually they were losing control of their lives.

Even the treaty-making protocol revealed the changing dynamics. No longer was the calumet ceremony at the center of the ritual; the signing of a document was. The written word overtook oral diplomacy. Still, the Quapaws tried to absorb this new way within their own customs. Heckaton, the principal chief by 1818, saw the treaty in terms of traditional Quapaw diplomacy and held his copy of the document as sacred.[17]

The 1818 treaty, which saw the Quapaws cede all but two million acres of their vast claims south of the Arkansas River, would further a policy that had been devised in a world before the Louisiana Purchase— before the wholesale removal of Indians seemed possible. Unlike the treaties with eastern tribes, this agreement did not specifically mention a broader policy objective, the "civilization" of Indians, but it clearly had that intent. While a great deal of cultural interchange had occurred between Quapaws and Europeans, Americans saw adaptation as moving in a single direction. Beginning with the Indian Trade and Intercourse Act of 1790, the U.S. government campaigned for revolutionary change in Indian societies in order to assimilate them into American culture. Quapaw women had traditionally been the farmers, while men were the hunters and warriors. The American plan called for Indian men to give up hunting for farming and herding and for Indian women to stop laboring in the fields and focus on work in the home, such as spinning and weaving. To aid this process of civilization, the government provided farm implements and training for Indian men.[18]

For the Quapaws this "civilization" program promised to do much more than simply reshuffle men's and women's economic responsibilities. It would require a radical reordering of Quapaw social and religious beliefs and a redefinition of manhood and womanhood. Work defined gender such that the meaning of Quapaw manhood was tied to hunting and womanhood to farming. By the late eighteenth century, the important role the men had played in the defense of the Louisiana colony had diminished. If they were no longer warriors and, under the civilization program, would no longer be hunters, would they still be men? U.S. policymakers, informed by their own gender ideology, had an easy answer. For the Quapaws, though, the answer was not so simple.

Work not only defined manhood and womanhood in Quapaw society but also shaped the ways Quapaws related to both the surrounding environment and the spiritual world. Women's ecological relationships were defined by farming and gathering edible plants. Men learned the environment a different way—through the work of hunting and fishing.[19] Reordering gender-based work could disrupt the reciprocity on which Quapaw society and spirituality rested. Women and men performed separate rituals to harness blessings for their labor, but each gender's rituals were understood to enhance the strength of all of the people. Women and men thus sustained the order and unity of the tribe by their complementary work. Rearranging their responsibilities would require a spiritual rebalancing of Quapaw society.[20]

The government's civilization program, then, demanded more than that men do women's work. By taking farming out of the hands of Quapaw women, it thus proposed to deny them the source of both their economic and their spiritual power (which was often hidden from U.S. officials). The Quapaw system denied women overt political power, and American authorities did not recognize what influence their distinct work and rituals did accord them.

For all its disruptive potential, some Quapaws were amenable to the Americans' urgings. When John Treat had finally been appointed agent to the Quapaws in 1807, one of his most important responsibilities had been "to encourage the Introduction of some of the arts of Civilization, the improvement of Agriculture and domestic manufactures." To carry out his duties successfully, he believed annuities should be employed to influence the Quapaws in the direction of acculturation and reward them for their agricultural and herding pursuits.[21] In a meeting with Treat, the Quapaws made it clear they knew that the government intended that they should "place less dependence upon the Chase for a Livelihood, and become more accustom'd to cultivating the soil." The Quapaws thought they could easily comply since they already raised enough corn and horses to trade the surplus to their white neighbors.[22] In light of the American goal, they had found it all the more extraordinary that the government would not consistently support but instead ignored them. In 1813 two Quapaws, Pa-He and She-Dusta, informed officials that they had no plows and only a few hoes for farming.[23]

While negotiating the treaty of 1818, the Quapaws clearly indicated that part of the payment for their land cession should be made in "necessary stock and other articles and . . . requested a temporary agent may be appointed to reside among them and instruct them."[24] The treaty provided for the sort of annuity that Treat had encouraged, but officials also hoped that immigrant Indians from the Southeast, who had nearly two decades of experience with the civilization program, would serve as role models for the western tribes. Treaty negotiators, including William Clark, governor of Missouri Territory and erstwhile explorer, saw the Cherokees as the vanguard: "Civilization is rapidly progressing among them and the influence of their example is so perceptibly diffusing itself among neighboring Tribes as to promise infinitely more success than could possibly be expected for that purpose conducted by white agents." The negotiators added that the Quapaws were "extremely desirous of adopting the habits and improvements of the Cherokees."[25]

Although some Quapaws accepted the government's plan, even they may not have interpreted the policy the way the Americans intended. Nowhere in official accounts is there a clear indication that these Quapaws understood that in placing "less dependence upon the Chase for a Livelihood," men would relinquish hunting completely and would replace women in the farm fields. The Quapaws, like many Cherokees, may have believed that the civilization program simply endorsed and enhanced women's role. In the late 1830s, after removal to the Indian Territory, some men continued to reject agricultural labor because it was women's work.[26]

As with the Cherokees, many Quapaws' willingness to embrace acculturation would not spare them displacement from Arkansas. The increasing settlement of white Americans in the territory changed the course of federal policy toward the Quapaws. As happened in the East, settlers' voracious appetite for land undermined the old policy of civilization and land cessions and narrowed the government's options to removal alone. Before the original policy of acculturation had a chance to succeed with the Quapaws, the growing importance of cotton and the declining trade in furs and deerskins began to threaten their homeland.[27]

The call for Quapaw removal began just a few years after the 1818 treaty. By the middle of the 1820s, their population had declined further to 455, which must have made them seem easier to deal with or to dispose of. Initially Robert Crittenden, as principal negotiator for the United States, reached an agreement with the Quapaws for a further land cession: the Quapaws would retain a strip of land along the Arkansas but relinquish their claims to land west to the Ouachita River. Soon after, though, Crittenden received orders from Secretary of War John C. Calhoun to negotiate not a land cession but complete removal. During the talks, Crittenden had written Calhoun requesting funds to buy all of the tribe's territory. Calhoun's removal order was, accordingly, based on his understanding of the wishes of Arkansas's white population. Crittenden, not surprisingly, did not proceed with the land cession; instead he pressured the Quapaws to sign a removal treaty of the sort he and other territorial officials had desired all along. Persuaded by territorial delegate Henry Conway, Congress appropriated the necessary money.[28]

In this 1824 treaty the Quapaws agreed to move to Caddo lands in northeastern Louisiana and southwestern Arkansas. Several métis and their families, who already lived apart from the villages, were allowed to stay on land grants in the cession. Of these, only Sarasin, who had received a medal from territorial governor James Miller, did not accept his grant; he instead chose to go with the people. By this time, however, even the grantees, as well as their French and métis neighbors, were viewed by American newcomers as having "gone native" and were gradually excluded from the emerging political and legal system.[29]

Reluctant to leave, the Quapaws by the next year wanted to renegotiate. The hold of the land of their fathers was still strong. The land had not only been shaped by their ancestors but also was a real and active force in their spiritual lives. In burial their ancestors had become a part of the land, making the land itself kin.[30] But the pleas of Heckaton, the principal chief, fell on deaf ears. Although the exact words were those of an interpreter, his message was clear: "The land we now live on, belonged to our forefathers. If we leave it, where shall we go to? All of my nation, friends and relatives, are there buried. Myself am old, and in the same place I wish to deposit my bones. . . . To leave my natal soil, and go among red men who are aliens to our race, is throwing us like outcasts upon the world."[31]

Having lost their place in the economy and culture of Arkansas, the Quapaws had held one thing vital to their life as a people—their land, their physical place, which gave them ties to their ancestors and their history. Now, however, they literally found themselves without a place.

The Quapaws' journey was not as dangerous as some other removals would be. Their problems really began when they arrived unexpected by the Caddos or their agent, George Gray. The Caddos were none too happy to see them.[32] Although these lands were not entirely unknown to the Quapaws, their unfamiliarity with the topography of the Red River valley soon became apparent. They settled on the Caddo Prairie, which straddled the Arkansas-Louisiana line. Below them was the Great Raft of the Red River, a giant mass of uprooted trees and vegetation. As the raft grew, it diverted the river onto the floodplain and created a large swamp.[33] In the spring of 1827, a combination of the growing raft and the rising waters of the Red flooded Caddo Prairie. Without natural levees like those on the south bank of the Arkansas, Quapaw fields twice were flooded and ruined. Making matters worse, the government's mismanagement and indifference denied them even the annuity supposed to be paid for their homeland. Sixty of the 455 Quapaws died of starvation.[34]

This first wholesale removal of Indian peoples with the support of the federal government was a preview of coming tragedies. But it was also noteworthy for something unique in the history of Indian removal: the Quapaws returned home. The spiritual pull of place worked with tragedy's shove. In 1827 Sarasin led one-third of the nation back to the Arkansas River. It was an unprecedented act of defiance on the part of the Quapaws, with their tradition of peace. By 1830 the rest of the nation had returned. Sarasin, later joined by Heckaton, began a campaign to turn the Quapaws into Americans. They wanted to use the annuity to buy agricultural implements, to educate their sons in the ways of the whites, and most controversial of all, to buy land like "their white brothers." But there was more to the effort than remaking the Quapaws into whites; it was a way in which the Quapaws could use the law and customs of the new order to heal the broken ties of kinship with the land and their ancestors.

In making this effort, Sarasin continued the traditional Quapaw strategy for dealing with whites. He tried to draw the Americans into the network of kinship, both by referring to his white brothers and by recounting his own métis bloodline (now elderly, he had been born in a different world, the son of a Quapaw woman and a French man).[35] At the same time, Sarasin and the other chiefs offered a vision of kinship with Americans that demanded protection and support in their time of need. The chiefs implored the secretary of war:

From our wish to become citizens and to be amenable to the laws of the United States We wished our Father Gov[ernor] Izard to expend of this money one Hundred Dollars to purchase us Ploughs, Hoes, & Axes and two hundred Dollars a year to the teacher who was teaching our Children the balance we wished him to keep in his hands for the Purpose of bying the Lands we had settled upon in Arkansas as soon as it would be offered for sale Our Father & friend Gov[ernor] Izard was called for by the Great Spirit and he left us He left Colo[nel] Ashley and Colo[nel] Bernard Smith (who both live at Little Rock) to take charge of his property the Ploughs, Hoes and Axes arrived and these men sold them at public auction as the private property of Gov[ernor] Izard and one cent of the Fifteen Hundred Dollars we have not recd.[36]

As Sarasin and Heckaton negotiated with federal and territorial officials, their people tried to find a new place for themselves in the growing cotton economy. Despite the government's earlier civilization program and the efforts of Sarasin and other Quapaw leaders, traditional gender roles persisted among many Quapaws, though in a very different setting. Women worked at agriculture, but some did so as field laborers picking cotton. They rebuilt homes and replanted cornfields. Some men still hunted for trade with merchants and ran horses, possibly stolen, from the Red River valley to the Arkansas, while others hunted and provided meat for white farm families. But the foodways of white settlers reduced opportunities for trade. A printer for the *Arkansas Gazette,* writing to his brother about Little Rock, exclaimed: "We live entirely on corn bread and salt pork, which are the staples of the country. The Indians sometimes bring deer and buffalo meat to town and try to sell it, but the folks are such intolerants that they seldom purchase any. They think there is nothing like a dead hog."[37]

As the Quapaws struggled to survive, some challenged the chiefly leadership and the order of the tribe. Heckaton, writing to the secretary of war, attributed this confrontation to a breakdown in gift exchange and, therefore, his ability to lead. "For what you will not give the annuity to the Quappaws my children," he asked,

All know that you have drawn it since last March. Col. Rector informed me last April that he was coming in 10 or 15 days and pay the annuity to us he came according to his promise but no

money with him he came a second time as he did before. . . .
[W]hat deceitful man? We cannot believe in him no longer he
had his tongue to [sic] much forked; but you, my dear Brother,
you should come and pay us the annuity, you know yourself
that we are indebted to Mr. F[rederick] Notrebe and to Mr.
[Antoine] Barraque and by not paying them I have no more
credit her[e], we are also indebted to Mr. [Wigton] King for the
tuition of my children, etc. and by not having the money in time
the Quappaws dissatisfied have attempted on my life several
times and will do so yet if you don't come and put stop by
paying them their money if I can not fulfil my promise, I will
be oblige to make a full statement of all facts concerning our
situation and send it to Washington.[38]

Heckaton's critics, though, blamed his drunkenness for some of the
Quapaws' troubles. In an 1831 letter to Pres. Andrew Jackson, other
Quapaw leaders chided Heckaton for agreeing, under the influence of
"spirits" and congressional delegate Ambrose Sevier, to the appointment
of Col. Wharton Rector as Quapaw agent. Other of the chief's decisions
left him open to charges of poor leadership. He had agreed to the use of
$900 of the Quapaws' $2,000 annuity for the education of four boys at
the Choctaw Academy in Kentucky run by and located on the plantation
of Sen. Richard M. Johnson. To make matters worse, the annuity was
scheduled to be reduced to $1,000 in just two years.[39]

The schooling of the four boys suggests in another way the extent to
which many Quapaws had embraced the earlier federal emphasis on
acculturation. Founded in 1825, the Choctaw Academy served Choctaw
and other Indian children whose education was financed by tribal annuities and the Civilization Fund, a government program for Indian education. The academy intended to shift Indian children away from traditional
patterns in work. Boys were taught agriculture and the "mechanical arts,"
while girls learned the pleasures of weaving, spinning, and sewing. Two
of the Quapaws enrolled at the academy in 1830 were, like Choctaw students, given names that sounded more civilized: Washington Eaton and
Rufus King.[40] The hope of government officials was that these few children would return to their peoples and spread the gospel of white
American culture.

Not every Quapaw agreed with the government's plan for education.
But even those who did not object to the schooling of their sons protested
this use, or misuse, of their annuities. Wigton King, a local teacher, had

taught a group of Quapaw boys for less expense than the Choctaw Academy.[41] Yet the use of annuity funds for the education of Quapaw children instead enriched Arkansas political elites and their extended families. As a member of Congress, Senator Johnson of Kentucky made sure there was financial support for Indian education and, therefore, his academy. His ties to the Family through his brother Benjamin only ensured support for his efforts from Arkansas. Sevier was able to squelch the Quapaws' protest against diversion of their annuity to the Choctaw Academy.[42]

More objectionable still to many Quapaws was that their growing dependence on the annuities was causing some of their leaders to follow the desires of a government program that challenged their customs. Annuities were not like the gifts of French or Spanish officials; nor were they part of a reciprocal exchange. American officials used them as a means to bind Indians to the government as wards, not partners or allies.

The Quapaws were being forced to rely on the kindness of others. By 1832 their challenge was not merely how to live and trade in a changing environment—now they struggled to survive. White settlers moving into the river valley increasingly pushed the Quapaws out of their homes and into the swamps.[43] The Quapaws were "outcasts upon the world," as Heckaton had once feared, and they were outcasts in Arkansas. Territorial officials, many of them members of the Family, continued to thwart Quapaw efforts to remain. They withheld annuities and supplies due the Quapaws and opposed their petitions to buy land. By 1833 the Quapaws were desperate. The new territorial governor, John Pope, a Jacksonian, got the Jackson administration's attention by supporting the Quapaws' efforts to buy land in Arkansas, but the government instead renegotiated removal. Impoverished and politically divided by the changes that had undermined their place in Arkansas for three decades, the Quapaws again agreed to depart, this time to the Indian Territory.[44]

The consequences of removal would haunt the Quapaws for the next several decades. Divisions within the tribe between the followers of Sarasin and Heckaton created by the first effort at removal lingered, and some groups did not immediately move to the Indian Territory. Those who followed Heckaton had to contend with bureaucratic confusion over the exact location of their new land and suffered one final removal within the Indian Territory in 1839. In time the remnants made their way to the new Quapaw home, ending the tribe's long sojourn in Arkansas.[45]

The Quapaws' exile from their homeland should remind us of the variety of experiences within the larger tragedy of Indian removal and demonstrates that for native peoples the Louisiana Purchase was not a story of progress and opportunity, but a darker tale of dispossession and forced migration. The Louisiana Purchase and the arrival of American settlers rapidly undid the Quapaws' well-developed system of trade and marital alliances with other peoples. As the white population increased and its political control expanded, it directed its power and its own familial connections to reenvision and reshape the Arkansas landscape for new purposes, especially the growing of cotton.

The Louisiana Purchase and the Black Experience

CHARLES F. ROBINSON II

For many Americans the bicentennial of the Louisiana Purchase marked a time for festive celebration. Throughout the thirteen states of the South and the plains that emerged from this vast territorial acquisition, institutions both public and private scheduled elaborate commemorative activities. Almost without exception, these events lauded the purchase as representing a "rebirth of America" and setting the stage "for the nation to become the superpower that it is today."[1] This tendency to view the acquisition of the Louisiana territory as a positive good is nothing new. Since 1803, Americans have heralded it as a great and progressive event. In June of that year, the editor of the *Boston Independent Chronicle* wrote, "we hope this highly excellent event will contribute to unite the candid and honest of every party and increase the peace, liberty, and safety of this favored country."[2] After signing the treaty of cession, Robert Livingston, one of the two American ministers sent to Paris, solemnly declared: "We have lived long, but this is the noblest work of our whole lives. . . . For this day the United States take their place among the powers of the first rank. . . . The instrument which we have signed . . . prepares ages of happiness for innumerable generations of human creatures."[3] Thomas Jefferson echoed this sentiment, praising the purchase for "enlarging the empire of liberty" and affording "a government so free and economical as ours the opportunity to extend happiness to many."[4]

Yet neither today's effusive nostalgia or yesterday's rhetorical optimism tells the whole story of the Louisiana Purchase. Acquiring the territory might have extended liberty for some, but for many others it signified the continuation and even expansion of an egregious and oppressive bondage. Although African Americans might join the majority in celebrating the purchase, in many respects to do so requires either that they don historical blinders or juggle history in such a way as to value the national good over the racial evil fostered by the purchase. Far from benefiting from this seminal event in American history, blacks already in the Louisiana territory found themselves shackled with new taskmasters, while many slaves east of the Mississippi would be transported away from their families and places of birth to grow cotton in the newly acquired American territory. And despite Americans' rhetorical embrace of liberty, Louisiana's new rulers would prove less compromising than the former ones when it came to the laws governing race and slavery.

The French established African slavery in Louisiana long before Americans took control of the area. Between 1719 and 1731, almost six thousand Africans were brought to Louisiana, quickly coming to outnumber whites. Many would work as slaves on the tobacco and indigo plantations at the southern end of the vast French claim.[5] The French attempted to model slavery in Louisiana on the institution as it existed in the French West Indies. Thus in 1724 the Code Noir, implemented in 1685 by Louis XIV to regulate slavery throughout the colonial empire, was extended to Louisiana. The code detailed the Crown's expectations of both slaves and masters, requiring strict obedience of the former while limiting the latter in the infliction of punishments. It also obliged owners to provide slaves with religious instruction, mandated certain standards in feeding and clothing them, and prohibited the separation of married couples.[6]

Although designed to protect the slave system, the Code Noir allowed manumissions. Masters over the age of twenty-five could free slaves, though only with the permission of the Superior Council, the colony's governing body. But while Article 54 declared that emancipated slaves had the same rights as freeborn persons, other articles limited equality before the law and subjected them to reenslavement for a number of offences. The code denied free blacks the right to inherit the property of or to receive gifts from former owners. Neither could freed blacks intermarry with whites.[7]

If the Code Noir legislated limits on masters in their handling of slaves, in practice it offered very little protection to either slaves or free persons of color in Louisiana. The treatment slaves received and the material conditions in which they lived seem to have been governed much more by the changing fortunes of staple-crop agriculture than by the letter of the law. The rural territory's dispersed populations worked against enforcement of the code, and slave masters routinely breached it with impunity.[8] Even when violations came to the attention of the Superior Council, masters often avoided severe punishment. Such was the case in 1730 when Amyault D'Auseville, a plantation owner, charged his lessee, Jacques Charpentier, with causing slave women to miscarry by his cruel beatings. D'Auseville also claimed that Charpentier violated other portions of the code by forcing himself sexually on female slaves and requiring them to work on Sundays. Although other whites confirmed some of D'Auseville's accusations, the Superior Council merely fined Charpentier. The code allowed for the confiscation of slave property in such cases, but the Superior Council chose not to do so. Instead, the abused slaves would continue to have to endure their brutal master.[9]

Another example of the limited protection the Code Noir afforded slaves can be seen in the experiences of a runaway slave named Guela. In 1737 authorities apprehended Guela and charged him with violating the code with his frequent, unauthorized absences from his plantation. Guela defended himself by blaming his penchant for running away on the cruel treatment he received at the hands of his master, who he claimed beat him frequently and failed to provide him with adequate food. Instead of investigating Guela's charges, as seemingly required by the Code Noir, the attorney general sentenced the slave to be punished by branding and having his ears cut off. Although no evidence exists to confirm that the sentence was carried out, Guela probably received the harsh penalty.[10]

Because of the brutality and rigor of their lives under French rule, blacks in the lower Mississippi valley often attempted to escape their condition. Some committed suicide rather than submit to enslavement, while others, like Guela, ran away. Throughout the French period, abandonment remained a persistent problem plaguing French masters in southern Louisiana.[11] Volunteering to assist either French colonials or their Native

American adversaries served as another means by which some slaves found freedom. In 1729, after the French had tried to seize the best lands of the Natchez Indians, the latter struck back and, with the help of some runaway slaves, killed about two hundred whites. The French feared that the attack signaled the beginnings of a potentially deadly alliance between natives and slaves. Therefore the French governor, Étienne Périer, recruited a small group of slaves, offering them emancipation if they helped in an assault on a nearby peaceful Indian village. The slaves agreed and participated in the massacre. From that point on the French continued to employ black freedmen in a limited way against native groups. A genuine Indian-slave alliance never fully materialized.[12]

French control of Louisiana came to an end in 1763, when Britain forced France to cede the colony to Spain. This change in colonial rulers meant that slaves and free people of color would now have new regulations governing them. Some historians have argued that Spanish slavery was a milder form than that imposed elsewhere in the Americas, such as by the English and subsequently in the United States. Citing the important role the Catholic Church played in colonial governance in Iberian societies, Frank Tannenbaum contends that Spanish slaves enjoyed greater legal and religious protections.[13] Other historians have disagreed, suggesting that Spanish law did not always translate into practice. In their view there existed few differences in the actual treatment of slaves in the various systems.[14] For the colony of Louisiana, the latter point of view appears to be the stronger one. Slave runaways remained as persistent a problem for the Spanish as it had been for the French. Logic would suggest that if the Spanish system had been more tolerable, then slaves would have been less inclined to flee. Some even attempted to violently overthrow the Spanish system. In 1795 slaves belonging to Julien Poydras, a Pointe Coupée planter with a reputation for being a kind master, began organizing to free themselves. Authorities discovered the plot and disrupted it, executing fifteen alleged conspirators.[15]

If Spanish rule cannot be shown to have immediately affected the material conditions of Louisiana slaves, one important factor set this era apart from the earlier French and later American periods. Spanish laws offered slaves many more opportunities to earn their freedom. Under this system, slaves abandoned by their masters or allowed to conduct themselves as free people for a number of years automatically became free. The Spanish generally liberated people of color who performed special services for the colony. Also, they recognized and encouraged slaves to purchase their freedom. This practice, known as *coartación*, empowered slaves to petition a tribunal for manumission once they had acquired a sum of money equal to their value. The state could then force a master, however reluctant, to accept the money in return for the slave's freedom.[16]

This liberal emancipation policy definitely increased the number of people of color who escaped slavery. Between 1769 and 1785 the free black population in lower Louisiana grew from 165 to 1,300. By the end of the century there were at least 2,000 free blacks there. In New Orleans alone some 1,500 blacks secured their freedom by means of *coartacíon* during the years of Spanish rule.[17] These free people of color often worked as artisans and craftsmen, making them vital to the expanding commercial economy of the region.[18] Further, because the Spanish feared that the French in Louisiana might attempt to usurp their authority, officials allowed free blacks to organize a separate militia. Service in the militia became a badge of honor to free blacks, and the force was an important component of regional stability for Spanish authorities.[19] Hence, by the time Americans took control over Louisiana in 1803, free blacks in what would become the state of Louisiana enjoyed higher social status and greater privileges than those elsewhere in the United States.[20]

This is not to say, however, that free people of color did not find their positions in society circumscribed by Spanish rules and practices. Like the French, the Spanish forbade intermarriage. They also frowned on interracial cohabitation. Spanish colonials even limited the types of dress that free women of color could wear to ensure that white women maintained a finer appearance. As historian Ira Berlin has suggested, "By the beginning of the nineteenth century, racial lines had been drawn so taut that free Negroes of property and rank feared to challenge the lowliest of whites."[21]

When the Americans acquired Louisiana in 1803, they inherited a territory in whose southern reaches slavery had been entrenched for almost a century. In fact slavery had been burgeoning there late in the Spanish period, with the increased cultivation of sugar and cotton and the importation of many more bondsmen directly from Africa.[22] One might think that the system's long tenure in the region, coupled with the fact that the United States was a slaveholding republic, ensured its continuation in Louisiana after the 1803 purchase. But in fact this was not the case, according to scholar Roger Kennedy. He argues that Americans had a real opportunity to end slavery in the region. In 1805–6 the Senate debated the very question of whether the inhabitants of Louisiana had a right to own slaves. Proponents of slavery believed that Article 3 of the purchase agreement, a clause guaranteeing residents of the territory the "rights, advantages, and immunities" of citizens of the United States, assured that slavery would continue in the region. Opponents, led by James Hillhouse of Connecticut, held that the clause conveyed no such right. Kennedy contends that during these debates, Thomas Jefferson had a meaningful opportunity to throw his prestige and political weight behind the antislavery cause but failed to do so. In Kennedy's view, had the president acted decisively, the southern portions of the Louisiana territory might have become a land of subsistence farmers rather than one of staple-crop planters.[23]

If anything, the laws governing slavery became harsher with the United States' acquisition of Louisiana. Early on, Americans' chief concern when it came to their new territory was securing control. From their prospective the population of the future state of Louisiana comprised a motley crew of disappointed Frenchmen, disaffected Spaniards, dangerous slaves, and potentially insurrectionary free blacks. For nine months after being named the first territorial governor, William C. Claiborne "followed orders to maintain the status quo" until Congress could create new governing provisions for the area. In March 1804 the first series of regulations arrived for the Territory of Orleans (that year the purchase had been divided into the Territories of Orleans in the south and Louisiana to the north; Orleans later became the state of Louisiana). Their focus was clear. Americans would attempt to stem the tide of slave imports from Africa to the region. Section 10 of the ordinance banned the entry of slaves from anywhere outside the boundaries of the United States. American citizens would have the exclusive right to introduce such slaves to the territory, and these slaves had to have been born in the United States or imported prior to 1798.[24]

These restrictions on the sorts of slaves allowed to enter Orleans Territory reflected Americans' growing concern over the racial revolution that had taken place in French-controlled St. Domingue. Since the beginning of the French Revolution in 1789, with its emphasis on "liberty, equality, and fraternity," free people of color on French-held Caribbean islands had been challenging their white rulers for more political and social power. By 1793, with the backing of the new French Republic, free people of color took effective control of St. Domingue. Yet the troubles were not over. Soon slaves began warring against their free black rulers in an attempt to win their freedom. Americans feared slaves from that region because they viewed them as probable insurrectionists who could spread French notions of universal equality.[25]

Governor Claiborne favored the prohibitions and sought to enforce them. Yet he soon discovered that the majority of area planters did not agree with him. Throughout the spring and summer of 1804, planters held special meetings to protest the restrictions. They also sent a memorial to Congress signed by two thousand heads of families registering their opposition to the measure. These actions of Orleans whites along with others reminded Claiborne of the tenuous nature of American control of the region. Fearing possible insurrection now on two fronts, the governor and other American leaders decided to bring a greater measure of security to the territory by nurturing a potential ally, free people of color—as the Spanish had before them.

The treatment of black militia might serve as a useful indicator of the fate of the free black community more generally under the American regime. During the Spanish period black members of this force had attained an elevated social status. Upon the arrival of the Americans, they quickly registered their loyalty to the United States. The garrison commander, Gen. James Wilkinson, noted three weeks after the Americans took the helm: "The Jelousies of the People of Color & the whites seem to be increasing, & if I may judge from what I see & hear, the former are most to be relied [sic] by us for they have universally mounted the Eagle in their hats & avow their attachment to the United States—while the latter still demonstrate their love for the Mother Country and do not conceal their fond Hope, that some incident . . . may return them to her bosom."[26] Free blacks generally believed that Americans would recognize them as full and equal citizens in accordance with their understanding of Article 3 of the cession treaty. Acting on this belief, leaders of the black militia requested on January 17, 1804, that their two companies be maintained under the new government.[27]

Governor Claiborne hesitated. He understood that refusing them could prove dangerous, but he fretted at the idea of having armed blacks at liberty in Louisiana's slave society. Secretary of War Henry Dearborn shared Claiborne's concerns about the militia. He directed the governor to maintain the force but to take cautious yet deliberate means to diminish its authority and size. Claiborne followed these orders and in June 1804 formally recognized the free black militia. He placed white officers in command of the company, however, even though its members initially resisted, arguing that such a move undermined their prestige in the black community and endangered company morale.[28]

This tenuous American alliance with free blacks for the security of Orleans proved to be only temporary. Not much time passed before white residents began complaining about the presence of the armed blacks. Initially Claiborne protected the right of the company to function, but after virulent protests from whites, he eventually caved in to the political pressure to dissolve them. This merely set the stage for a full-fledged assault on the rights and powers of free blacks by the government of the territory. In 1806 the legislature denied free blacks the right to carry guns without permission from a justice of the peace. It also empowered slaves to testify against free blacks in a court of law and required free blacks to be punished like slaves for certain crimes. A new law even mandated deference toward whites.[29] Subsequent legislation would attempt to control the numbers of free blacks by preventing their emigration from Spanish and French Caribbean islands.[30] By the end of 1808, the status of free blacks in the Territory of Orleans seemed bleak. Their militia had been dissolved and their rights had been scaled back.

Several events would provide some temporary reprieve from this legal assault. First, in January 1811 a group of slaves near New Orleans rose to rebellion. Startled and frightened by the prospects of the insurrection becoming more widespread, Governor Claiborne accepted the services of some free black men who offered to help quash the uprising. These men served the territory "with great exactitude and propriety," according to those whites who testified before the territorial legislature about their actions.[31]

The second thing that temporarily bolstered the importance of free blacks in the eyes of whites was the international tension surrounding the War of 1812. As American and British relations worsened, Spain, a British ally, began positioning soldiers near the border of the new state of Louisiana. Among the first units was a company of 150 black soldiers. Rumors persisted that the Spanish had corresponded with free black leaders in Louisiana in order to solicit their assistance when hostilities began. Claiborne feared that unless the state used a "certain portion of the chosen men among the free men of colour" in her defense, the foreign free black soldiers might incite slaves to rebel and to join the Spanish (who still held Texas and the Floridas) in warring against the United States. Therefore he convinced the newly formed state legislature to reorganize four companies of free blacks composed of sixty-four men each. All of the men, including the junior officers, would be from the propertied ranks of free blacks. As before, however, white commanders would lead the companies.[32]

Although Louisiana whites mustered some free blacks to the front, they remained nervous and hesitant about doing so. When leaders of the black militia approached Claiborne and requested that their numbers be expanded to include some six hundred additional men, the governor balked out of fear that such an increase would imperil the state's security rather than enhance it. In the minds of whites, free blacks and slaves shared common bonds of color and ethnicity that transcended their class differences and made them potentially dangerous allies. Even in the presence of a foreign enemy, white Louisianans never lost sight of the need to guard against the perceived enemy within.[33]

Nevertheless, desperate times produced desperate measures. By late 1814 the war was going badly for the Americans, and a British invasion of Louisiana appeared imminent. Needing troops badly, Gen. Andrew Jackson issued a message to free blacks requesting and welcoming their participation in what he called "the glorious struggle for natural rights." The general declared that past policies to exclude freed men had been "mistaken policy," and he assured them a relative equality of treatment with white soldiers. As a result more free blacks joined the militia. When Jackson fought the British at the Battle of New Orleans, approximately six hundred free blacks served in his ranks.[34] After the battle free blacks won copious praise from white Americans for their gallantry. Jackson lauded them for their "courage and perseverance," as did state lawmakers.[35]

The laudatory comments would soon cease. Once the emotional aftermath of the battle had passed and the foreign threat subsided, white Americans returned to a repressive normality that did not bode well for people of color in the state. Steadily Louisiana whites elaborated on the legal discriminations visited upon free blacks, carrying them well beyond the sumptuary laws and limitations on intermarriage imposed during the French and Spanish periods. For example, although the practice of segregating blacks in theaters and public exhibitions had long been tradition, in 1816 the City of New Orleans codified the social separation by forbidding "any white person to occupy any of the places set apart for people of color; and the latter are likewise forbidden to occupy any of those reserved for white persons." During the 1840s, when New Orleans established a new public school system, educators denied admission to the children of free blacks. In the use of a number of other public facilities, such as restaurants, saloons, streetcars, hospitals, and city cemeteries, Louisiana whites also segregated free blacks by custom or local ordinance.[36] In other enslaved portions of the old purchase territory—those that did not have a free black population of several generations' standing—free people of color would fare even worse in the eyes of the law. In Arkansas, for example, free blacks not only could not testify against whites or own guns but also had to post a $500 bond. In 1859 the Arkansas legislature went so far as to simply to order their expulsion from the state.[37]

Hobbled by the law, free people of color lacked the economic opportunity and resources that whites possessed. In fact, depending on the decade, the property assets of whites in New Orleans were five to ten times greater in value than those of blacks. Forced mostly into skilled-laborer positions, free blacks could not earn as much as their white counterparts, who had advantages in inherited wealth, education, and social standing. Free black women suffered greater economic disadvantages than did black men, for antebellum society usually placed special encumbrances in the way of female opportunity.[38]

Of course, slaves faced far more severe legal restrictions than free people of color. During the French and Spanish periods, as noted, the protections slaves enjoyed in the eyes of the law often did little to improve their actual condition. But as Americans restructured the institution in the future state of Louisiana to resemble that in other parts of the South, slaves lost even many of the legal rights granted under the French and Spanish. For example, slaves lost the right to legally marry, to hold property, and to testify against whites in a court of law. Under American regulations slaves had no right to religious instruction. The only reference in the new codes made to religion stipulated that slaves who fell ill be allowed "temporal or spiritual assistance which their situation may require." Most importantly, that aspect of the colonial code of clearest actual benefit to slaves, the Spanish practice of *coartacíon,* was done away with. In the state of Louisiana, slaves could not simply earn their freedom —they could be manumitted only by special act of the legislature.[39]

With regard to material conditions, white Americans often forced slaves to endure extremely harsh treatment in Louisiana. Most subsisted on a diet consisting chiefly of pork and cornmeal. According to historian Joe Gray Taylor, the average adult received a little over three pounds of meat and seven quarts of meal a week. Children, generally described as slaves under the age of ten, received less. In fact masters commonly used food as an incentive to get rapidly developing children to go out into the fields sooner than they would otherwise. The allotments given to slaves could be hardly sufficient to stave off pangs of hunger. Some masters allowed slaves to supplement their diets through hunting, fishing, and/or gardening. Others simply ignored their persistent hunger.[40] In response, slaves sometimes resorted to stealing, often with grave consequences. One jarring example of this can be found in the WPA interview with former slave Henrietta King. King told of an incident in which she stole a piece of candy:

Well, here's how it happened. She put a piece of candy on her wahstan' one day. I was 'bout eight or nine years ole, an' it was my task to empty de slop ev'y mornin'. I seed dat candy layin' dere, an' I was hungry. . . . I seed dat peppermint stick layin' dere, an' I ain't dared go near it 'cause I knew ole Missus jus' waitin' for me to take it. Den one mornin' I so hungry dat I cain't resist. I went straight in dere an' grab dat stick of candy an' stuffed it in my mouf an' chew it down quick so ole Missus never fin' me wid it. Nex' mornin' ole Missus say: "Herietta, you take dat piece o' candy out my room?" "No mam, ain't seed no candy." "Chile, you lyin' to me. You took dat candy." "Deed, Missus, I tel de truf. Ain't seed no candy." "You lyin' an' I'm gonna whup you. Come here." "Please, Missus, please don't whup me. I ain't seed no candy. I ain't took it." Well, she got her rawhide down from de nail by the fireplace, an' she grabbed me by de arm an' she turn me 'cross her knees whilst she set in de rocker so's she could hol' me. I twisted an' turned till finally she called her daughter. De gal come an' took dat strap like her mother tole her and commence to lay it on real hard whilst Missus holt me. I twisted 'way so dere warn't no chance of her gittin' in no solid lick. Den ole Missus lif' me up by de legs, an' she stuck my haid under the bottom of her rocker, an' she rock forward so's to hol' my haid an' whup me some mo'. I guess dey must of whupped me near a hour wid dat rocker leg a-pressin' down on my haid. Next thing I knew de ole doctor was dere, an' I was lyin' on my pallet in de hall, an' he was a-pushing' an' diggin at my face, but he couldn't do nothing at all wid it. Seem like dat rocker pressin on my young bones had crushed 'em all into a soft pulp. . . . Artar a while it was over jes' whar it is now. An I ain't never growed no mo' teef on dat side. Ain't never been able to chaw nothin' good since.[41]

Sometimes whites treated Louisiana slaves like livestock. Octavia George, born in Mansieur, Louisiana, remembered how masters fed slave children. She recalled that the children "were fed in boxes and troughs under the house. They were fed corn meal mush and beans. When this was poured into their box they would gather around it the same as we see pigs, horses, and cattle gather around troughs today."[42]

Slave children in Louisiana lived under the constant fear of being separated from parents. Although Louisiana had a law that ostensibly forbade the separation of children under the age of ten from their mothers, it applied only to those purchased from other states. It did not affect intrastate trading, neither did it circumscribe the right of masters to isolate parents and children from one another on a farm or plantation.[43] J. W. Terrell, the son of his master and a slave woman, experienced such a separation. He recalled how his father had taken him from his mother when he was six weeks old and placed him under the care of his aged maternal grandmother. The grandmother died shortly thereafter, leaving Terrell under the care of his father. Terrell described his father as a cruel man who subjected him to harsh punishments for the most trivial offenses. Eventually the man grew tired of rearing the boy and gave him to his sister. The father's sister treated Terrell kindly, but the father insisted that the child wear a bell strapped to his shoulder both day and night until he reached the age of twenty-one. He informed Terrell that the bell was "punishment for bein' born into the world a son of a white man."[44]

Louisiana slaves, like those elsewhere, also suffered from inadequate clothing. Although considerable variation could exist, adult males generally received two cotton shirts and two pair of cotton trousers for the summer and denim or blanket overcoats along with cotton shirts and jeans for the winter. Masters typically allotted adult females two cotton dresses for the summer and denim or blanket overcoats and a wool dress for the winter. Slave children received even less clothing, for masters regarded long shirts as adequate for slaves less than seven years of age. Shoes were provided only in the winter.[45]

Slave quarters in Louisiana, Taylor writes, consisted of shacks, with a family of seven or more often occupying a residence measuring no more than sixteen by eighteen feet square. These cabins had few furnishings if any, but they usually had a chimney that allowed slaves to cook and to attempt to stay warm. If masters provided bedding, the mattresses were often stuffed with corn shucks. The poor material conditions of slaves made them susceptible to a number of ailments. They often fell ill from intestinal worms, being forced to walk most of their lives barefoot on land where farm animals defecated. Louisiana slaves also suffered from "looseness of the bowels" and a number of respiratory diseases.[46]

Available evidence does not permit us to conclude that material conditions for Louisiana slaves were actually worse in the American era than under the French and Spanish. Despite the legal limitations placed on owners, there is plenty of evidence, as indicated above, of cruel treatment by French and Spanish masters. Working conditions were notoriously harsh in regions cultivating sugar, which became the staple of lower Louisiana's slave economy by late in the Spanish period. But the Louisiana Purchase certainly brought many more black people to the territory to live as slaves and spread them across a much greater expanse as American cotton agriculture pushed itself relentlessly across the Mississippi. Slaves had been a substantial part of the population in what would become the state of Louisiana during the colonial period, but in many other places in the Trans-Mississippi, slavery really blossomed only after the purchase opened the West to American slaveowners. In French and Spanish Arkansas, for instance, slaves had existed only in small numbers; perhaps sixty of the nearly four hundred residents of Arkansas Post in 1798 were black. Some did farm labor, but others worked in mercantile enterprises or as rivermen in a region whose market economy was still based on the products of the hunt.[47] By contrast, in the fifty-eight years between the Louisiana Purchase and Arkansas's secession, many thousands of African Americans would be either brought or born there as plantation agriculture became entrenched in the lowlands and slave labor became the sine qua non of the state's biggest business—cotton.[48]

The Louisiana Purchase, though a grand and joyous event for many, brought little positive change for blacks in the region. Instead, it extended slavery's reach. Prior to American occupation, the French and Spanish enslaved the vast majority of blacks in the territory. After the raising of the Stars and Stripes, most people of color retained their slave status while losing much of what opportunity had existed for them to become free. But free blacks arguably lost the most with the arrival of the Americans. Spanish rule had afforded them a measure of opportunity that U.S. hegemony fairly quickly took away.

So how should African Americans today respond to the commemorations of the Louisiana Purchase? Many ethnic groups are faced with this dilemma when reflecting upon one or another chapter of the American story. It is sometimes easy for the majority to overlook or dismiss wrongs in the nation's past since their ancestors often benefited from them. But African Americans and others find themselves constantly struggling to rectify their "two-ness" and accomplish the quite arduous task of fully celebrating America's history without excusing its most egregious aspects.[49] The only practical way for Americans to make the celebration of racially charged events from the past palatable to the nation's minority communities is to create a society in which the vestiges of past wrongs no longer negatively affect them. As long as color and ethnicity are perceived as liabilities in American society, then remembrances of the Louisiana Purchase's vicious racial reality will continue to grind exceedingly small and produce hurt and alienation. Society cannot undo its past, but by using the lessons of history, the nation can construct a more positive and progressive present and future.

8

The First Years of American Justice

Courts and Lawyers on the Arkansas Frontier

LYNN FOSTER

The Louisiana Purchase annexed millions of acres of land west of the Mississippi to the United States. In the Territory of Louisiana, stretching from what is today Arkansas up to Canada, the common-law legal system of the United States replaced the civil-law systems of France and Spain, the previous sovereigns at the scattered posts and settlements. The common-law framework of court, judge, attorneys, and juries was thus imposed on the "wild" frontier. In the years that followed, white Americans, French traders, Native Americans, and slaves petitioning for freedom would all appear in the territory's new courts, which some have characterized as "discouragingly primitive" and "crude."[1]

The record books and court files of the Arkansas Post courts from 1808 to 1814 reveal how this new judicial system operated in that remote community and the surrounding territory.[2] Studying these court records and documents not only sheds light on the practice of law on the southwest frontier but also opens a window on life in Arkansas during the first two decades after the Louisiana Purchase, a period about which we know relatively little.[3]

Within a year of the purchase, Congress created what would effectively become the state of Louisiana, naming it the Territory of Orleans. It annexed the remainder of the purchase, including Arkansas, to the Territory of Indiana as the District of Louisiana. As such, its laws were enacted by the Indiana territorial legislature, comprising Gov. William Henry Harrison and Indiana's territorial judges (in the first stage of territorial government, the governor and judges served as the legislature). A year later Congress established the District of Louisiana as a territory in its own right. Arkansas made up the southernmost portion of the Territory of Louisiana, just north of the Territory of Orleans. In 1812, when the Territory of Orleans achieved statehood and took the name of Louisiana, for clarity's sake the old Territory of Louisiana was renamed the Territory of Missouri. Arkansas remained the southernmost part of Missouri until it was granted territorial status in its own right, as the Territory of "Arkansaw," on July 4, 1819.[4]

The Louisiana Territory was subdivided into five districts in 1804.[5] Over the next decade, Arkansas was sometimes part of a larger district or county, sometimes a district or county in its own right with its own county government—a confusing state of affairs that was not conducive to the administration of justice. Even compared to other frontier jurisdictions, the Arkansas legal system would be distinguished by the frequency with which territorial governors shut down its courts, the ones farthest from the seat of government in St. Louis.

In 1804 Arkansas was part of the huge District of New Madrid. The court of record for the district sat at the town of New Madrid, over two hundred miles from Arkansas Post. The first District of Arkansas was created in 1806 by Gov. James Wilkinson and abolished in 1807 by Acting Gov. Frederick Bates. Gov. Meriwether Lewis reestablished the District of Arkansas in August 1808.[6] The Courts of Common Pleas and General Quarter Sessions of the Peace for the Arkansas District, the first functioning courts of record, convened at Arkansas Post, the district's seat of government, intermittently from December 1808 to March 1814.[7] The District of Arkansas was abolished a second time and annexed back into the new County of New Madrid in 1812 by Gov. Benjamin Howard because of the difficulty of keeping the offices at the distant Post filled and staffed.[8] But in 1814 Arkansas finally regained a permanent separate status as the County of Arkansas. Once more the Post was the seat of a court of record, now called the General Court. In 1819 the Territorial Superior Court, the highest court of the new Territory of Arkansas, was established and met briefly at Arkansas Post until the seat of government moved to Little Rock in 1821.

Although the record books of these territorial courts have been available to researchers at the Arkansas History Commission, for many years historians believed that all of the case files had been lost.[9] But during the spring of 2001, library assistant Louise Lowe discovered territorial case files mingled with the Arkansas Supreme Court Records and Briefs Collection at the University of Arkansas at Little Rock (UALR)/Pulaski County Law Library. Profs. Kathryn Fitzhugh and Lynn Foster, together with research assistants, identified twenty-five files from the period of 1808 to 1814. Coincidentally, files from Missouri territorial appellate courts housed at the Missouri State Archives were indexed and made available to remote researchers at about the same time. Some of the cases tried at Arkansas Post had been appealed to the General Court, which sat in Ste. Genevieve and St. Louis. Thus for a few of the earliest cases, an unusually large quantity of information is available from three sources: court-record books from Arkansas Post, documents filed with the Arkansas court, and appellate documents filed in Missouri. These records reveal much about courts and lawyers in Arkansas during the first years of U.S. rule.

Then as now, the common-law judicial system of the United States—inherited from England—differed markedly from those of France and Spain, the previous sovereigns over Arkansas. France and Spain, along with most nations, are "civil law" countries, whose legal systems derive from Roman law.[10] In "civilian" legal systems, the judge assumes a greater role—more a fact-finder than a referee—and attorneys do not play as prominent a part in court proceedings. The dispenser of justice in colonial Arkansas was the commandant at Arkansas Post. During the last four decades of colonial government, commandants had civil and probate jurisdiction over cases where small amounts of money were at issue (though historian Morris Arnold believes that commandants at Arkansas Post often exceeded their jurisdiction and ruled on more significant disputes without interference from the governor general in New Orleans).[11] Dispute resolution at the Post did not involve pleadings, written records, or lawyers. Indeed, "[t]he Spanish officers would not have tolerated the technicalities and quibbles of an American lawyer," William F. English has written. "All kinds of forensic disputation was discouraged, whether in the courts or in the community gatherings."[12] The jury, the right to refuse to incriminate oneself, and the writ of habeas corpus were nonexistent under the rule of France and Spain. But spouses had more equal rights in marital property because of the community property system, and generally parents could not disinherit their children under the civil law. Instead of consulting written statutes and case law, as would common-law judges, commandants at the French and Spanish posts used as authority a few volumes of laws from the civil codes and relied heavily on unwritten practices and usages of the local communities.[13]

The former French, Spanish, and American inhabitants of the Louisiana Purchase territory were ambivalent about the U.S. takeover. On the one hand, protection from Indian attacks improved with the increased number of soldiers and forts and the gradual westward movement of the frontier. On the other hand,

> [i]t was clearly perceived by the people and landowners, both French and Americans, that under the new government they would have to pay taxes, work the roads, render military service, furnish their own rifles, powder and ball, knapsacks and even provisions, in order to protect themselves against the inroads of the Indians; that the settlement of land titles provided by the Act of 1804 would take a long time, and that the method of doing business in a summary and quick way, with which they were familiar under the Spanish government, would be followed by a slower, more expensive and technical system. It was apparent that the system of litigation introduced by the Americans in upper Louisiana checked trade and hence arose great dissatisfaction. People preferred the quick judgment of one man to twelve.[14]

The French citizens of Arkansas Post would surely have noted the aspects of this new judicial system that made it slower and more cumbersome. First, there was the multiplicity of courts: common pleas, quarter sessions, oyer and terminer, orphans, and probate—all took the place of the informal meeting, without written petitions, before a single commandant. Second, the American system required far more officials. Judges, justices of the peace, prosecuting attorneys, clerks, treasurers, sheriffs, constables, coroners, recorders, and notaries public, at a minimum, administered the judicial system at the county level. Third, lawyers were a sine qua non of the new order. The American system also imposed new duties on the residents of the Post. White male citizens had a legal obligation to participate as both grand and petit jurors. Yet as inconvenient, mysterious, and confusing as public trials, especially jury trials, could be, they provided consistently entertaining theater for the community.

When the first Arkansas courts of record began operation in 1808, the Louisiana territorial statutes in force called for dual courts in each district: the Court of Common Pleas and the Court of General Quarter Sessions of the Peace. Each would hold three terms per year.[15] Their terms were set so as to allow lawyers enough time to travel a circuit from court to court (though no St. Louis or Ste. Genevieve lawyers traveled to Arkansas Post as it was simply too distant).[16] For most intents and purposes, the two courts really were one; they met on the same days and were administered by the same judges. They differed only as to their subject-matter jurisdiction and by the fact that separate record books for each were kept by the clerk. Court met six days a week, Monday through Saturday.

In the legal parlance of the times, the Court of Common Pleas could "hold pleas of assize, scire facias, replevins, and hear and determine all manner of pleas, suits, actions and causes civil, personal, real and mixed according to law."[17] This court exercised jurisdiction over civil matters (that is, suits between private parties).

The Court of General Quarter Sessions had jurisdiction over all criminal cases except for capital crimes. Originally only the General Court had jurisdiction over these, but by 1808 jurisdiction had been decentralized to special courts of oyer and terminer.[18] A judge of the General Court would travel from St. Louis to the appropriate district and sit with the judges of the Court of Common Pleas to hold the court of oyer and terminer to try capital offenses, but the record book contains no evidence that any such court ever convened at the Post.[19] Only one indictment of murder was ever issued, and the district was dissolved before the case could be tried. The Court of General Quarter Sessions issued a writ of venire—literally, a command to come—to the sheriff before and during each of its terms, requiring him to summon a grand jury. Petit juries, however, seem to have been called much more informally, probably simply from men in the vicinity of the courthouse.

The criminal law enforced by these courts was notable in numerous respects. Under a criminal statute enacted by the Louisiana territorial legislature, courts could order that the bodies of executed murderers be "delivered to a surgeon for dissection."[20] The punishment for rape was castration, "to be performed by the most skilful physician, at the expense of the territory, in case the party convicted shall not have sufficient property to pay the same and costs."[21] Other penalties for noncapital crimes included imprisonment, fines, whippings, and the pillory. It was a crime for children or servants to refuse to obey the lawful commands of their parents or masters, and if found guilty by a justice of the peace, offenders would be sent to a jail or house of correction until "they shall humble themselves to the said parent's or master's satisfaction."[22] Those convicted of capital crimes could not avail themselves of the "benefit of clergy," a legal device dating back to medieval times that enabled clergy at first—and later anyone—to escape capital punishment if they could read a passage from the Bible.[23] Slaves were largely removed from the criminal-justice system. They had the right to a jury only in cases of murder and arson; otherwise they were punished at the discretion of the court.[24]

In addition to administering the criminal law, the Court of General Quarter Sessions, like other courts of the period, had responsibilities that would fall to Arkansas county "quorum courts" today.[25] It adjusted claims regarding property tax assessments; managed the county's money; issued licenses; levied taxes on businesses such as taverns, merchants, and ferries; and authorized the planning and construction of roads, bridges, and government buildings such as courthouses and jails. During this period the welfare of the needy was the responsibility of local governments, and thus the court could also provide for the support of the indigent. The only example of this function being carried out in the period 1808–14 came in the spring of 1810, when the grand jury decided that John Taylor, an inhabitant of Arkansas who had been ill for several years, was unable to support himself. The court ordered the sheriff "to provide at as low a Rate as possible his maintenance, clothing washing and mending."[26]

The judges of the courts of common pleas and of general quarter sessions in each district were not required to be lawyers but merely "respectable inhabitants."[27] Although the statute required between three and five judges per court, only two had to be present to conduct business. Judges served terms of four years and received three dollars' pay for each day they attended court.[28]

Below these courts were the "justice of the peace courts." These had jurisdiction over "small causes" involving less than sixty dollars, mostly actions of debt. They could not hear criminal cases; actions of slander, replevin, or trespass; or cases involving title to land. The officer of the court, who carried out the orders of a justice of the peace, was not a sheriff but a constable. Appeal could be had to the Court of Common Pleas.[29] The statutes also established orphans' courts, with jurisdiction over orphaned children, which were to be held by justices of the courts of common pleas, but there is no record of such a court at Arkansas Post during this period except for one brief entry in the record book.[30] Probate courts, with separate judges and jurisdiction over the estates of deceased persons, were created as well. Probate judges could not render final judgments—those had to issue from common pleas judges—and their decisions were appealable to the General Court. There is no evidence in the record books as to whether the Probate Court met during this period.

Appeals from the various courts of common pleas and of general quarter sessions were heard in Missouri by the General Court. Originally the General Court met twice a year in St. Louis, but by 1808 the spring term had been moved to Ste. Genevieve.[31] The General Court had concurrent jurisdiction over civil and criminal cases and was the court of last resort in the Territory of Louisiana. The right to appeal ended at the boundaries of the territory; disappointed litigants could not "take a case all the way to the Supreme Court." From its inception the General Court's judges were all lawyers.

The first glimpses of this new judicial system in operation in Arkansas come from 1808. In July of that year, Territorial Secretary Frederick Bates (the equivalent of the lieutenant governor) visited Arkansas Post. Bates, who also served on the Land Commission, had traveled to Hopefield to hear persons claiming land grants from Spain.[32] Perplexed at the lack of claimants—only Joseph Stillwell, a settler along the Arkansas River, appeared—he ventured onward to Arkansas Post to attempt to collect more claims, even though they would be late. Bates did indeed find a number of claimants and their agents at the Post.[33] He had brought with him to Arkansas two blank justice-of-the-peace commissions from Gov. Meriwether Lewis. After meeting numerous men, he commissioned Benjamin Fooy, an early settler who had emigrated from Holland, to be justice of the peace at Hopefield and Capt. George Armistead, a military officer at Fort Madison at the Post, for the same position at Arkansas Post.[34] They held their positions for only a few months since they were replaced by new officials after Arkansas was made a district.

On Monday, December 5, the first session of the new courts convened at Arkansas Post. Situated near the mouth of the Arkansas River, the Post was the most populous white settlement in Arkansas from 1803 to at least 1820. It had been established in 1686, and though having fluctuated in size and changed location several times, by the first decade of the nineteenth century, it numbered around five hundred persons.[35] Cherokees lived in a number of settlements to the north along the

St. Francis River. Estimates as to their number in this location vary, for during this time there was an intermittent flow of Cherokees across the Mississippi, west through these settlements, on into northwestern Arkansas, and back. Indeed, there may well have been even more Cherokees at the largest settlement along the St. Francis than there were whites at the Arkansas Post.[36] Quapaw villages lay relatively close to the Post, upstream along the Arkansas, and Osages lived much farther to the northwest, along the Arkansas and Osage Rivers, in present-day Missouri and Oklahoma. Many of the French descendants at the Post were also descended from Quapaws, but neither Quapaws nor Osages per se appear in the early record books of the Arkansas courts. Cherokees, however, and whites living among them are mentioned with some frequency during this period. (As will be discussed later, the Cherokees actually seem to have manipulated the justice system for their own purposes.)

One caveat is in order here, however. The terms "French," "Quapaw," and "Cherokee" may conjure up images of three distinct populations, but that was far from the case. There had been extensive intermarriage between the French at the Post and the Quapaws. This led to both French-Quapaw families at the Post and Quapaw-French families at the Quapaw villages. A number of whites also lived and intermarried with the Cherokees. Many of the Cherokee leaders were part white; one, John D. Chisholm, immigrated to the United States from Scotland. This intermingling caused problems within a legal system in which one's "race" and free or slave condition—free black, mulatto, slave, Indian, white—determined one's legal status. Actual ancestry and choices of lifestyle did not fit neatly into the pigeonholes of the law.[37]

Arkansas judges and other officials were all commissioned by Gov. Meriwether Lewis and accordingly presented their commissions for the record. François Vaugine was the presiding, or chief, judge. A merchant then in his mid-forties, Vaugine was a member of a prominent French family. He had grown up in Louisiana and had lived at Arkansas Post for sixteen years.[38] Joseph Stillwell, an associate judge, had lived at the Post for ten years. Originally from New Jersey and in his mid-fifties, Stillwell had received a fifteen-by-forty-arpent grant of land from Gov. François Luis Hector, the Barón de Carondelet and had come to Arkansas to perfect this claim in 1797. He located it along the Arkansas River about four miles upstream from the Post.[39] Charles Refeld was to be the third judge, but he declined his commission. Benjamin Fooy from Hopefield accepted a commission as judge but was not present during the first term. These longtime settlers, titled "esquire" in the record book, definitely fit the statutory requirement of respectability.

The clerk of the court, John W. Honey, moved to Arkansas Post from Missouri. Honey, though, would stay in Arkansas for less than a year before returning to Missouri, where he would later hold various official posts. Besides the clerkship, Honey also held the positions of treasurer, recorder, and judge of the Probate Court. Harold Stillwell, brother of Joseph, served as sheriff.[40] During its first session the court appointed Isaac Fooy, Benjamin's brother, constable for Hopefield and Michel Pringle constable for Arkansas Post and Little Prairie.[41] André Fagot served as coroner, justice of the peace, notary public, and official interpreter for the numerous French citizens of Arkansas. At this time there were far more French than Americans living at the Post, though the ratio was changing rapidly.[42]

During the first term the Court of Common Pleas had no cases on its docket. On the criminal side the Court of General Quarter Sessions convened the Post's first grand jury. The grand jury was to hear complaints brought by anyone, including its own members, and to return "true bills" of indictment when it determined that a person most likely had committed a crime; the Sixth Amendment of the Constitution guarantees the right to indictment by a grand jury. Recently enacted statutes required a grand jury to be drawn by lot from a pool of names of "sixty honest and intelligent householder, farmers, merchants and traders . . . not being clergymen, practitioners of physic, or attorneys of any court, sheriffs, or their deputies, ferry-keepers, or constables, or such as be, or be reputed, persons of ill fame, but altogether such as be of the best fame, reputation and understanding and credit in there [sic] district."[43] Grand jurors, like petit jurors, were also required to be free white male citizens over the age of twenty-one.[44] The record book is silent as to how the jurors were selected. It is hard to believe, however, that a pool of sixty such men existed at that time at the Post.

The diversity of the white male residents at Arkansas Post is clearly seen in the composition of the first grand jury.[45] At least eight of the twenty-four men summoned were of French extraction, several others had German names, and the rest were English and Irish. The ethnic composition of the jury, though, was not proportional to the makeup of the Post's general population. Morris Arnold theorizes that the French *habitants* were reluctant to involve themselves with the court system.[46] Of the men who had been summoned, four did not appear and were subject to fines unless they could show cause for their absences.[47] Although the grand jury could consider anyone's complaint, at this first session no one came forth, and the jury was discharged the first day. Before the court adjourned, planning was begun for roads from the Post to "the Bayou" and to the "Arkansas Prairie."[48]

Following the establishment of American courts came American lawyers. Lawyers filled many roles. As judges they rendered justice (though at first few judges except those of the highest court were attorneys because a practice offered the possibility of much greater income).[49] Lawyers often served the courts in other capacities, such as justices of the peace, sheriffs, and clerks. As attorneys at law they provided the interface between courts and suitors. They functioned in other roles too, such as conveyancers, personal representatives of decedents' estates, commissioners, agents, and auditors. In the course of their activities, many of them became wealthy in land and slaves. Many also speculated in land. Since money was scarce on the frontier, lawyers accepted payment in peltries, land, slaves, and notes.

We know little about Arkansas's first attorney at law. Perly Wallis appeared before the judges during the December 1808 term and was admitted to the bar. In order to practice as an attorney at law before any court in the Territory of Louisiana, statutes required the applicant to present a license from one or more of the judges of the General Court (the highest bench in the territory).[50] Wallis produced "sufficient document of his good and Moral Character and of his having been a practising Attorney in a former Court of this District."[51] This court was probably the justice-of-the-peace court of Capt. Henry Armistead.[52] In September 1808 Wallis had written to Frederick Bates, after the latter's visit to Arkansas Post, reporting the apprehension of some felons and an alleged murderer and stating that he had lent Armistead "every assistance in my Power which Perhaps was very imperfect as we have not the Laws of the Teritory."[53] Because Wallis was not admitted to practice by the General Court until the following year, and therefore unlikely to have been licensed by one of its judges, Morris Arnold has concluded that Wallis was illegally admitted to practice during that first term.[54] This seems to be true, but the actions of the judges become more understandable when one recalls that none of them were lawyers. Based on his skill at pleading and his success rate, Wallis was almost certainly an experienced lawyer. Bates stated that Wallis was from nearby "Ouachita."[55] He had already been practicing law within the district. Surely it would have been desirable to have at least one lawyer around. An attorney at law was necessary to prosecute criminal cases, and as compared with his first competitors, Wallis displayed a superior knowledge of the law.

In early Arkansas, as now, public opinion of lawyers was ambivalent. Although most were effective and performed valuable and necessary services, many lawyers were perceived as unscrupulous. They were closely identified with land speculators, who were also the objects of public fear and derision. The practice of law could be violent, owing not only to the general lawlessness of frontier communities but also to the "code duello." Judges and lawyers settled personal and political disagreements by dueling, even as far north as St. Louis, and judges routinely sat armed in the courtroom.[56] Some of these dueling jurists, however, rose to prominence in their communities and became the namesakes of Arkansas towns and counties. But how did these frontier attorneys build a practice in the first place? Perly Wallis's appearances in the early courts of Arkansas are illuminating.

The Court of Common Pleas opened its first session in December 1808 but adjourned after three days for lack of cases to hear. During the next session, which convened on Monday, April 3, 1809, Perly Wallis, being the only attorney at law, represented four plaintiffs—François Michel, George Hook, William Hickman, and William Bradford—in five actions of debt and trespass on the case.[57] The amounts at stake ranged from $207 to $2,754. Two of the suits were discontinued by his clients, resulting in their having to pay the costs of the defendants. The others were continued over until the August term.[58] The record book does not list Wallis as attorney for any civil defendants; plaintiffs were more promising clients.

On the criminal side, in the Court of Quarter Sessions of the Peace, Perly Wallis presented a commission from "John Scot Esquire Attorney General of the Territory of Louisiana" that appointed Wallis deputy attorney general for the District of the Arkansas, and he was sworn in.[59] As deputy attorney general, Wallis would bring charges before the grand jury and prosecute criminal cases. During this term he had a wide-open field, being the only attorney on either the criminal or the civil dockets. Parties not represented by him either represented themselves, appearing in their "own proper person," or granted a power of attorney to another person who then represented them in court as an "attorney in fact" (as opposed to an attorney at law).[60]

During the April 1809 term the court held six jury trials and three bench trials. There being only a small number of adult white males at Arkansas Post available to participate in the judicial system, the record books bring to mind the game of musical chairs. A defendant could be dismissed from charges one day and sit on someone else's jury the next. Three men on the jury in one of Wallis's cases were Wallis's clients in other cases already begun and continued until the next term.[61] Trials were held with dispatch—often several would take place in a single day—with the same jury sitting all day long. During this term all of the charges were assault and battery except for two. In one, John Berry was charged with "treating Indians with whiskey and getting them drunk." He was found guilty and sentenced to court costs and ten days in prison.

The second charge of the grand jury was against Wallis himself. On the second day of term, John Breck Treat, the Indian agent at the Arkansas Post factory, brought a complaint to the grand jury against Perly Wallis.[62] In the instrument filed with the grand jury, Treat claimed:

> A number of Suits suppos'd ten, or eleven have since the last Court been commenced at this place. At this time by inquiry at the Clerk's office eight of those Suits are quashed, or directed to be discontinued. One Lawyer, or Attorney: or one pretending to be such Perly Wallis it is believed is the only person who in those different causes has been consulted and employ'd.—In one cause it can be proven, and if required shall be proven by both Plaintiff and Defendant that in the Causes then particularly depending between them each party have as his Client paid him Fees as demanded by said attorney to quash and discontinue the suit as has been done.—
>
> This conduct is judg'd to be highly improper as it tends to destroy all confidence that any Citizen could wish, or ought to have when employing or advising with any counsel in matters relating to his personal liberty, reputation, or interest, that the man who will take fees on both sides cannot be of sufficient moral principle or integrity and therefore deserves not the Confidence of any public body as a Lawyer, or Attorney, and ought not to be admitted to practice as such.[63]

Treat seems to be accusing Wallis of representing both plaintiff and defendant in the same lawsuit, of perhaps instituting the lawsuit and later urging the parties to discontinue the case in court and settle. In such an instance Wallis would have been entitled to attorney's fees. The record book, which at this time listed the names of counsel, does not bear out the allegation.[64]

Treat had a personal complaint as well—that between terms of the court, Wallis had issued a summons to him to attend some depositions at "Ouachita, a place out of the territory."[65] Only a judge had the power to issue a summons. Treat's charge against Wallis, though not stated, seems to be usurpation of authority.[66] The clerk's treatment of this case is interesting. In the space where the crime would normally be written, the page is blank.[67] Instead of the grand jury finding a "true bill," it found the complaint "just."[68] Since Treat's assistant at the factory, James B. Waterman, was a grand juror, perhaps his presence partially explains why the jury was persuaded by the plaintiff.[69] At Wallis's motion, the court graciously postponed consideration of the presentment until the next day.

On April 5, after four trials earlier that day, Wallis's case was called. Again, unusually, the record book does not indicate the charge. Wallis moved that the case be thrown out of court for lack of a prosecutor (he being the prosecutor), whereupon Treat came forward and was permitted by the court to prosecute his own case. Twelve jurors were sworn in: Daniel Mooney, Jeremiah Monroe, Joseph Dardenne, Pierre Pertuis, Joseph Bion, John Hadley, Samuel Prior, Morgan Donoho, Swanson Yarborough, Martin Surrano, Nathaniel Porter, and James Scull. (Wallis was simultaneously serving as prosecutor against Pertuis and Hadley, which brings to mind an interesting ethical question—if you were a defendant serving on a jury trying your prosecutor, would you be less likely to find him guilty?) Wallis moved that the jury be "composed of Men entirely who understand the English language." Treat objected, and Wallis withdrew the motion. The jury found the deputy attorney general not guilty.[70]

The following week, after the adjournment of court, Perly Wallis promptly filed suit against John Treat for slander based on the latter's complaint to the grand jury and public remarks that he had reportedly made about Wallis. Wallis alleged that Treat had defamed him because his client George Hook had sued the factor, and added, "if what the said Treat had so maliciously stated been true and his said cause in the Common Pleas been just he had nothing to fear." Wallis claimed damages of two thousand dollars. Pursuant to the complaint, the court issued a writ of capias on April 15.[71] Not to be outdone, on the seventeenth, after being brought in by the capias writ, Treat filed a complaint against Wallis for detention and false imprisonment.[72] Both of these cases were set to be heard at the next term of the court in August. But by then John Honey had left Arkansas, and for want of a clerk, the court did not meet.

In October 1809 the General Court issued a subpoena for both John Treat and the records of the *Wallis v. Treat* lawsuit to be brought before the court in Ste. Genevieve on the "first Monday in May next." Treat's brother Samuel, his attorney in fact, produced the two writs at the December term of the Court of Common Pleas at the Post. They would have had the effect of removing the case to the General Court. Removals in civil cases were allowed "when either of the parties shall fear that he will not receive a fair trial, in the court wherein it is depending on account of one of the judges of the court where the suit is depending is interested or prejudiced, or that the sheriff, or (if he be of party) the coroner is interested or prejudiced, or that the adverse party has an undue influence over the minds of the inhabitants of the district where the suit is depending or that the petitioner is so odious that he cannot expect a fair trial."[73] But the judges refused the writs, incorrectly stating that the term of the General Court had expired.[74]

Wallis faced his first, albeit weak, competition during the December 1809 term in the person of Patrick Darby, who presented a power of attorney to represent George Hook (whom Wallis was also representing). Also at this term, James B. Waterman (Treat's assistant Indian factor) assumed the position of court clerk.[75] Waterman's holding of two positions was not unusual at the time: a single position was seldom full-time and usually did not pay enough to support a person.

At the following term in April 1810, more would-be attorneys appeared. Hezekiah Kirkpatrick and J. L. Henderson were licensed in the Territory of Orleans, though not apparently in any state or in the Louisiana Territory. They petitioned the court to be able to represent parties "pro tempore until a sufficient number of licensed attornies shall appear in the said Court to enable each of said parties to engage some regular attorney in his favor."[76] The court refused "for reason that no atty shall be allowed to plead until he comes forward qualified as the law directs."[77] Once again Perly Wallis served as prosecuting attorney and also represented parties before the civil side of the court. At this term Samuel Treat moved to postpone the slander case against his brother till the next term, for "he is ignorant of the law himself and had not the benefit of counsel."[78] Ironically, in his attempt to obstruct the first lawyer at the Post, John Treat found himself in need of a lawyer. The court appointed J. L. Henderson to represent him, even though this was a civil trial.[79] When the debt case of George Hook against John Treat was called for trial, an evidentiary question arose. Henderson requested the court to admit oral evidence of a judgment, which the court properly refused. The jury found Treat liable for the debt of $1,377 and costs, a total of $1,800.[80] During this term Henderson again presented a writ of certiorari and a writ of habeas corpus from the General Court in the cases of *Wallis v. Treat* and *Treat v. Wallis,* and again the court refused to act on them. Shortly thereafter, however, the judges changed their minds. A week after the end of term, the clerk certified the record and sent it off to the General Court.[81] Meanwhile, though, the cases were continued in the Court of Common Pleas. In addition, Treat appealed his loss to Hook.[82] The outcome of the appeal is not known, but a later entry in the record book reveals that Treat lost title to 117,000 arpents of land to pay off Hook's judgment.[83]

Wallis and his competition continued to harass one another during this term. Patrick Darby complained to the grand jury—unsuccessfully—that Wallis was wrongfully assuming the authority of deputy attorney general, and Wallis complained to the grand jury—successfully—that Darby had wrongfully accused him. Darby pleaded not guilty and "put himself upon God and his Country," in other words, he requested a jury.[84] The trial occurred on the morning of Wednesday, April 4, with Darby found guilty.[85] He was fined five dollars and the costs in both actions.[86]

At the August 1810 term, the grand jury brought a presentment against Wallis for selling two hats without a license—but this time Wallis was successful in quashing it for lack of a prosecutor, since he could hardly prosecute himself.[87] On August 10 the judges ordered that Patrick Darby be "Excluded in future from Pleading at this bar under any Pretence whatsoever under Power of attorney or otherwise for his repeated contempt of the court."[88] Their ire was short lived, however. On the following day, on motion of Kirkpatrick, the court reversed its order, "the said Darby having made such acknowledgments as are satisfactory to the Court."[89]

In a subsequent term François Vaugine accepted an official license from the General Court for Perly Wallis to practice and another commission authorizing Wallis to serve as deputy attorney general. But with Vaugine the only judge present at the December 1810, April 1811, and August 1811 terms, the court could do no business, and it swiftly adjourned, illustrating one of the problems of frontier courts—distance and the difficulty of travel.[90] Judge Joseph Stillwell's plantation was out of town several miles upriver, and Judge Benjamin Fooy at Hopefield lived even farther away. Roads were little more than paths; watercourses were the chief highways. Even if roads were passable, malaria and other illnesses characterized as "agues" and "fevers" often incapacitated people and prevented them from traveling.

In December 1811 two new judges joined the bench: Samuel Mosely and Henry Cassidy.[91] In addition, three more attorneys were admitted to practice: Anthony Haden, Alexander S. Walker, and John Miller. Walker later achieved prominence as a territorial legislator, but little is known about the other men.[92] During this session *Wallis v. Treat* (the slander case) was tried.[93] One juror, Sylvanus Phillips, was a client of Wallis, which in modern times would have disqualified him.[94] Haden represented Treat. Again the jury was composed of men of French, German, English, and Irish extraction, albeit with fewer Frenchmen.[95] This jury found for Wallis, holding Treat liable for $750 plus costs. Treat moved for a new trial, which was granted.[96] Wallis responded with a bill of exceptions, which was used at common law to record the objections to decisions, rulings, or instructions of the judge. It would be signed by the judge, if accurate, and entered in the record for purposes of appeal.[97] In this case the bill of exceptions is significant because, in the words of the record book, "Plaintiff Tendered a bill of exception to the opinion of the Court in granting the New trial which the Court refuses to sign because it stated that the Court would not suffer the Plaintiff to Proceed nor read the Law in his behalf, which is false as the objection was argued by mister Wallis— Miller & Tayler and Several Cases Cited."[98] Wallis complained that the court would not let him argue precedent as authority, but the court disagreed, and the clerk even noted the name of one case argued by Wallis. This is the first and only mention of any case authority during the period 1808–14. The record book and court documents occasionally mention statutes as authority but give no citations, and the name of the statute is referred to only rarely. Today, of course, any legal argument supported by authority must cite that authority. In the first half of the nineteenth century, though, freewheeling frontier lawyers seldom offered such citations. Much less authority existed, and few sizable collections of law books could be found on the frontier.

During the April 1812 term, both trials were finally put to rest. Miller, representing Wallis in *Treat v. Wallis* (the false imprisonment case), moved to quash the suit, and the court granted his motion. Treat was granted his new trial in the slander case and was again found guilty.[99] Three years after their instigation, the litigation ended. By this time Treat was no longer even at Arkansas Post; he had been appointed to head the Indian factory at Chickasaw Bluffs in 1810.[100]

Wallis's actions at the Post illustrate several aspects of frontier legal practice. The attorney did not limit himself to practicing law but also acted as a land agent. He held a government position, that of deputy attorney general, and attempted to represent so many parties that conflict of interest was a clear problem and led to his prosecution at the hands of the Indian factor. Yet, at least during this time period, Wallis was successful. He won his cases.

Another notable aspect of this frontier legal system was the ethnic mix encountered in Arkansas Post juries and proceedings. It extended beyond French, German, and Anglo-American. By 1810 there was increased involvement with the courts by the Cherokees from the settlements along the St. Francis, including one of the most prominent figures in Arkansas Cherokee history—Connetoo, or Connitue, also known as John Hill, who had led the Cherokee migration to the St. Francis in the 1790s.[101] During the December 1811 term, "John Hill" served on two juries, one for an alleged assault and battery.[102] At the very same term, Jesse Isaacs filed suit for Robert Clary against John Hill, "alias Connitue," for an action of trespass on the case. Isaacs alleged an injury worth $408 and damages of $1,000.[103] The case was continued over until the next term, during which Hill again appeared in court as a juror, this time for a trial in which the defendant was found guilty of robbery.[104] Three days later Hill appeared as the defendant in the civil case brought by Isaacs. He told the court that he was a Cherokee and thus not subject to its jurisdiction. The court agreed and dismissed the case.[105] Once sued, Hill/Connetoo chose to be a Cherokee. While that status precluded him from further jury service (he not being a "white male citizen"), it also protected him from further lawsuits.

Whites living among the Cherokees also appeared in court. John W. Hunt was a white trader who had lived with the Chickamaugas in Tennessee and crossed the Mississippi with some Cherokees when they moved to the St. Francis River around 1796. He remained with them despite being whipped by a government agent at one point as part of the futile effort to keep whites off of Indian lands.[106] As early as April 1809 he served as a juror in several criminal trials.[107] He also served on grand juries and on at least one civil petit jury during the April 1810, December 1811, and April 1812 terms.[108]

John D. Chisholm, another well-known figure in Cherokee history, also turns up in the records. Born in Scotland, he emigrated to the United States in the 1790s and was involved in a number of questionable speculative land deals. He had several wives (perhaps at the same time), at least one of whom was a Cherokee. He represented the Cherokees on a number of occasions at treaty signings.[109] In January 1811 Robert Clary filed suits against John D. Chisholm and Dennis Chisholm (probably the former's son) for debt.[110] Ultimately Clary discontinued the suit against Dennis but won the suit against John.[111] Information regarding the nature of Dennis's debt has not survived, but a list of supplies purchased by John between March and September 1810 does exist. The list contains such items as "2½ Gallons Whiskey" ($5.00), "104 lb porke" ($7.28), "one sow and pigs" ($10.00), "50 lb Salt" ($5.00), "3 1/2 yd callico" ($7.00), "1 Drest Deerskin" ($2.00), "2 Hats" ($10.00), "16 Bushels Corn" ($16.00), "6 lb powder" ($6.00), and "1 Boat" ($30.00).[112]

A Peggy Chisholm was indicted for assault and battery in December 1811. She was not arraigned until April 1812 but, like Connetoo, used her Cherokee identity to evade the jurisdiction of the court and was discharged.[113] Other Cherokees from the St. Francis settlements and farther west may well have been involved in lawsuits and trials at the Post. The Indians' hitherto unexamined relationship with this court indicates not only a desire for involvement with, and an understanding of, white institutions but also a willingness to use their distinct status to their advantage.

African Americans had much less, if any, opportunity to "work" the justice system to their own benefit. Slaves had been introduced at Arkansas Post by John Law's French colonists in 1721.[114] In 1805 Treat wrote to his superior, "divided amongst those in this Neighbourhood, are sixty Blacks, seldom more than three in a Family, and with one, or two exceptions, the whole of them are Slaves."[115] A territorial statute gave these slaves the right to petition for freedom, "stating the ground on which the claim to freedom is founded."[116] But the justice system remained weighted against them.

On December 6, 1811, Perly Wallis appeared as counsel for a man offering a freedom petition, Martin Barker. Wallis had "a paper said to be signed by a certain Louis Barker a former Master of said Negro," but ex-judge Joseph Stillwell claimed Barker as his slave. Wallis moved that Barker be allowed to sue "as a poor person" (thus not having to pay costs) for his freedom. The court declined to rule Barker free, stating, "there are not sufficient matters set forth in said petition to authorize the interference of the Court."[117] This was the only freedom petition at the Post from 1808 to 1814. Unfortunately the file has not survived, and the only extant evidence of its occurrence is the record book. Perhaps Barker was Stillwell's property. Or perhaps, as happened frequently, Barker was really free and Stillwell was seizing the opportunity to enslave him.[118]

The status of a slave was an element in another series of proceedings, the Miller-Cassidy dispute, that further illustrates some of the weaknesses of the American justice system in a small frontier community. As noted above, Henry Cassidy and John Miller both appear for the first time in the record book of the court at the December 1811 term, Cassidy as judge and Miller as attorney. Miller, though, did not present his license until the April 1812 term, in the form of a letter from Judge B. C. Lucas of the General Court; Miller was also appointed deputy attorney general for the term.

The origin of the Miller-Cassidy dispute is not clear. During the April term the case of *Peeler v. Phillips* was called. Richmond Peeler was an agent for James Killgore, a planter along the Bayou Boeuf in Rapides Parish in the Territory of Orleans. Killgore, through Peeler, claimed that his slave Sam had been enticed or stolen away by a man named Moses Harris. Phillips, who claimed to be Sam's current owner, was possibly what lawyers today would call a bona fide purchaser, or "bfp." He pleaded that Robert Clary had obtained a writ of execution against Moses Harris, a constable had sold Sam at auction, and he had purchased Sam at the auction with no knowledge of Sam's status. Peeler sued Phillips for "detention of a negro." Ultimately Phillips would be tried and found not guilty twice. This case would be appealed to the General Court.[119]

Henry Cassidy sat as a judge in the *Peeler v. Phillips* trial, but he had served as the security for Richmond Peeler's bond in the same case. Anthony Haden represented Peeler; Perly Wallis and John Miller were counsel for Phillips. Miller objected to Cassidy acting as judge because he had served as the security and thus conceivably might be biased toward an outcome in favor of Peeler. As the case continued, each time it was called, Cassidy apparently attempted to remain on the bench, for each time Miller had to object before Cassidy would step down.[120] Another cause for animosity between the two men was their competing claims upon a potentially huge tract of Arkansas land that had been granted by the Spanish governor of Louisiana to Elisha Winter and his sons in 1797.[121] The grant was an issue in Miller's allegation of slander against Cassidy a few weeks after the end of term:

on the Tenth day of May one thousand Eight hundred and
twelve at village of arkansas in the District and Territory afsd

[aforesaid], in a certain Discourse which he the afsd Henry
Cassidy then and their had with a number of the good Citizens
of the district of Arkansas & Territory afsd of and concerning
the aforesaid John Miller Esqr in the Presence and hering of
Divers good and respectable Citizens of the District aforesaid,
then and their falsely and maliciously Said, rehersed and
Proclaimed and Loudly Published these false, feigned, and
Scandalous, malicious, and opprobrious English words following, to, of and concerning the Said John Miller, in the Presence
and hering of those Citizens that is to say he (meaning the said
John Miller Esqr) is a thief, and stole my table (meaning a table
of his the afsd Henry Cassidy) and I meaning himselfe will
Prosecute the afsd Miller for stealling my table (and he Still
meaning the afsd John Miller Esqr is a thief and Stoat [stole] all
the Books he has in his Library marked with the name of Peter
Walker from the Shelves of the afsd Peter Walker Decd and
meaning him selfe will Prove it (And he still meaning the afsd
John Miller Esqr is a theaf and Stoat [stole] two Deeds the one
for twenty Thousand acres of Land given to Peter Walker Esqr
by Elisha Winters the other an agreement for the Quantity afsd
given by the afsd Henry Cassidy to the aforesaid Peter Walker
Esqr and he still meaning the afsd John Miller Esqr Stoat [stole]
the afsd Books and Deed from amongst the effects of Peter
Walker, and I meaning him selfe will Prosicute him meaning the
afsd Miller for Larceny, and he Still meaning the afsd Miller is a
Swindeller and obtained a negrow named Sam from Sylvenus
Phillips by Swindelling and Perjury and I meaning him sefe the
afsd Henry Cassidy will Prove it And after wards (to wit, on the
Same day and year aforesaid at village of Arkansas in the
District and territory afsd in a certain other Discourse which
the said Henry Cassidy then and their had with Divers other
good and worthy Citizens of the District and Territory aforesaid
of and Concerning the Said John Miller Esqr, Then and their
falsely and maliciously Said, rehersed, and Proclaimed, and
Loudly Published these other false feigned Scandalous, mali-
cious and opprobrious English words following of and
Concerning the Said John Miller he meaning the Said John
Miller Esqr is a pretender and imposter and no Lawyer, and he
Still meaning the afsd John Miller Esqr is a thief and Stoal his
License from the Honorable John B. C. Lucas one of the Judges

of the general Court authorised to grant Licenses to all those
who are Duely Quallified to Practice in the territory afsd (and
he Still meaning the afsd Miller is a Pretender and no regular
Lawyer which I can make appear well knowing that he the afsd
John Miller Esqr was then and Long previous Duely Licenced
to Practice Law in the Superior and inferior Courts of the
Territory of Lousiana (and he still meaning the afsd John Miller
Esqr is a Soundrel and Perjured villan and has done enough to
Send him to the State Prison, and I meaning him selfe will
Prosecute him still meaning the afsd John Miller Esqr and Send
him to the State Prison and I still meaning him selfe the afsd
Henry Cassidy will Prove the afsd John Miller Esqr a thief
Scoundral and Perjured vallan and I Still meaning him selfe will
dig up or cause to be Dug up the Dead Body of Phebe Miller
Decd the wife of the afsd John Miller Esqr and I meaning him
selfe will tie a roap round the neck of him meaning the afsd
John Miller Esqr And if he meaning the afsd John Miller Esqr
opposes me meaning him selfe in Diging up the Dead Body of
his wife meaning the Dead Body of Phebe Miller Decd the Late
wife of the afsd John Miller and In tying the afsd roap Round
his neck meaning the afsd John Miller and in Beating him until
he meaning the afsd John Miller owens himselfe Guilty of
Stealing Swindelling and Perjury I meaning him selfe the afsd
Henry Cassidy will take the Life of him meaning the afsd John
Miller Esqr.[122]

In other words, Cassidy, among other things, accused Miller of stealing
his claim to the Winter grant.[123] Before the next term of the court, which
would be in August 1812, the disagreement between the two men esca-
lated. Miller alleged:

Henry Cassidy on the Eighth Day of July in the year of our
Lord one thousand Eight hundred and twelve at the Clerks [the
clerk was Patrick Cassidy, Henry's brother] office in the village
and District of Arkansas and Territory aforesaid and within the
proper Jurisdiction of this Court an assault did make in and
uppon the Body of him the aforesaid John Miller and with a
certain gun commonly called a shot gun which he the Said
Henry Cassidy then and there held in both his hands loded with
Powder and Shot did then and there Deliberately Shoot at [and]

wound him the said John Miller in the Left Breast Side neck and Sholder of him the aforesaid John Miller making in all twenty one wounds by Reason of which Said Shooting and wounding he the said John Miller was in great Danger of Losing his Life and still continued Disabelled in his Left arm and Breast and he the aforesaid John Miller was then & there putt to great expence and Cost by Reason of the aforesaid shooting and wounding.[124]

Miller filed a charge of libel against Cassidy before the grand jury at the August term. The judges present were François Vaugine, Samuel Mosely, Henry Cassidy himself, and a new judge, James Scull, a trader.[125] The grand jurors delivered three indictments against Cassidy: one for "a libell against John Miller and his wife Phebe Miller" and two others for assault and battery (the victim's name is not listed).[126] No doubt Miller was able to assist the grand jury in its deliberations, for during this term of court he was again the prosecuting attorney. Cassidy pled guilty to the charge of assault and battery and was fined twenty-five cents—clearly a miscarriage of justice if this was the penalty for the shooting. Cassidy pled not guilty to the second charge of assault and battery, was tried on August 5, and was found not guilty the same day. Later that day the grand jury presented charges of perjury and felony—apparently assault—against John Miller. It was the last day of term, and thus the libel, perjury, and felony cases would be continued at the December term. Before adjourning "until Court in Course," the judges ordered that Anthony Haden serve as prosecutor in the proceedings involving John Miller.[127]

The Court of Common Pleas had not adjourned, however, and on August 7 Cassidy appeared to make bond for four hundred dollars premised on his keeping the peace "towards all the good citizens of the United States & more especially towards John Miller of the District of Arkansas."[128] On August 13 Miller petitioned the court to divide the Winter grant and designate twenty thousand arpents for him, which he claimed under a deed from Winter to Peter Walker and assigned by Walker to Phebe Thornburg, Miller's late wife. Cassidy, another claimant to the Winter grant, objected that Miller had no right to the land "because the assignment said to be made from said Walker to the aforesaid Phebe is not proved according to law, the Court have concluded not [to] decide either for or against the motion till they can get advice."[129] On September 12 Miller sued Cassidy for trespass on the case and for slander.

In the meantime, Judge Henry Cassidy decided to become a lawyer. At that time there were three routes open to those who wished to practice. First, they could attend a law school. Although a law degree is required in virtually all jurisdictions today, in 1812 there were only a handful of schools offering study in law; the closest one to the Arkansas Post would have been Transylvania University in Lexington, Kentucky. The second route, followed by Abraham Lincoln, was to read law on one's own. The third and most common was to apprentice to a lawyer. But there was still only a handful of lawyers at the Post and no law-trained judges. Thus on October 27, 1812, Perly Wallis addressed a letter to "all whom it may concern" recommending Henry Cassidy to study law in St. Louis. The following day "A.H.," certainly Anthony Haden, wrote a similar letter.[130] Cassidy had studied with both of these lawyers, and the letters found their way to Rufus Easton, a prominent St. Louis attorney and judge, who wrote the following April to William Sprigg that Henry Cassidy had studied law with him for two months.[131] This two-month course of study—bolstered, of course, by the time Cassidy had spent on the bench—was sufficient to allow Cassidy to obtain admission to the bar from Judge John B. C. Lucas.

Meanwhile, on November 30 John Miller appeared in court at Arkansas Post to defend himself against Cassidy's lawsuits.[132] But the courts did not meet for the December term; the required quorum of two judges was not present. In fact the next time a court of record would hold trial at the Post would be nearly two years later, in September 1814, as the General Court of Arkansas County under Judge George Bullitt. Thus for the time being, Miller and Cassidy could not pursue their litigation at the Post.

Not to be deterred, Miller attempted to remove his lawsuits to the General Court in St. Louis. He filed both the slander and assault declarations, seeking ten thousand dollars in damages for the assault, together with affidavits stating that a fair trial could not be had in the District of Arkansas, where the cases were pending, because "the said defendant being one of the judges of the said court of Common Pleas of the said District of Arkansas is both interested and prejudiced and has undue influence over the other judges and because the Sheriff of the Said District is related to the Said defendant & the Clerk of the said court is a brother of the Defendant and because Samuel Moseley—one of the judges of the said Court is prejudiced against the said plaintiff."[133]

A sheriff tried to serve process on Henry Cassidy twice. The first time he looked for Cassidy in the County of St. Louis and could not locate him.[134] The second time, in the spring of 1814, the outcome appears in the sheriff's return on the cover sheet of the capias: "I could not Execute this writ the Defendant keept me off with force and arms and his Brother Patrick Cassady told the Defendant that I was the Sheriff and to take care of himself."[135] It appears from the General Court file as though the cases were never tried before that bench. Interestingly, on this capias at the bottom is written "Miller, Carr and Scott attorneys." Most likely the two latter names are those of William C. Carr, one of the most prominent attorneys in St. Louis at the time, and John Scott, former attorney general for the territory.[136] It does not appear as though Miller remained to practice in St. Louis, however.

The old courts of common pleas and general quarter sessions met one more time in March 1814 under Judges Joseph Stillwell, Samuel Mosely, and François Vaugine, though a regular term of court was not held because of "the parties not being timely noticed." Henry Cassidy duly presented his license from Judge Lucas to practice law in all the courts of record in the territory and was admitted to the bar. Cassidy also was commissioned to serve as deputy attorney general.[137]

In 1814 Congress established a unique court for the new Arkansas County. Styled the General Court (by now the Missouri Territory's highest court had been renamed the Superior Court), it had full jurisdiction of both common pleas and superior court matters. Appeal was allowed to the Superior Court.[138] On September 5, 1814, the General Court was called to order. Judge George Bullitt was a lawyer who previously had presided over a court at Ste. Genevieve and was not a member of the Arkansas Post community. Henry Cassidy was still deputy attorney general, but he and Miller had not abandoned their litigation. The suits were both called and continued over until the next term.[139] On April 4, 1815, however, Judge Bullitt discontinued all suits and process that were begun prior to the dissolution of the District of Arkansas.[140]

Henry Cassidy went on to a successful legal practice for the next few years. He later represented Arkansas County in the Missouri territorial legislature. Miller never appeared as counsel again in the Arkansas General Court. Given his alleged injuries, his health may have prevented him from practicing law. And yet there is one tantalizing bit of evidence, which can perhaps serve as an epilogue. Page 401 of volume 19 of *Territorial Papers of the United States* begins a letter from a John Miller to Josiah Meigs, then commissioner of the General Land Office. Miller corresponded from Phillips County on February 4, 1822, at the "fourth Chickey Saw Bluffs." He claimed forty thousand acres of the Winter grant—the same amount that Cassidy claimed John Miller stole in 1812—and was willing to give up his claim if his two sons could be granted "a certain Island Known by the name of Millers Island Number 34 on the missippi river and one Thousand acres opposit the Lower point of sd [said] Island on the Arkensaw Shore." In return he was also willing to share information about the Winter grant. It seems somehow fitting that his letter ends with a nota bene: "If I have no Chance of receiving a Donation I wish you to Destroy my Letter as I have been advised to write in this way to you under the impression that I would Get my request complyed with J Miller."

The Miller-Cassidy dispute prominently displayed many of the characteristics of Arkansas's frontier courts in the first years of American justice. Lay judges and a shortage of attorneys made for simpler pleading and procedure. The court met only intermittently due to the twin difficulties of traveling long distance and the illnesses that plagued Arkansas settlers. Conflicts of interest were endemic because of the small size of the community, though one suspects that some of them could have been avoided. Finally, even during this period, the Miller-Cassidy dispute evidences the resort to revenge (in this case a shooting) outside of the legal system for perceived wrongs that the courts could not or would not punish. With the increased influx of southern "gentlemen" into the territory, this method of dispute resolution would ripen into the duel, which would prove deadly to a good number of Arkansas lawyers and government officials.[141]

PART THREE

Remembering
THE
Purchase Era

Dancing into the Past

*Colonial Legacies in Modern
Caddo Indian Ceremony*

GEORGE SABO III

The bicentennial of the Louisiana Purchase is an appropriate moment to consider the different ways the peoples of the Louisiana territory have remembered their history. One group of indigenous inhabitants —the Caddo Indians who, at the beginning of the colonial period, occupied a homeland extending across present-day southwestern Arkansas, northwestern Louisiana, northeastern Texas, and southeastern Oklahoma —use a particular ceremony, the Turkey Dance, to recall the past. To understand Caddo history within the context of their knowledge system, one may begin with a story of Caddo origins:

> The original home of the Caddo was on lower Red River in Louisiana. According to their own traditions . . . , they came up from under the ground through the mouth of a cave in a hill which they call *Cha' kani'na*, "The place of crying," on a lake

close to the south bank of Red river, just at its junction with the
Mississippi. In those days men and animals were all brothers
and all lived together under the ground. But at last they discovered the entrance to the cave leading up to the surface of the
earth, and so they decided to ascend and come out. First an old
man climbed up, carrying in one hand fire and a pipe and in the
other a drum. After him came his wife, with corn and pumpkin
seeds. Then followed the rest of the people and the animals.
All intended to come out, but as soon as the wolf had climbed
up he closed the hole, and shut up the rest of the people and
animals under the ground, where they still remain. Those who
had come out sat down and cried a long time for their friends
below, hence the name of the place. Because the Caddo came
out of the ground they call it *ina,* mother, and go back to it
when they die. Because they have had the pipe and the drum
and the corn and pumpkins since they have been a people, they
hold fast to these things and have never thrown them away.[1]

The fact that Caddo Indians today hold to this account of their origins suggests that their concepts of history differ from those held by folk
in societies partaking of western European traditions. In the latter case,
history is often regarded as a linear, chronological narrative concerning
flesh-and-blood personages, real events, and actual circumstances that
help us understand the past and its connection with the present. For
Caddos (and for most other American Indians), history likewise provides
an account of how present circumstances developed. But the inclusion of
their emergence and separation from underground worlds shared with
animal kin as part of that history betoken an altogether different perception of reality. Belief in return *to* the earth following passage through life
on the earth also suggests this, reflecting the Caddos' eternal as well as
chronological frameworks. At the same time, references to links between
emblematic goods and Caddo existence as "a people" suggest a second
important function of history, identity formation.[2]

So it is that every society creates history according to its own under-
standings of the world and of time-space relationships. Different groups
use their past for distinctive purposes. The means by which communities
maintain their histories are varied too. Social structures, political and economic arrangements, ceremonial performances, storytelling, and recogni-
tion of special places and emblematic objects all may be used to maintain
ties with the past. The preservation of historical information in written

accounts is important in Western or European-derived societies, but such sources are less important or are absent altogether among other groups. Many American Indian communities, for example, embed historical knowledge into a variety of "texts," including those spoken, crafted, and danced.[3] This suggests the need for alternatives to universal definitions of history, ones that understand history in terms of multiple systems of socially constructed "ways of knowing."[4]

The Caddo Turkey Dance is an excellent example of a nonwritten historical text. Connections with the past are maintained in the dance's three primary components: the beat of the drum, the chant of the singers, and the movement of the dancers. The Turkey Dance articulates two forms of historical knowledge, which we may label "traditional" (based on legendary or "mythic" sources) and "conventional" (based on events and experiences that occur within the context of day-to-day or phenomenal reality).[5] Caddo Indians bring these multiple forms of historical knowledge to performances that provide a profound sense of identity in today's complex social world.

The Turkey Dance is one of a larger series of dances that relate features of Caddo culture and history.[6] But of this greater collection, the Turkey Dance alone is devoted entirely to historical exposition.[7] Much of that content recalls people, events, and circumstances associated with the colonial era and, more specifically, the decades leading up to and following the Louisiana Purchase.

Women perform the Turkey Dance. Since it must be completed during daylight hours, it is always the first dance performed at gatherings that begin in the afternoon and continue late into the night. It is considered a survival or victory dance because the words of many of the accompanying songs relate events in which ancestors triumphed over adversity. The dance proceeds in four phases, and while every performance has its own character, the following description identifies the basic sequence.[8] Unfortunately no combination of words can adequately convey the experience participants derive from the visual sensation of swirling colors in rhythmic movement, the mesmerizing effect of feet hitting the ground in time with the beat of the drum and the chant of the singers, and the heightening of perceptual faculties through participation in a sacred and inspirational event.

As with all Caddo dances, the Turkey Dance can be adapted to different venues. The basic requirement is an outdoor or indoor space large enough to accommodate the gathered participants. There is a circular indoor dance arena at the Caddo nation complex near Binger, Oklahoma.

Elsewhere, community halls, school gymnasiums, classrooms, and other indoor spaces are used as necessary. Outdoor dancing at the complex takes place in a dirt arena surrounded by arbor-covered benches, with a flagpole at one side and an elevated announcers' booth on the opposite side. At other sites a simple circle of folding chairs can be used to demarcate a dance area.

In the first phase, four to eight drummers-singers take their seats around a drum placed in the center of the dance ground. The southern-plains-style big drum used today is typically two to three feet in diameter and twelve to eighteen inches in depth, made of hides stretched tightly over a decorated cylindrical wooden frame. Formerly smaller water drums were used.[9] Drums are considered sacred objects and treated with great respect. For example, children learn very early that they should not run up and play on the instrument. The beat of the drum is said to represent the earth's heartbeat. They usually contain pieces of flint, or charcoal from a fire ignited by flint, to symbolize the fire brought to the earth's surface by the first Caddo man. The drum and its beat, therefore, connect dance participants (drummers-singers, dancers, and observers) to one another through common descent from the first people and with the earth to which they eventually return.

As the first drumbeats are sounded, the singers begin a series of short songs in different dialects that call the dancers ("Come, you turkeys") and invite them to "kick, kick the dirt" in time with the beat. The head dancer leads the others in a slow, stately movement encircling the drum. Younger dancers and little girls join the adult women as the movement proceeds.

While the dance ground fills, the second phase begins. It is marked by the longest series of songs, those relating ancestral events that take place both in chronological and eternal timeframes. Throughout this sequence the women, in single file, follow the lead dancer's steps, which imitate both the wandering path of the turkey as well as its gait, with the feet shooting one after the other quickly forward and then back before touching the ground.

The dancers' movements change during the third phase. The women skip or use a hop-step and follow the lead dancer away from the drum toward the edge of the dance ground and back, alternately turning from left to right and right to left. After repeating this pattern, the dancers shift to a toe-heel step and resume the circle around the drum for the final phase of the dance. One by one the women walk out to the perimeter, where they select a male who will join them for the fourth phase, in which partners alternately face toward and away from each other. They rotate when the drumbeat changes tempo so that one partner is always dancing backward. Changes in the tempo also signal the beginnings of new songs.

Earlier accounts indicate that men were required to give up an article of clothing (such as a hat) or pay money (usually a dollar) should they refuse a woman's request to join her in the dance. Money or another small gift could also be exchanged in return for the relinquished clothing. (This practice seems to have eroded, however, as I have observed no cases of men refusing to take part in the Turkey Dances I have witnessed over the past twenty years.) Dancers are supposed to choose men who are not close relatives, but today there seems to be no hard rule against a woman selecting her husband, son, or brother.

The Turkey Dance ends when this phase concludes.

Caddo people regard the Turkey Dance as one of their oldest surviving traditions. Nobody knows how old the dance is, but the song cycle narration of victories over former antagonists (Indian and white) suggests that the women's victory dance observed among the "Cenis" (Hasinai) by Henri Joutel in May 1687 may well have been an example.[10] Joutel was lieutenant and post commandant on La Salle's disastrous 1685 venture to establish a French colony along the Gulf Coast.[11] La Salle's ships landed the colonists in Matagorda Bay near present-day Victoria, Texas, but food and material shortages, disease, and Indian hostilities quickly prompted searches for an overland route to the Mississippi River so that the party could reach trading posts in the Illinois country. Joutel took charge of a small group of survivors during the third and last expedition in 1687, after La Salle was murdered by two of his associates. A few days after the killing, Joutel and his companions reached Caddo villages along San Pedro Creek near its confluence with the Neches River (near present-day Crockett, Texas), where they were permitted to lodge in the "hut" of one of the chiefs and trade some of their wares for food supplies needed to continue their journey. Most of the able-bodied Caddo men, joined by one of the Frenchmen, went off to wage war. In his journal, Joutel wrote:

> We were all uneasy until the 18th of that month when, to our great surprise, we saw one morning at daybreak a troop of women enter our hut who were painted and smeared. When they had all entered, they began to sing various songs in their language at the tops of their voices; after which, they began a kind of circle dance holding each other's hands. For what purpose were they performing this ceremony that lasted a good

two or three hours? We learned that it was because their people
had come back victorious over their enemies. As soon as the
village had heard it, they all gathered in the way that I have
told. Their dance ended with a few presents of tobacco that
those in the hut made to the women who had come. I noticed
during their dance that, from time to time, some of them took
one of the scalps that was in the hut and made a show of it,
presenting first from one side, then the other, as if to jeer at the
tribe from which the scalp had come. At noon, one of the warriors also arrived at our hut, apparently the one who had
brought the news of the enemies' defeat.[12]

Following the return of the warriors a day later, the villagers again gathered in the chief's residence, where they performed ceremonies to honor
the men killed in battle and present the scalps of vanquished enemies.
Once more the women danced "in an unclosed circle formation. They set
a sort of rhythm that they stamped with their feet and waved with fans
made from turkey feathers; in this way they adapted all this to their songs
which seemed too long to me because I could not understand anything."[13]

If we compare Joutel's account with the preceding description of the
modern Turkey Dance, we can identify several continuities along with a
few changes. The women's exclusive charge to perform the dance, the
daytime scheduling of the performance, its thematic emphasis on victorious events (typically male warfare exploits), the circular choreography
accompanied by a distinctive rhythm and song lyrics, and the association
with turkeys all remain unchanged across the intervening centuries. Scalps
are no longer displayed, though the choreography of the modern dance's
third phase corresponds to Joutel's description of the side-to-side movements of the seventeenth-century women when they displayed scalps in a
taunting manner. The fourth phase of the modern dance, in which the
women call upon men to join them, is evidently a new addition, though
again it recalls the presence of seventeenth-century warriors (who were
only symbolically represented in the first performance witnessed by the
French).

Joutel did not mention the use of a drum to set the dancer's cadence,
but it is certain that Caddo Indians—like many other southeastern Indian
groups—were using water drums or drums made from ceramic pots or
brass trade kettles at that time. In fact one evening two months later,
when Joutel and his companions were approaching the Arkansas River en
route to the Quapaw villages, they "heard a noise in the night that

sounded like a drum." Immediately following that observation, Joutel noted that the "Indians cover a pot with a dressed skin stretched over the top, and they beat it as a drum or rather as a kettle drum."[14] He could only have acquired this knowledge during the time he spent participating in La Salle's venture, which included his trek across Caddo country. Drums made from kettles were observed among Caddo Indians by members of Martin de Alarcón's 1718–19 expedition to Texas, and Father Isidro Espinosa witnessed Caddo women using a hollow-log drum during his 1715–18 visit to Texas.[15]

If Joutel's account suggests the enduring significance of turkeys to the ceremony, how might that association be accounted for? According to the late Vynola Beaver Newkumet, who was an active participant in Caddo cultural activities and an expert in Caddo history, it is explained in a frequently recounted story of the dance's origins: "A young warrior was hunting in the woods one day, when he heard beautiful songs. Tracing the sound to its source, he discovered a number of turkey hens dancing around a group of gobblers. He watched and listened until he had fixed the dance in his memory. After he returned to his village, he related what he had learned. The villagers began to use it and it became a fundament of Hasinai historiography."[16]

Many Caddos believe the Turkey Dance preserves a legacy of former times when village locations were chosen partly in relation to nearby turkey roosts. One explanation for this practice is that if enemies approached by night, the turkeys would be awakened, and their consequent stirring would provide an alarm to sleeping villagers.[17] Perhaps more significantly, such places were also handy sources of food. Turkeys have been a staple in the diets of southeastern and southern-plains Indians for thousands of years, and during early historic times Caddos continued to make use of this species.[18]

Consistent with the value attached to turkeys as food is the way they are featured in two "trickster" stories, both collected during the first decade of the twentieth century by George A. Dorsey. In the first story Wild-Cat attacked Rabbit and had him down, about to kill him, when Rabbit convinced his foe that some nearby turkeys might provide more tasty fare. Rabbit instructed Wild-Cat to lie as if dead and then called the turkeys by singing the Turkey Dance song. As the birds performed a victory dance around Rabbit's supposedly defeated foe, Wild-Cat jumped up to grab one of them and Rabbit escaped.[19] Coyote is the protagonist of the second story, in which he kills and eats one of his sons in retribution for his carelessly letting a sackful of turkeys escape while a fire for cooking them was being prepared.[20] The first story makes explicit reference to the Turkey Dance and its victory theme, while both identify turkeys as a preferred food source.

Although we can never determine with certainty what ideas or knowledge prompted ancient Caddos to associate one of their most important ceremonies with a particular animal species, these traditional references to turkeys as highly valued food sources furnish an important clue. The two endemic subspecies of turkeys in eastern Texas—the Rio Grande and the Eastern Wild—both prefer open, mixed oak-pine forest stands interspersed with grassy and brushy areas. These habitats provide adequate cover and roost areas as well as ready supplies of food: acorns in winter and soft mast foods, such as berries and seeds, along with insects, in the summer. Indians could manage these habitats with two activities that tend to increase turkey populations: using fire to maintain and renew forest openings supporting grassy and brushy vegetation, and selectively culling oak stands to maintain spacing and thus increase the acorn yields of productive middle-aged trees.[21] Archeological and paleoenvironmental data indicate that precontact southeastern Indians engaged in both of these practices, the latter partly to increase acorn yields for their own consumption needs.[22] White-tailed deer—another important food source for ancient as well as historic Caddo populations—are also associated with the same habitats and respond favorably to the same management practices.[23] Further, the distribution of these habitats within river and stream valleys corresponds to the distribution of the best soil resources for agricultural production. In sum, the readily identifiable locations of turkey roosts are excellent indicators of the presence of habitat and species matrices best suited for supporting the hunting, gathering, and agricultural subsistence economies of ancient and historic Caddo Indians. As such, turkeys then as now are appropriate symbols for ceremonies dedicated to celebrating victories on which the life and livelihood of Caddo communities depend.

For at least three hundred years—and probably much longer than that—the Turkey Dance has endured as an important women's ceremony for renewing community solidarity and for projecting identities on occasions when threats to survival have been overcome. Central to this function are the accompanying song lyrics, which refer to historical circumstances. In 1995 funds provided by the National Park Service permitted Caddo historian Cecile Elkins Carter and several others to complete a Turkey Dance documentation project, which produced a videotape of the dance and a booklet describing patterns and other details of the dresses

Caddo women wear for that ceremony. An audiotape of forty-nine Turkey Dance songs recorded earlier by four Caddo elders was transcribed during the project by University of Oklahoma linguist Alice Anderton, using the Caddo alphabet developed by University of California, Santa Barbara, linguist Wallace Chafe. Accompanying the transcription are comments that Carter obtained from the late Lowell "Wimpy" Edmonds, who at the time was head drummer and singer. Anderton and Chafe also transcribed Turkey Dance song texts obtained from several other Caddo elders (both male and female) and produced a concordance and master list of the entire song collection. (Copies of these materials are on file at the Caddo Heritage Museum, located at the Caddo Nation complex.)[24]

The lines of the first seven Turkey Dance songs, each repeated several times (with elaborations), call the dancers to the arena:

Hayhah náwwah, Hayhah náwwah. [OK, turkeys!]
Hawkaa náwwah, yaawanay hanitsiwaa. [Turkeys; they're gathering.]
Yawwaa haynay. [translation unknown]
Haynawwaahah, haynawwaahah, haynawwahah. [translation unknown]
Haynawwaahah, haynawwah. [translation unknown]
Yaawah nikitsiaawah. [They're in a bunch!]
Waynay kuchaawaaway. [translation unknown]

According to interview notes, Vynola Beaver Newkumet identified an alternative translation of the opening songs:

"Come, you turkeys! Kick, kick [the dirt]."
Repeat Song 1 in an old [Haish?] dialect.
Mentions the growing number of dancers in the old Neche dialect.
"Come on, you Hainais [Neche dialect]."
"Come on, Yona."
Repeats Song 4 in Kichai dialect.
Repeats Song 5 in Kichai dialect.[25]

In this translation the opening songs clearly refer to the historical situation of the Caddos. The Hainais were the head group of the Hasinai alliance, comprising communities distributed along the Neches and Angelina Rivers in eastern Texas. The Yona, or Yowani, were a band of Choctaws who left Mississippi during the eighteenth century and settled along the Neches River near the Nacogdoches, another group belonging to the alliance. Kichais joined the Hasinai to fight Osages and Apaches during the late seventeenth and early eighteenth centuries before amalgamating with Wichita-speaking relatives in Indian Territory. The opening songs thus call on Caddos and their historical allies to participate in celebrating their heritage and continuing existence as a people.

Songs chanted during the second phase of the Turkey Dance refer to ancestral events in which heroic Caddos achieved victories over treacherous foes. At any given dance the head singer-drummer chooses an appropriate selection of songs from the repertoire he and his accompanists have mastered. Songs that refer to specific groups with whom modern Caddos now enjoy friendly relations (such as Osages and Comanches) are not sung when members of those groups are present.

Among the victory songs used today are several that can be tied to specific eras and documented circumstances. One, for example, refers to retribution against a Tonkawa Indian.

> Witu? Náttih dawkaywab,
> Witu? Náttih dawkaywaabah. [All right, women, listen.]
>   [repeat]
> Nihaynaayuh ha?ahat. [When he followed, it was all right.]
> Nihayniyuudih ha?ahat. [When he caught up with us, it was all right.]
> Tayawkudah Tankaway. [The Tonkaway whooped.]
> Sawt'anaayah kutsini?ah. [He thought, "They'll be afraid of me."]
> Nidimbi?nah na sik'uh. [They beat him with a rock.]
> Ana shuuwi? Ta?iyaasa? [It's because a warrior was there.]

Related to this song is another that refers to a Yuwani (Yojuane) enemy.

> Yaawanitay kaniki?ah. [The Yuwani got killed.]
>   [repeat five times]
> Nidimbinah haay hah shúuwi? kaduhdáachu? [The Kadohadacho
>   brave beat him.]
> Yaawanitay kaniki?ah. [The Yuwani got killed.]
> Yaawanitay kaniki?ah.

The Tonkawa people consisted of several autonomous bands of nomadic buffalo hunters occupying the central Texas plains along the Brazos and Colorado Rivers west of the Hasinai region. Their language has been difficult to classify, but some have suggested a relationship with Coahuiltecan languages spoken by other groups in the western Gulf region of northern Mexico and southwestern Texas.[26] Consistent with the lyric, Father Francisco Casañas de Jesus Maria identified two Tonkawa bands, the Yojuanes and the Mayeyes, as Caddo enemies in 1691. By 1745, however, Tonkawan groups along with their Atakapan neighbors had befriended the Hasinais, from whom they were now able to purchase weapons. Throughout the rest of the colonial era, relationships between the Tonkawas and Caddos wavered but on the whole were peaceful. From this we can conclude that the reference in the song texts to Tonkawa enemies probably predates the mid-eighteenth century, making these among the oldest songs still part of the Turkey Dance repertoire.[27]

A half-dozen songs on the master list tell of victories against Osages.

Hay Washaash sawk'aybawnah? [Osage, have you heard?]
  [*repeat five times*]
Kiba?nah na nisiki?ah. [A person got killed.]
Kusi ?wan?ti? ta?aawkuudah. [Everyone whooped.]
Waashaashi kiba?nah na saniki?ah? [The Osage say . . . killed?]
Kusah náttih ?anti saayah. [A woman got (stood) up.]
Habakisa t'aybaw?ah. [She said, "I'll go see."]
Waashaashi, kunahina kaniki?ah. [There the Osage lies, where they
  killed him.]

Throughout the eighteenth century and during the first decades of the nineteenth century, Osage Indians were the Caddos' foremost enemies. Raiding expeditions from Missouri villages took Osage warriors all the way to the Red River.[28] The transfer of Louisiana territory from France to Spain in 1763 served only to exacerbate the longstanding hostilities between the Caddo and Osage tribes. Licenses for the lucrative Osage trade were monopolized by merchants operating out of St. Louis, much to the irritation of Arkansas Post traders. This led to an increase in illicit trade with Osages on the part of merchants, hunters, and other "malefactors" operating in the Arkansas River valley upstream from the Post. Osages were able to use the increased supply of firearms and ammunition so acquired to drive indigenous occupants, including several Wichita-speaking tribes, from the region. These groups were forced to relocate farther south into Caddo territory. Attempts by Spanish officials in New Orleans to prohibit Osage trade along the Arkansas River were ineffective, and attempts by Quapaws to halt Osage intrusions had only a limited effect. If anything, these actions increased the Osages' determination to extend their hegemony.[29]

The resulting lawlessness and turmoil turned the Arkansas River valley, in the words of Upper Louisiana's Lt. Gov. Athanase de Mézières, into a "pitiable theatre of outrageous robberies and bloody encounters."[30] These encounters included several with Caddo Indians in which men were killed, women and children were abducted, and horses stolen. In response to one instance of theft, the powerful Kadohadacho leader Tinhioüen pursued a group of Osage miscreants and killed them at the house of an Arkansas River trader. After a brief lull the Osages resumed their depredations in 1777. During one raid upon the Kadohadachos, Osage marauders stole a large number of horses and killed five men and two women. Tinhioüen retaliated by killing five Osages. It is these events that are referred to in the series of Turkey Dance songs praising victorious strikes against Osages.[31]

Another song that can be dated to the late eighteenth century refers to the Kichai alliance with Caddos, which brought for both groups an increased measure of defense.

> Waashashii nikin?at hawkanih. [They were taking the Osage.]
>   [*repeat three times*]
> Sawt'anaayah, kuybataay, niudisa? [They thought they wouldn't catch up with him.]
> Kahanaabah kichahih. [They said it was the Kichai.]
> We kitaynah
> Wishiyah wa kitay niudisa? [They got that Osage and]
> Waashashii ta?in?ah
> Ni daahawn daawah. [they took him back.]

The Kichais were Caddoan-language speakers whose eighteenth-century villages originally were located in eastern Texas between the Brazos and Red Rivers. Kichai villages, along with those of their Caddo and Wichita neighbors (another group of Caddoan-language speakers), suffered the brunt of Osage attacks in the years following the transfer of Louisiana from France to Spain. The presence of unlicensed traders elevated the level of raiding for horses and other goods, which in turn incited rivalries between the tribes inhabiting the land between the Arkansas and Red Rivers. Attempts to increase their share of European goods flowing into the region brought Caddos and Kichais into conflict with one another and with the Wichita-speaking Norteños tribes.[32]

By 1770 these troubles became sufficiently disruptive to move the Irish-born governor of Spanish Louisiana, Alexander O'Reilly, to take action. O'Reilly urged de Mézières to bring the leaders of the warring tribes together in order to arrange for peace. De Mézières first invited the leaders of several Caddo communities to Natchitoches, whereupon he used gifts of supplies and grants of increased access to licensed traders to rekindle their support. Then he encouraged Caddo leaders to settle their differences with the other tribes. Tinhioüen succeeded in gathering Norteños and Kichai representatives at his village in September 1770. In the negotiations that followed, the men came to an accord about the root causes of their internecine conflict, but no treaty was concluded. Following a winter of devastating Comanche and Osage attacks, the Hainai leader Bigotes traveled to the Norteños and Kichai villages, succeeding where Tinhioüen had failed in securing terms of peace. Thereafter, Caddos and Kichais focused more on fighting against the Osages than with each other.[33]

Osage raiding continued throughout the 1770s, and their military advantage increased with every successful capture of goods. Caddos, Kichais, and neighboring groups meanwhile suffered ongoing decline. Spanish administrators for their part continued to pressure the Caddos and their allies to resist Osage incursions. Caddos and Kichais mounted successful campaigns against the Osages from 1781 to 1783, the results of which were praised by Spanish officials in addition to being celebrated in Turkey Dance songs like the one given above. Trade for armaments and other supplies, however, forced Caddos ever deeper into debt. Tinhioüen complained to de Mézières's successor, Étienne de Vaugine, who offered to ease the Caddos' plight by supplying lower-priced goods. When these failed to materialize, Osages regained the upper hand over the Caddos and their allies, and Spanish officials in Texas and Louisiana were powerless to alter the outcome. When in 1788 the Kadohadachos were forced to relocate their villages farther down the Red River, the Kichais threatened to leave the area altogether. In one of his last accomplishments before his death in 1789, Tinhioüen persuaded Spanish officials at Natchitoches to extend assistance to the Kichais, resulting in the relocation of their village closer to the Caddos.[34]

An interesting set of songs that generally occur in unison identifies a range of antagonists—Cheyennes, Comanches, Shawnees, "soldier chiefs," and whites—that reflects conditions on the southern plains in the years just before Caddo removal from their homelands to reservation lands, first in Texas, later in Oklahoma.

Siya naabaw kaniki?ah. [They killed the Cheyenne.]
  [*repeat four times*]
Kan?ikawnah sii tanaahah. [He bellowed like a buffalo.]
  [*repeat both lines two more times*]
Kahdii sawt'uh kaniki?ah. [They killed the Comanche chief.]
  [*repeat*]
Kahanaabah kaduhdáachu?. [They say it was the Caddos.]
  [*repeat both lines*]
Náttih sawt'uh, kan?ikiyah. [A Comanche woman was killed.]
  [*repeat two times*]
Kinhanaabah kichahi. [They say it was the Kichais.]
  [*repeat two times*]
Kahdii súnda kaniikíi?ah. [The soldier chief was killed.]
Kahanaabah kaduhdáachu?. [They say it was the Caddos.]
?íkinishi kaniikíi?ah. [The white man was killed.]
Kahánáabah Shawanuh. [They say it was the Shawnees.]

Expansion of white American settlement east of the Mississippi River following the Louisiana Purchase, combined with an increase of Hispanic settlements in the American Southwest, displaced a number of Indian tribes onto the Great Plains.[35] The war for Mexican independence, which began in 1810, pushed several refugee groups onto the southern plains, where they encroached on lands occupied by other Indians, including Comanches and Cheyennes. Meanwhile, Caddo homelands south and west of the Red River also absorbed groups, including Alabamas, Cherokees, Delawares, Kickapoos, and Shawnees, all of whom were displaced from homelands east of the Mississippi by white American settlers.

This convergent process produced still more cultural and environmental stress. Some of the new groups shared a characteristic that set them apart from—and often against—the region's indigenous populations: a much closer association with Hispanic and Anglo institutions with which they shared a centuries-long history. Such associations pitted the newcomers and their aspirations for land grants against groups like the Caddos, now increasingly displaced within their own homelands. While Caddos still managed to hold the respect of many immigrant groups as well as that of many U.S. officials in the decades immediately following the Louisiana Purchase, the influx of new Indian and white settlers exacerbated contests for lands and elevated the incidence of hostilities referred to in these songs.[36]

While some Turkey Dance song lyrics clearly refer to identifiable historical circumstances, there are others that modern informants cannot translate precisely but for which the general storyline is known. These lyrics generally reflect dialects no longer used within the dwindling community of Caddo-language speakers. Earlier descriptions suggest the subject matter often represents events more appropriately ascribed to eternal, rather than chronological, frameworks. Vynola Beaver Newkumet, for example, has identified song references to events "long before" the relocation to Oklahoma, the most notable example of which tells of the flood that created Caddo Lake in northwestern Louisiana and northeastern Texas:

> It begins with the people dancing in the evening. More than one
> village was present during the night's dancing. As the dancers
> continued, the water began to rise. Two brothers went to higher
> ground because they were worried about the rising water. But
> the dancers in the valley continued on without distraction. The
> older of the two brothers called out: "Let's go to higher
> ground—we might all drown." But the others went on dancing
> despite his effort. The brothers looked to the east and saw a
> ridge of land moving around as if it were a great snake. The
> undulating form was holding back the water. Others came and
> saw the snakelike movement, while the lake formed upstream.
> The dancers were no longer above the surface of the water.
> They were lost to the lake, only to reappear as fantastic crea-
> tures. The dawn allowed those people who had gone to high
> ground to see the natural levee and the lake that had formed
> behind it.[37]

In all, the series of victory songs representing the core of Turkey Dance performances consists both of those that celebrate illustrious occasions memorialized in chronological frameworks (and documented in chronologically ordered Euro-American accounts) and of those that refer to primordial events involving "mythic" culture heroes. These latter stories occur within an alternative, eternal structure that for Caddos exists alongside the temporal.

To close the Turkey Dance, another short series of songs similar to the opening sequence follows. The key phrases are "They're gathering" and "They're still dancing." According to the late Lowell "Wimpy"

Edmonds, "That's [like saying] you all got there—you survived."[38] The end of the dance brings to a close a celebration of cultural persistence in an ever-changing and often-threatening world.

This consideration of the Turkey Dance's major components—the beat of the drum, the chant of the singers, and the movement of the dancers—illustrates how Caddo Indians use their own mode of history to construct and transmit a unique social identity. As noted above, their history makes use of two sources of understanding: traditional knowledge based on "mythic" stories concerning primordial events understood in terms of eternal frameworks (that is, an ever-present and unchanging "time out of time") and conventional knowledge based on actors and events that exist in linear time and are documented in written accounts shared with non-Indian or Western historical traditions. The Turkey Dance drumbeat, representing the heartbeat of the earth, to which all Caddos eventually return, reflects traditional knowledge and its emphasis on the enduring ties and cyclic repetitions that connect cosmological communities. This form of understanding is also represented in aspects of dance choreography and in song lyrics that memorialize primordial events and associated culture heroes. Conventional knowledge is reflected in choreography and lyrics that relate events understood in chronological sequence, alternative accounts of which exist elsewhere. Within the Turkey Dance performance, both forms of knowledge are seamlessly integrated, thus permitting Caddo Indians to construct and transmit identities that maintain connections with the past while responding simultaneously to the realities of the present and the uncertainties of the future. Rituals like the Turkey Dance provide people living within day-to-day temporal mindsets a means of access to the eternal, allowing them to experience primordial events and make those events and the works of associated culture heroes a vital part of the ongoing historical process through which the community sustains its identity and viability.

To perform the Turkey Dance, then, is to enact in the here and now the historical process of survival and persistence. It serves not merely to portray where the community came from in a chronological sense: through their performance, the drummers, singers, and dancers bring into the arena what Mircea Eliade called an "eternal return" where past/present and here/there distinctions collapse in the repetition of archetypal or "epitomizing" events.[39] Figuratively and literally, Turkey Dance participants relive hallowed survival events with every performance and in this way experience and sustain the history of their community. As this history unfolds in rhythm, movement, and song, the lyrical series indexes and memorializes what we can assume were important moments of identity transformation.

When we consider *which* transformations are memorialized, we confront a striking fact: with the exception of songs pertaining to primordial subjects, the remaining series all deal with events that took place in the decades immediately preceding and following the Louisiana Purchase. How can we explain the lack of song references to precontact and early postcontact events (that is, events before the contacts with La Salle and Joutel) and to events from times that follow the colonial era?

This absence may well be a function of the way oral traditions are used to index chronological events. With successive generations, new stories replace old stories, but the new stories continue to preserve thematic information that defines what it is to be a member of the community. The current repertoire of Turkey Dance songs thus preserves stories that resonate enduring values within the modern community. These happen to dwell on events of the colonial era that undoubtedly replaced an earlier repertoire.

But given this process, how can we explain the retention of colonial-era songs? Why are there no songs from subsequent times? As we have seen, Caddo Indians achieved noteworthy victories in the era extending from the establishment of Texas and Louisiana through the subsequent transfers of those territories between French, Spanish, and American dominions. Many losses were suffered to be sure, but strong governing institutions and the political skills of leaders like Tinhioüen and Bigotes maintained a dominating and respected position for Caddo communities. The history experienced by these Indians following the Louisiana Purchase, by contrast, provides less cause for celebration. In a series of events, Caddo communities suffered unprecedented cultural losses.[40]

From the time of the Louisiana Purchase up to the 1830s, Caddos living along the Red River and to the south and east—in the Sabine, Neches, and Trinity river basins—found their homelands increasingly encroached upon by other Indians and white settlers. Competition for land increased among the expanding number of occupying groups, leading to increased hostilities exacerbated by illegal traders who, among other things, brought large quantities of alcoholic beverages into the region. The consequences of these events for the Caddos included population declines and displacement within their homelands. Seasonal hunting excursions now also took them farther west into Texas, where they experienced frequent clashes with other Indian and white groups.

Caddo leaders—like the famed early-nineteenth-century Kadohadacho headman Dehahuit, who greeted the Freeman-Custis expedition of 1806—

continued to play time-honored roles working to quell disturbances in the region by brokering alliances between willing Indians and whites. But Caddos (along with other native groups) were regarded by U.S. officials as part of the so-called Indian problem that had to be addressed to make way for the advance of American civilization. Another circumstance affecting Caddos during this era was a decline in food and other material resources, creating desperate need. In this context Kadohadacho representatives gathered on June 25, 1835, at the Caddo Agency along the Red River at the request of U.S. Agent Jehiel Brooks. Over the next few days, Brooks convinced the Kadohadachos to sell nearly six hundred thousand acres of their lands to the United States for eighty thousand dollars. Faced with no viable alternative, the Kadohadachos signed the treaty on July 1 and agreed to vacate their homelands within one year.[41]

Before the move took place, however, the revolution for Texas independence from Mexico broke out. This thrust the Kadohadachos and their other Caddo relatives, many already in Texas, into a limbo that lasted until 1839, when Caddo communities were relocated along the upper Trinity and Brazos Rivers. There they coexisted uneasily with Delaware, Kichai, Wichita, and Waco Indians, but hostilities with white Texan settlers quickly developed. Treaties between the Republic of Texas and the Caddos, which included additional relocations for the purpose of providing protection from white depredations, brought no lasting peace to Caddo villages. Conflicts with whites were only exacerbated when Texas joined the United States in 1845, and supervision of Indian affairs was transferred to the federal government. In 1847 U.S. Army major Robert S. Neighbors was appointed special agent for Indian affairs in Texas, and he later gained fame—and the gratitude of the Caddo people that continues to this day—for his heroic efforts to end the growing epidemic of Indian-white hostilities in Texas. Neighbors suggested in 1849 that the federal government establish a permanent reservation where Indians could live separately from whites. Five years later the Texas legislature designated land with which the United States could create such a reservation, and the Caddos moved to an area along the Brazos River fifteen miles downstream from Fort Belknap. There, auspicious beginnings toward the establishment of a successful agricultural economy were made, but hopes of regaining a livelihood were dashed by continuing attacks from white settlers. Consequently in 1859 U.S. troops escorted the Caddos on yet another removal, this time to land in Indian Territory along the Washita River in present-day Caddo County, Oklahoma.[42] They shared assigned lands there with Wichita Indians and with Delawares who were intermarried with Caddos and Wichitas.

The outbreak of the American Civil War brought renewed violence to the region, and Caddos were forced again to flee their villages, many seeking refuge in Kansas. In 1867, Caddos returned to the Washita River, where they set to work reestablishing their settlements. They discovered, however, that the U.S. government had made treaties giving their lands south of the river to the Kiowas and Comanches and lands north of the river to the Cheyennes and Arapahos. The Caddos persevered nevertheless, first on lands shared with the neighboring tribes and later on individual allotments following passage of the Dawes Act in 1887.[43]

The cultural changes that took hold during these hard times, extending from 1835 to the beginning of the twentieth century, were erosive and disruptive of former traditions in ways altogether different from earlier experiences of transformation, or ethnogenesis, in which new cultural forms, such as production of hides for commodities exchange or increased intertribal marriages, were at least derivative of earlier economic and social institutions.[44] Hardly an era of victories, the lack of corresponding Turkey Dance song celebrations for this period is perhaps not surprising.

The passage of the Indian Reorganization Act of 1934, which reversed a decades-long U.S. policy of assimilating American Indian cultures, prevented the Turkey Dance from disappearing altogether. That legislation, along with passage of the Oklahoma Indian Welfare Act two years later, led to the creation in 1938 of the Caddo Indian Tribe (now Caddo Nation) of Oklahoma.[45] The cultural resurgence that followed included many returns to traditions long submerged, including ceremonies like the Turkey Dance, that are now used to preserve historical knowledge and maintain the beliefs and practices that define what it is to be Caddo.

Despite these efforts, the number of Caddo speakers continued to drop through the twentieth and into the twenty-first centuries to the point where today only a few remain. This also helps explain the absence of references to events after the colonial era. While precedent exists for adding new events to those celebrated and memorialized in Turkey Dance songs, the declining number of Caddo-language speakers possibly accounts for the fact that no songs have been added recently. As a result the current Turkey Dance song series, resurrected and maintained from earlier times, has become something of a "closed canon"—not unlike the Latin in the Roman Catholic mass. The Turkey Dance still serves its traditional function as a ceremonial mechanism for constructing and transmitting social identities that preserve ties to the past, but that function rests almost exclusively on a legacy of events linked in time to the Louisiana Purchase era.

The main point to be drawn from this consideration of the Turkey Dance is that Caddo history is *enacted*—in dance and song, in the telling of stories, and in other celebrations. History is neither mute nor static; it is a dynamic component of Caddo culture that people use today—just as their ancestors did in times past—to shape identities and transfer those identities from generation to generation, even in the face of disruption and loss. History as action keeps alive what it is to be Caddo, even as that understanding responds to the opportunities, demands, and impositions of a larger, changing world. Ceremonies like the Turkey Dance make it possible for Caddo Indians to experience directly the historical process through which their identity and culture persist.

Notes

Introduction. A Whole Country in Commotion

The epigraph is taken from Dan L. Flores, ed., *Jefferson and Southwestern Exploration: The Freeman and Custis Accounts of the Red River Expedition of 1806* (Norman: University of Oklahoma Press, 1984), 174.

1. Elliott West, "Why It Matters that Lewis and Clark Did Not Get Sick" (lecture, University of Arkansas, Fayetteville, Sept. 29, 2003).

2. Flores, *Jefferson and Southwestern Exploration,* 30–31, 35–38.

3. Allan Kulikoff, "Uprooted Peoples: Black Migrants in the Age of the American Revolution, 1790–1820," in *Slavery and Freedom in the Age of the American Revolution,* ed. Ira Berlin and Ronald Hoffman (Charlottesville: University Press of Virginia, 1983), 152.

4. Foster's song in fact seems to have been directly inspired by *Uncle Tom's Cabin.* See Ken Emerson, *Doo-dah! Stephen Foster and the Rise of American Popular Culture* (New York: Simon and Schuster, 1997), 189–200. By all appearances, when crowds at the Kentucky Derby launch into "My Old Kentucky Home," they are largely unaware that they are singing about slaves sold south to Louisiana, perhaps because they never make it to the third verse: "The head must bow and the back will have to bend / Wherever the darkey may go. / A few more days, and the trouble all will end / In the field where the sugar canes grow." Kentucky, in adopting the song as its state anthem, has retained that verse but changed "darkey" and "darkeys" to "people" wherever the offending words occur in the lyric.

5. As Henry Adams trenchantly observes of the purchase, "the prejudice of race alone blinded the American people to the debt they owed to the desperate courage of five hundred thousand Haytian negroes who would not be enslaved." Henry Adams, *History of the United States of America during the First Administration of Thomas Jefferson, 1801–1805* (1889; New York: Library of America, 1986), 316.

1. Lewis and Clark: Kidnappers

1. Richard White, "Frederick Jackson Turner and Buffalo Bill," in *The Frontier in American Culture,* ed. James R. Grossman (Berkeley: University of California Press; Chicago: The Newberry Library, 1994), 7.

2. David R. Francis, *The Universal Exposition of 1904* (St. Louis: Louisiana Purchase Exposition, 1913), 257.

3. Ibid.

4. Thomas Jefferson, "The Limits and Bounds of Louisiana," in *Documents Relating to the Purchase and Exploration of Louisiana* (New York: Houghton, Mifflin, 1904).

5. Quoted in Jon Kukla, *A Wilderness So Immense: The Louisiana Purchase and the Destiny of America* (New York: Alfred A. Knopf, 2003), 327.

6. Warren L. Cook, *Flood Tide of Empire: Spain and the Pacific Northwest, 1543–1819* (New Haven: Yale University Press, 1973), 450–55.

7. Donald Jackson, ed., *Letters of the Lewis and Clark Expedition, with Related Documents, 1783–1854* (Urbana: University of Illinois Press, 1962), 63.

8. John L. Allen, "Geographical Knowledge and American Images of the Louisiana Territory," in *Voyages of Discovery: Essays on the Lewis and Clark Expedition,* ed. James P. Ronda (Helena: Montana Historical Society Press, 1998), 44–46. For an accessible look at maps of the period illustrating this perception, see Paul E. Cohen, *Mapping the West: America's Westward Movement, 1524–1890* (New York: Rizzoli, 2002).

9. Frank Norall, *Bourgmont, Explorer of the Missouri, 1698–1725* (Lincoln: University of Nebraska Press, 1998).

10. Alfred Barnaby Thomas, *After Coronado: Spanish Exploration Northeast of New Mexico, 1696–1727* (Norman: University of Oklahoma Press, 1935), 33–39.

11. David B. Gracy II, *Moses Austin: His Life* (San Antonio: Trinity University Press, 1987), 55.

12. Quoted in Kukla, *Wilderness So Immense,* 328.

13. Cook, *Flood Tide of Empire,* 443.

14. Ibid., 60–72.

15. Surprisingly there remains only one competent work on Pike, now more than fifty years old: W. Eugene Hollon, *The Lost Pathfinder: Zebulon Montgomery Pike* (Norman: University of Oklahoma Press, 1949).

16. Elliott Coues, *The Expeditions of Zebulon Montgomery Pike . . .* (1895; reprint, Minneapolis: Ross and Haines, 1965), 2:382.

17. Cook, *Flood Tide of Empire,* 479.

18. Still the only good account of the expedition is Dan Flores's excellent introduction to his edited version of the expedition's journal in *Jefferson and Southwestern Exploration: The Freeman and Custis Accounts of the Red River Expedition of 1806* (Norman: University of Oklahoma Press, 1984), 3–90.

19. Ibid., 85–90.

20. John D. Unruh Jr., *The Plains Across: The Overland Emigrants and the Trans-Mississippi West, 1840–60* (Urbana: University of Illinois Press, 1962), 84.

2. Jefferson's Grand Expedition and the Mystery of the Red River

1. John Francis McDermott, ed., "The Western Journals of Dr. George Hunter, 1796–1805," *Transactions of the American Philosophical Society* 53 (1963): 5.

2. Jefferson to Lewis, Washington, Nov. 16, 1803, in *Letters of the Lewis and Clark Expedition, with Related Documents, 1783–1854,* ed. Donald Jackson (Urbana: University of Illinois Press, 1962),136–38.

3. Thomas Jefferson, "The Limits and Bounds of Louisiana," in *Documents Relating to the Purchase and Exploration of Louisiana* (New York: Houghton Mifflin, 1904), 7–45; Pedro Cevallos to Messrs. Charles Pinckney and James Monroe, Aranjuez [Spain], Feb. 24, 1805, in *Annals of Congress,* 8th Cong., 2d sess. (1805), 1391.

4. A discussion of Humboldt's sources and a detail of his map portraying the confusion appears in Dan L. Flores, ed., *Southern Counterpart to Lewis and Clark: The Freeman and Custis Expedition of 1806* (1984; Norman: University of Oklahoma Press, 2002), 20–21. See also John L. Allen, "Geographical Knowledge and American Images of the Louisiana Territory," *Western Historical Quarterly* 2 (Apr. 1971): 151–70. There was other evidence buttressing the American assumption about the Red River's course as well, including a claim by noted Louisiana trader Jean Brevel that in 1764–65 he had ascended the Red to the Continental Divide and visited Santa Fe. Indian Agent Dr. John Sibley of Natchitoches had forwarded this story to the president in 1805.

5. For the Vial, Mares, and Fragoso journals describing their travels using the rivers of the southern plains, along with interpretive commentary putting these journeys in historical context, see Noel Loomis and Abraham P. Nasatir, *Pedro Vial and the Roads to Santa Fe* (Norman: University of Oklahoma Press, 1967). The Spanish unease over Vial's report is covered especially on pages xvii and 413–14.

6. James Wilkinson to Henry Dearborn, Washington, July 13, 1804, War Department, Letters Received, Main Series, Record Group (RG) 165, National Archives and Records Administration (NARA).

7. Thomas Jefferson to William Dunbar, Washington, May 25, 1805, in *Life, Letters, and Papers of William Dunbar of Elgin, Morayshire, Scotland, and Natchez, Mississippi: Pioneer Scientist of the Southern United States,* ed. [Eron Opha Moore] Rowland (Jackson: Mississippi Historical Society, 1930), 177.

8. Mitchill's report is in *Annals of Congress,* 8th Cong., 1st sess. (1805), 1124–26. Dunbar's comments came in a letter to Jefferson from Natchez dated June 9, 1804. See Rowland, *Life, Letters, and Papers of William Dunbar,* 133–35. Stories of unicorns along the Red got added support with

the discovery of La Harpe's journal in Natchitoches in 1805, with its purported description of one. Representations of the horned water serpent appear in rock-art panels, particularly the Rocky Dell site, as far east as the Texas Panhandle. Elsewhere I have argued that the meteorites that fueled the "silver ore" tales are the actual source of two generations of "silver mine" expeditions into Texas. A sixteen-hundred-pound meteorite was hauled in from the Texas plains by traders in 1810. See Dan L. Flores, ed., *Journal of an Indian Trader: Anthony Glass and the Texas Trading Frontier, 1790–1810* (College Station: Texas A&M University Press, 1985), 85–99.

9. John Sibley, "Historical Sketches of the Several Tribes in Louisiana South of the Arkansas River and between the Mississippi and the River Grand," in Thomas Jefferson, *Message from the President of the United States, Communicating Discoveries Made in Exploring the Missouri, Red River, and Washita, by Captains Lewis and Clark, Doctor Sibley, and Mr. Dunbar* (New York: Hopkins and Seymour, 1806). Scholars have debated which peoples the term "Hietan" referred to, but there is no question that the early American traders, Sibley, and the Jefferson administration applied it to the Comanches.

10. The copy of this southwestern letter of instructions eventually addressed to Thomas Freeman and presented to him in November 1805 is published as appendix 1 in Flores, *Southern Counterpart to Lewis and Clark,* 319–25. The copy in the Thomas Jefferson Papers, Library of Congress, was never addressed. Jefferson's letter to Lewis is published in Jackson, *Letters of the Lewis and Clark Expedition,* 60–66.

11. The official report is most accessible in *Annals of Congress,* 9th Cong., 2d sess. (1806), 1106–46. Dunbar's daily journal appears without editing or commentary in Rowland, *Life, Letters, and Papers of William Dunbar.* The most substantial scholarly work published on the expedition is McDermott, "Western Journals of Dr. George Hunter."

12. *The Forgotten Expedition,* produced by Dale Carpenter and Larry Foley (Conway: Arkansas Educational Television Network, 2002).

13. Dunbar to Henry Dearborn, Natchez, May 4, 1805, in Rowland, *Life, Letters, and Papers of William Dunbar,* 148–49. For information on the candidates considered and rejected for various reasons, see Flores, *Southern Counterpart to Lewis and Clark,* 39–49.

14. Freeman to Jefferson, Washington, Nov. 10, 1805; and Thomas Jefferson, letter of introduction and credit for Thomas Freeman, Washington, Nov. 16, 1805, Thomas Jefferson Papers, 1st ser., Library of Congress, Washington, D.C.

15. Freeman to John McKee, Philadelphia, Nov. [?], 1805, John McKee Papers, Library of Congress.

16. Wilson first mentions his bird project in a letter to the president, telling Jefferson that one hundred drawings were completed. Then, "hearing that

your Excellency had it in contemplation to send travellers this ensuing summer up the Red River, the Arkansaw and other tributary streams of the Mississippi . . . , I beg leave to offer myself for any of these expeditions; and can be ready at a short notice to attend your Excellency's orders. Accustomed to the hardships of travelling; without a family; and an enthusiast in the pursuit of Natural History, I will devote my whole powers to merit your Excellency's approbation; and ardently wish for the opportunity of testifying the sincerity of my professions." Alexander Wilson to Thomas Jefferson, Kingsessing, Feb. 6, 1806, quoted in *The Journals of Zebulon Montgomery Pike*, 2 vols., ed. Donald Jackson (Norman: University of Oklahoma Press, 1966), 2:389 n. 1. But while Bartram's cover letter is in the Jefferson Papers, I have never been able to find Wilson's there and believe that Jefferson either did not receive Wilson's letter or lost it.

The other pertinent letters are Wilson to William Duncan, Feb. 26, 1806; and Wilson to William Bartram, Philadelphia, Apr. 22, 1806, in Clark Hunter, ed., *The Life and Letters of Alexander Wilson* (Philadelphia: American Philosophical Society, 1983), 232–48.

17. Because of a continuing confusion about these applications, see particularly Jefferson to Rafinesque, Washington, Dec. 15, 1804; and Bartram to Jefferson, Philadelphia, Feb. 6, 1806, Jefferson Papers, 1st ser. See also Hunter, *Life and Letters of Alexander Wilson*, 79. Additional documentation along with the fuller story is in Flores, *Southern Counterpart to Lewis and Clark*, 56–61; and Dan L. Flores, "The Ecology of the Red River in 1806: Peter Custis and Early Southwestern Natural History," chap. 2 of *The Natural West: Environmental History in the Great Plains and Rocky Mountains*, ed. Dan L. Flores (Norman: University of Oklahoma Press, 2001). Custis was related by marriage to the Byrd, Randolph, and Lee families, as well as to George Washington.

18. Dunbar to Dearborn, Natchez, Mar. 18, May 6, 1806, in Rowland, *Life, Letters, and Papers of William Dunbar*, 332, 341.

19. See Flores, "Ecology of the Red River in 1806."

20. "Muster Roll of a Company of Infantry under the Command of Capt. Richard Sparks in the 2nd Regiment of the United States, commanded by Col Thos. H. Cushing, from 30 April, when last Mustered, to 31 May 1806, and 31 May to 30 June," Records of the Adjutant General's Office, 1780s–1917, RG 94, NARA; Dunbar to Dearborn, June 15, 1804, and Dunbar to Jefferson, Natchez, May 6, 1806, in Rowland, *Life, Letters, and Papers of William Dunbar*, 138–39, 194–95.

21. Where I quote either Custis or Freeman in the following section, my sources are Custis's four reports to the War Department written during the expedition and the portions of Freeman's journal that are still extant. All the above were assembled for and appear in Flores, *Southern Counterpart to Lewis and Clark*, 99–279.

22. For recent scholarship on the Nolan story, see Flores, *Journal of an Indian Trader,* 10–15; and Maurine Wilson and Jack Jackson, *Philip Nolan and Texas: Expeditions to the Unknown Land, 1791–1801* (Waco: Texian Press, 1987).

23. The council's decision on the boundary was sent to Provincias Internas officials in a communication from Andres Lopes Armesto, Chihuahua, Apr. 22, 1804, Bexar Archives, Center for American History, University of Texas, Austin. Wilkinson's letter is reproduced in "Reflections on Louisiana," in *Louisiana under the Rule of Spain, France, and the United States, 1785–1807: Social, Economic, and Political Conditions of the Territory Represented in the Louisiana Purchase,* ed. and trans. James Alexander Robertson (Cleveland: Arthur H. Clark, 1911), 2:325–47.

24. Donald Jackson discusses Spanish efforts to intercept Lewis and Clark in *Thomas Jefferson and the Stony Mountains: Exploring the West from Monticello* (1981; reprint, Norman: University of Oklahoma Press, 1993), 154. The journal and documents of Vial's first attempt to intercept Lewis and Clark appear in Abraham Nasatir, "More on Pedro Vial in Upper Louisiana," *The Spanish in the Mississippi Valley, 1762–1804,* ed. John Francis McDermott (Urbana: University of Illinois Press, 1974), 100–19; Donald Jackson, "What if the Spaniards Had Captured Lewis and Clark?" in *Among the Sleeping Giants* (Urbana: University of Illinois Press, 1987), 10–22.

25. Marques de Caso Calvo to Juan Bautista de Elguezebal, New Orleans, June 17, 1804; and Antonio Cordero to Nemecio Salcedo, San Antonio de Bexar, Oct. 23, 1805, Bexar Archives.

26. Salcedo to Cordero, Chihuahua, Apr. 13, 1806, Bexar Archives; Fecundo Melgares to Real Alencaster, Santa Fe, June 2, 1806, the Spanish Archives of New Mexico, New Mexico State Archives and Records Center, Santa Fe.

27. I have elsewhere argued that Lucas Talapoon seems to have been Philip Nolan's guide into Texas in the 1790s and thus is the individual to whom Daniel Clark Jr. referred when he had written Jefferson, "In company with [Nolan] is a Person a perfect master of the language of signs." See Flores, *Southern Counterpart to Lewis and Clark,* 131–32 n. 14.

28. David Stahle and Malcolm Cleaveland, "Texas Drought History Reconstructed and Analyzed from 1698 to 1980," *Journal of Climate* 1 (Jan. 1988): 59–74.

29. Francisco Viana to Antonio Cordero, Nacogdoches, June 3, 1806, Bexar Archives.

30. The tabulated costs for the exploration appear in Flores, *Southern Counterpart to Lewis and Clark,* 295–96 n. 25.

31. The manuscript of Clark's map and the printed version may be compared in Carl I. Wheat, comp., *1540–1861: Mapping the Transmississippi West* (San Francisco: Institute of Historical Cartography, 1957–63), vol. 2,

maps 291, 316. Freeman and Custis's route and Viana's route of interception appear on Fray Jose Maria de Jesus Puelles, *Mapa Geographica de la Provincias Septentrionales de esta Nueva Espana (ano de 1807),* copy in the Map Collection, University of Texas, Austin.

32. On the proposed Arkansas River expedition, see particularly Jefferson to Dearborn, Washington, Feb. 14, 1807, Jefferson Papers, ser. 1; Dearborn to Dunbar, Washington, Mar. 30, 1807, in Rowland, *Life, Letters, and Papers of William Dunbar,* 197–98; and Freeman to Dearborn, Natchez, June 15, 1807, War Department, Letters Received, Main Series, RG 165, NARA. Freeman's later career is reconstructed from a plethora of documents in Flores, *Southern Counterpart to Lewis and Clark,* 313–16.

33. Item on Edwin James's death, Louis H. Pammel Papers, University Archives, Iowa State University Library, Ames.

34. The best recent discussion of the discovery of these is in Gary E. Moulton, *The Journals of the Lewis and Clark Expedition,* vol. 2 (Lincoln: University of Nebraska Press, 1986), app. B, 530–48.

35. See especially Flores, "Ecology of the Red River in 1806."

36. Peter Custis, "Observations Relative to the Geography, Natural History, & etc., of the Country along the Red-River, in Louisiana," *The Philadelphia Medical and Physical Journal* 2, pt. 2 (1806): 43–50; Peter Custis, "Bilious Fever of Albemarle County" (MD thesis, University of Pennsylvania, 1807); Custis to Barton, Drummond Town, Va., May 21, 1807, Benjamin Smith Barton Collection, Library of the American Philosophical Society, Philadelphia.

37. [Nicholas King], *An Account of the Red River in Louisiana, Drawn Up from the Returns of Messrs. Freeman & Custis, to the War Office of the United States, Who Explored the Same, in the Year 1806* (Washington, D.C.: N.p., [1807]). The original 142-page manuscript of this redaction, replete with many dozens of errors made in transcribing Custis's Latin binomials, is in the Peter Force Collection, Library of Congress. Only ten copies of the printed version are known to exist today. According to the Library of Congress, its copy came bound to the *back* of King's redaction of Pike's 1805 Mississippi River account. See Thomas Streeter, *Bibliography of Texas, 1795–1845* (Cambridge, Mass.: Harvard University Press, 1960), vol. 2, item 1040.

38. On Custis's later life, see Custis to Barton, New Bern, Oct. 29, 1808, Barton Collection; notice of marriage, Dr. Peter Custis to Mary Pasteur, daughter of Dr. Edward Pasteur, Apr. 20, 1809, in *Raleigh Register,* Apr. 27, 1809; and Alan Watson, *A History of New Bern and Craven County* (New Bern: Tryon Palace Comm., 1987), 323. On his later (1818) marriage to Katherine Carthy, daughter of Dr. Daniel Carthy, see Craven County Marriage Bonds, North Carolina State Archives, Raleigh.

The characterization of his personality is in the Stephen Miller Memoir, Recollections of Physicians in Early North Carolina, Collection 371, East

Carolina Manuscript Collection, J. Y. Joyner Library, East Carolina University, Greenville.

Other sources on Dr. Custis's post-exploration life include Peter Custis Will and Testament, June 30, 1840, Craven County Original Wills, North Carolina State Archives (which lists his children as Linnaeus, Peter, Sally, Betsey, Pennan, and Park); Custis Family Bible, New Bern Historical Society; and Dr. Peter Custis, Certificate of Death, May 1, 1842, Craven County, N.C., Superior Court, "Will Book D," 54–55.

39. Jackson, *Exploring the West from Monticello,* 234.

40. *(New Orleans) Louisiana Gazette,* May 16, 1811. On the widespread suspicion of Jefferson's knowledge of the Burr Conspiracy, see Dearborn to Wilkinson, Washington, Jan. 21, 1807, War Department, Letters Sent, Main Series, RG 165, NARA.

41. Dan L. Flores, "The River That Flowed from Nowhere," in *Horizontal Yellow: Nature and History in the Near Southwest* (Albuquerque: University of New Mexico Press, 1999), 37–80. Custis appears as "Dr. Raphael Bailey" in another fictional account of southwestern exploration that allows the expedition to penetrate New Mexico. See Donald Jackson, *Valley Men* (New York: Ticknor and Fields, 1984).

42. Randolph Marcy, *A Report on the Exploration of the Red River, in Louisiana* (Washington, D.C.: Government Printing Office, 1854). Scholars have never been able to locate the headwaters scenes Marcy describes, but his biographer, Eugene Hollon, speculated in 1955 that Marcy may actually have explored Tule Canyon. By comparing the captain's descriptions, and especially lithographs of the scene, with onsite examinations, I was able to demonstrate this in 1990. See Hollon, *Beyond the Cross Timbers: Travels of Randolph B. Marcy, 1812–1887* (Norman: University of Oklahoma Press, 1955); and Dan Flores, *Caprock Canyonlands: Journeys into the Heart of the Southern Plains* (Austin: University of Texas Press, 1990), 106–7, 114–15.

43. Ernest H. Ruffner, "Survey of the Headwaters of the Red River, 1876," in *Report of the Secretary of War,* 45th Cong., 2d sess., 1877, H. Exec. Doc. 1, vol. 2, pt. 2.

44. In 1808 a trading expedition sponsored by Jefferson's Indian agent, Dr. John Sibley, and led by Anthony Glass actually carried the U.S. flags from the Grand Expedition's stores to the tribes of the southern plains. See Flores, *Journal of an Indian Trader.*

3. Could Louisiana Have Become an Hispano-Indian Republic?

1. François Luis Hector, Barón de Carondelet, Military Report on Louisiana and West Florida, Nov. 24, 1794, in *Louisiana under the Rule of Spain, France, and the United States, 1785–1807: Social, Economic, and*

Political Conditions of the Territory Represented in the Louisiana Purchase, ed. and trans. James Alexander Robertson (Cleveland: Arthur H. Clark, 1911), 1:297; Spanish Ambassador to Paris to Francisco de Saavedra, June 12, 1798, quoted in Minister Alvarez to Captain-General of Cuba, June 26, 1798, ibid., 1:349.

2. Francisco Cruzat to Esteban Miró, Aug. 23, 1784, in *Spain in the Mississippi Valley, 1765–1794,* ed. and trans. Lawrence Kinnaird (Washington, D.C: Government Printing Office, 1946–49), 2:117.

3. Pierre François Xavier de Charlevoix to the Duchess of Lesoiguieres, Nov. 8, 1721, in *Histoire et Description Generale de la Nouvelle France, avec Le Journal Historique d'un Voyage fait par ordre du Roi dans l'Amérique Septentrionnale,* by Pierre François Xavier de Charlevoix (Paris: Rolin fils, 1744), 3:411; Paul Du Poisson to Father ——, Oct. 3, 1727, in *The Jesuit Relations and Allied Documents: Travels and Explorations of the Jesuit Missionaries in New France, 1610–1791,* ed. and trans. Reuben Gold Thwaites (Cleveland: Burrows Brothers, 1896–1901), 67:319; Pierre François de Rigaud, Marquis de Vaudreuil to Jean Frédéric Phélypeaux, Compte de Maurepas, Mar. 20, 1748, Box 3, LO 117, Vaudreuil Papers, Loudoun Collection, Huntington Library, San Marino, Calif.; Louis Vivier to Father ——, Nov. 17, 1750, in Thwaites, *Jesuit Relations,* 67:326; Henri d'Orgon to Pierre François de Rigaud, Marquis de Vaudreuil, Oct. 7, 1752, Box 8, LO 399, Vaudreuil Papers; Norman Ward Caldwell, *The French in the Mississippi Valley, 1740–1750* (Urbana: University of Illinois Press, 1941), 39; Jean Baptiste Truteau, Description of the Upper Missouri, 1796, in *Before Lewis and Clark: Documents Illustrating the History of the Missouri, 1785–1804,* ed. and trans. Abraham Phineas Nasatir (St. Louis: St. Louis Historical Documents Foundation, 1952), 2:384; attachment of Pierre Chouteau to Henry Dearborn, "Apercu de la population des diverses tribus du District de la Louisiane," Nov. 19, 1804, ibid., 2:759–60.

4. For more on Osage expansion, see Willard H. Rollings, *The Osage: An Ethnohistorical Study of Hegemony on the Prairie-Plains* (Columbia: University of Missouri Press, 1992); Gilbert C. Din and A. P. Nasatir, *The Imperial Osages: Spanish-Indian Diplomacy in the Mississippi Valley* (Norman: University of Oklahoma Press, 1983); Cecile Elkins Carter, *Caddo Indians: Where We Come From* (Norman: University of Oklahoma Press, 1995); and Kathleen DuVal, "'Faithful Nations' and 'Ruthless Savages': The Rise and Fall of Indian Diplomacy in the Arkansas River Valley, 1673–1828" (Ph.D. diss., University of California, Davis, 2001). The Spanish outlawed the slave trade but continued other commerce. Alejandro O'Reilly, Proclamation, Dec. 7, 1769, in Kinnaird, *Spain in the Mississippi Valley,* 1:125–26.

5. Bernardo de Gálvez to Fernando de Leyba, Jan. 13, 1779, in Kinnaird, *Spain in the Mississippi Valley,* 1:321.

6. François Luis Hector, Barón de Carondelet to Ignacio Delino, June 29, 1792, ibid., 3:56.

7. François Luis Hector, Barón de Carondelet to Zenon Trudeau, Dec. 22, 1792, ibid., 3:107.

8. François Luis Hector, Barón de Carondelet, draft order, [1793], ibid., 3:144; François Luis Hector, Barón de Carondelet to Zenon Trudeau, May 6, 1793, ibid., 3:149.

9. See, for example, Merchants of St. Louis to François Luis Hector, Barón de Carondelet, June 22, 1793, in Nasatir, *Before Lewis and Clark,* 1:181–84. St. Louis was founded in part for the purpose of controlling the Osages by centralizing trade and diplomacy. See Din and Nasatir, *Imperial Osages,* 56; and William E. Foley and C. David Rice, *The First Chouteaus: River Barons of Early St. Louis* (Urbana: University of Illinois Press, 1983).

10. Zenon Trudeau, trade report, entry for 1793, in Nasatir, *Before Lewis and Clark,* 2:530; log of *La Fleche,* Feb. 9, 1793, in Kinnaird, *Spain in the Mississippi Valley,* 3:119; Zenon Trudeau to François Luis Hector, Barón de Carondelet, Apr. 10, 1793, ibid., 3:148; St. Louis Merchants' Petition, Oct. 15, 1793, ibid., 3:195–98.

11. Morris S. Arnold, *Colonial Arkansas, 1686–1804: A Social and Cultural History* (Fayetteville: University of Arkansas Press, 1991), 62. The average agricultural output of wheat, corn, and tobacco was $4,120. The Osage fur trade averaged $18,750. Morris Arnold and Dorothy Jones Core, eds., *Arkansas Colonials, 1686–1804: A Collection of French and Spanish Records Listing Early Europeans in the Arkansas* (DeWitt, Ark.: Grand Prairie Historical Society, 1986), 47–91; John B. Treat to Henry Dearborn, Mar. 27, 1806, Letter Book of the Arkansas Trading House, 1805–10, Record Group 75, National Archives and Records Administration, Washington, D.C., M142.

12. Manuel Perez to Esteban Miró, Aug. 23, 1790, in Nasatir, *Before Lewis and Clark,* 1:134–35. Lt. Gov. Zenon Trudeau reported 16,000 pesos of trade with the Osages out of a total St. Louis trade of 30,799 pesos. Zenon Trudeau, trade report, entry for 1794, ibid., 2:530. When the St. Louis merchants allotted trading posts, the Osages got sixteen traders and an estimated 96,000 livres of trade goods, more than all other tribes combined. Zenon Trudeau, minutes of merchants' meeting, May 3, 1794, in Kinnaird, *Spain in the Mississippi Valley,* 3:278–79.

13. Manuel Perez to Esteban Miró, Oct. 5, 1791, in Kinnaird, *Spain in the Mississippi Valley,* 2:416; Manuel Perez to Esteban Miró, Nov. 8, 1791, in Nasatir, *Before Lewis and Clark,* 1:150; Merchants of St. Louis to François Luis Hector, Barón de Carondelet, June 22, 1793, ibid., 1:182; the Marqués de Casa Calvo to Ramón de Lopez y Angulo, May 8, 1801, in *The Spanish Régime in Missouri: A Collection of Papers and Documents Relating to Upper Louisiana Principally within the Present Limits of Missouri during the Dominion of Spain, from the Archives of the Indies at Seville,* ed. Louis Houck (1909; reprint, 2 vols. in 1, New York: Arno, 1971), 2:309–10.

14. Log of *La Fleche*, Feb. 9, 1793, in Kinnaird, *Spain in the Mississippi Valley*, 3:119.

15. Louis Lorimier, journal, Aug. 22, 1794, in Houck, *Spanish Régime*, 2:94.

16. Esteban Miró to Bernardo de Gálvez, Aug. 1, 1780, quoted in Esteban Miró to Marqués de Sonora, Feb. 1, 1781, ibid., 1:255.

17. Francisco Cruzat, "Report of the Indian Tribes Who Receive Presents at St. Louis," Nov. 15, 1777, in Houck, *Spanish Régime*, 1:144; Victor Collot, "State of the Indian Nations," 1796, in Nasatir, *Before Lewis and Clark*, 2:384; Stanley Faye, "The Arkansas Post of Louisiana: Spanish Domination," *Louisiana Historical Quarterly* 27 (July 1944): 637.

18. Zenon Trudeau to François Luis Hector, Barón de Carondelet, Sept. 28, 1793, in Nasatir, *Before Lewis and Clark*, 1:197.

19. Zenon Trudeau to François Luis Hector, Barón de Carondelet, Sept. 28, 1793, in Kinnaird, *Spain in the Mississippi Valley*, 3:206–7.

20. Jacobo Du Breuil to Esteban Miró, Dec. 29, 1786, ibid., 2:196.

21. Esteban Miró to Jacobo Du Breuil, Jan. 25, 1787, ibid., 2:197.

22. Luis de Blanc and Rousseau to Esteban Miró, Mar. 20, 1787, ibid., 2:199.

23. Esteban Miró to Joseph Valliere, Feb. 4, 1790, fol. 219, leg. 7, Papeles de Cuba, Archivo General de Indias, Seville, Spain.

24. Zenon Trudeau to François Luis Hector, Barón de Carondelet, Apr. 10, 1793, in Nasatir, *Before Lewis and Clark*, 1:171–73.

25. Louis Lorimier to François Luis Hector, Barón de Carondelet, Sept. 17, 1793, in Kinnaird, *Spain in the Mississippi Valley*, 3:204–5.

26. Ste. Genevieve Inhabitants to Esteban Miró, Apr. 9, 1790, fol. 338, leg. 7, Papeles de Cuba.

27. Zenon Trudeau to François Luis Hector, Barón de Carondelet, Sept. 28, 1793, in Nasatir, *Before Lewis and Clark*, 1:199. See also Carl J. Ekberg, *Colonial Ste. Genevieve: An Adventure on the Mississippi Frontier* (Gerald, Mo.: Patrice, 1985).

28. Bernardo de Gálvez, *Instructions for Governing the Interior Provinces of New Spain, 1786*, ed. and trans. Donald E. Worcester (Berkeley, Calif.: Quivira Society, 1951), 43.

29. Zenon Trudeau to François Luis Hector, Barón de Carondelet, July 25, 1792, in Nasatir, *Before Lewis and Clark*, 1:156–57; Zenon Trudeau to François Luis Hector, Barón de Carondelet, Sept. 28, 1793, ibid., 1:200.

30. Zenon Trudeau to François Luis Hector, Barón de Carondelet, July 25, 1792, ibid., 1:156–57.

31. Many historians of the Osages have taken the influential French traders Auguste and Pierre Chouteau at their word that the brothers created the Arkansas band by persuading a group of Osages to separate from the main groups and move to the Arkansas River region after the Chouteaus lost their

monopoly on Osage trade from St. Louis in 1802. As Willard Rollings points out, Osage establishments existed along the Arkansas earlier than this. Rollings, *The Osage,* 160, 194–98. See also Pedro Piernas to Luis de Unzaga y Amezaga, Apr. 24, 1773, quoted in Fernando de Leyba to Bernardo de Gálvez, Jan. 13, 1779, in Houck, *Spanish Régime,* 1:163; Athanase de Mézières to Luis de Unzaga y Amezaga, Sept. 4, 1774, in *Athanase de Mézières and the Louisiana-Texas Frontier, 1768–1780: Documents Published for the First Time, from the Original Spanish and French Manuscripts, Chiefly in the Archives of Mexico and Spain,* ed. Herbert Eugene Bolton (Cleveland: Arthur H. Clark, 1914), 2:110; Esteban Miró to Antonio Rengel, Dec. 12, 1785, in Nasatir, *Before Lewis and Clark,* 1:124; and Francisco Cruzat to Esteban Miró, Nov. 24, 1787, in Houck, *Spanish Régime,* 1:251.

32. Francisco Cruzat, "Investigation of Benito Vasquez' Activities among the Great Osage," June 22, 1787, in Kinnaird, *Spain in the Mississippi Valley,* 2:214–15.

33. Zenon Trudeau to François Luis Hector, Barón de Carondelet, July 25, 1792, in Nasatir, *Before Lewis and Clark,* 1:156–57; Esteban Miró to Alange, Aug. 7 [or 11], 1792, in *Documentos inéditos para la historia de la Luisiana, 1792–1810,* ed. Jack D. L. Holmes (Madrid: José Porrua Turanzas, 1963), 61.

34. Jacobo Du Breuil to Esteban Miró, Mar. 18, 1785, fol. 560, leg. 107, Papeles de Cuba; Esteban Miró to Bernardo de Gálvez, Aug. 1, 1780, quoted in Esteban Miró to Marqués de Sonora, Feb. 1, 1781, in Houck, *Spanish Régime,* 1:254–55; Rollings, *The Osage,* 167. While Osage chieftanships were not necessarily strictly patrilineal, the new chief apparently always came from the family and clan of the deceased. Carl Chapman, "The Indomitable Osage in Spanish Illinois (Upper Louisiana), 1763–1804," in *The Spanish in the Mississippi Valley, 1762–1804,* ed. John Francis McDermott (Urbana: University of Illinois Press, 1974), 293–94.

35. Esteban Miró to the Marquis de Sonora, Feb. 1, 1781, in Houck, *Spanish Régime,* 1:256–57; Jacobo Du Breuil to Esteban Miró, Mar. 18, 1785, fol. 560, leg. 107, Papeles de Cuba; Esteban Miró to Jacobo Du Breuil, Apr. 28, 1785, fol. 567, leg.107, ibid.

36. Terry P. Wilson, "Claremore, the Osage, and the Intrusion of Other Indians, 1800–1824," in *Indian Leaders: Oklahoma's First Statesmen,* ed. H. Glenn Jordan and Thomas M. Holm (Oklahoma City: Oklahoma Historical Society, 1979), 142.

37. Auguste Chouteau and François Luis Hector, Barón de Carondelet, contract, May 18, 1794, in Houck, *Spanish Régime,* 2:106–8; Rollings, *The Osage,* 191.

38. Zenon Trudeau to François Luis Hector, Barón de Carondelet, Apr. 18, 1795, in Nasatir, *Before Lewis and Clark,* 1:320.

39. See, for example, Chapman, "Indomitable Osage," 293; and Foley and Rice, *First Chouteaus,* 53.

40. Zenon Trudeau to François Luis Hector, Barón de Carondelet, Aug. 30, 1795, in Nasatir, *Before Lewis and Clark,* 1:346.

41. See, for example, Carlos Dehault de Lassus to Marqués de Casa Calvo, Sept. 25, 1800, in Houck, *Spanish Régime,* 2:301; and Marqués de Casa Calvo to Ramón de Lopez y Angulo, May 8, 1801, ibid., 2:309. For evidence of Arkansas Osage dislike for the Chouteaus, see Rollings, *The Osage,* 200, 211.

42. François Luis Hector, Barón de Carondelet to Zenon Trudeau, Jan. 26, 1797, folder 260, box 3, Correspondence and Papers of Francisco Luis Hector Carondelet: Outgoing and Incoming A–L, Louisiana Collection, Bancroft Library, Berkeley, Calif.

43. Foley and Rice, *First Chouteaus,* 56.

44. Zenon Trudeau to Manuel Gayoso de Lemos, Jan. 15, 1798, in Nasatir, *Before Lewis and Clark,* 2:538.

45. Zenon Trudeau to François Luis Hector, Barón de Carondelet, Apr. 18, 1795, ibid., 1:320.

46. Louis Lorimier, journal, Aug. 26, 1794, in Houck, *Spanish Régime,* 2:95.

47. François Luis Hector, Barón de Carondelet, Military Report on Louisiana and West Florida, Nov. 24, 1794, in Robertson, *Louisiana under the Rule of Spain, France, and the United States,* 1:300, 303, 309.

48. Rollings, *The Osage,* 127–28, 132.

49. Louis Lorimier, journal, Feb. 13, 1794, in Houck, *Spanish Régime,* 2:73.

50. Louis Lorimier, journal, Aug. 26, 1794, ibid., 2:95–96.

51. James MacKay, "Table of Distance along the Missouri in Ascending from the Mouth up to the White River," 1797, in Nasatir, *Before Lewis and Clark,* 2:486; Zenon Trudeau to Manuel Gayoso de Lemos, Jan. 15, 1798, ibid., 2:543. In the 1780s and 1790s, Spanish ambassador Diego de Gardoqui assigned a few large land grants to American citizens, including George Morgan, a Philadelphia speculator whose Ohio claims Congress had rejected. But Governor Miró refused Morgan the large grant, instead offering smaller plots of 320 acres for actual settlers. Thomas Perkins Abernethy, *The South in the New Nation, 1789–1819* (Baton Rouge: Louisiana State University Press, 1961), 62–63.

52. See Kathleen DuVal, "'A Good Relationship, & Commerce': The Native Political Economy of the Arkansas River Valley," *Early American Studies: An Interdisciplinary Journal* 1 (Spring 2003): 61–89.

53. James Bruff to James Wilkinson, Nov. 5, 1804, in *Territorial Papers of the United States,* ed. Clarence E. Carter and John P. Bloom (Washington, D.C.: Government Printing Office, 1934–75), 13:80.

54. See, for example, Martinde Navarro, "Political Reflections on the Present Condition of the Province of Louisiana," c. 1785, in Robertson, *Louisiana under the Rule of Spain, France, and the United States,* 1:238.

55. Marc Villiers du Terrage, *The Last Years of French Louisiana,* trans. Hosea Phillips, ed. Carl A. Brasseaux and Glenn R. Conrad (Lafayette: Center for Louisiana Studies, 1982), 434–37.

56. S. Charles Bolton, *Arkansas, 1800–1860: Remote and Restless* (Fayetteville: University of Arkansas Press, 1998), 75–77; Grant Foreman, *Indians and Pioneers: The Story of the American Southwest before 1830,* rev. ed. (Norman: University of Oklahoma Press, 1936), 63–79.

4. A Shifting Middle Ground

1. Richard White offered the middle-ground concept to describe what developed between Indians and whites in the Great Lakes region during the seventeenth and eighteenth centuries. For him it emerged with the "inability of both sides [Indian and white] to gain their ends through force. The middle ground grew according to the need of people to find a means, other than force to gain the cooperation or consent of foreigners. To succeed, those who operated on the middle ground had, of necessity, to attempt to understand the world and the reasoning of others and to assimilate enough of that reasoning to put it to their own purposes." White, *The Middle Ground: Indians, Empires, and Republics in the Great Lakes Region, 1650–1815* (Cambridge: Cambridge University Press, 1991), 52. Stephen Aron finds the middle-ground thesis a useful one for what transpired in Kentucky. Aron, *How the West Was Lost: The Transformation of Kentucky from Daniel Boone to Henry Clay* (Baltimore: Johns Hopkins University Press, 1996), 11. His chapter "The Meeting of Hunters" (5–28) describes how Indians and whites collaborated and borrowed from each other as the first white hunters appeared. A subsequent chapter, "The Parting of Hunters" (29–57), details the dissolution of this middle-ground relationship.

2. Daniel H. Usner Jr., *Indians, Settlers, and Slaves in a Frontier Exchange Economy: The Lower Mississippi Valley before 1783* (Chapel Hill: University of North Carolina Press, 1992). See also Usner, *American Indians in the Lower Mississippi Valley: Social and Economic Histories* (Lincoln: University of Nebraska Press, 1998).

3. Wayne Morris, "Traders and Factories on the Arkansas Frontier, 1805–1822," *Arkansas Historical Quarterly* 28 (Spring 1969): 32. Morris explains that "southern furs were from forty to sixty per cent less valuable than those of northern frontiers because the warmer climate produced lighter pelages and made them more susceptible to rot."

4. According to Morris S. Arnold, though, some lower Mississippi valley products did reach Europe, at least during the eighteenth century, when the area was nominally French. Arnold, *The Rumble of a Distant Drum: The Quapaws and Old World Newcomers, 1673–1804* (Fayetteville: University of Arkansas Press, 2000), 61.

5. W. David Baird describes the alliance between the Quapaws and the French and Spanish. He also traces the disintegration of the relationship between the Quapaw and those in control of Arkansas Post after the American takeover. Baird, *The Quapaw Indians: A History of the Downstream People* (Norman: University of Oklahoma Press, 1980), 39–60. Morris S. Arnold has elaborated further on the close association between the Europeans occupying Arkansas Post and the Quapaws. See Arnold, *Colonial Arkansas: A Social and Cultural History, 1686–1804* (Fayetteville: University of Arkansas Press, 1991); and Arnold, *Rumble of a Distant Drum.*

6. Quoted in Morris, "Traders and Factories on the Arkansas Frontier," 28–29. See also Kathleen DuVal, "'Faithful Nations' and 'Ruthless Savages': The Rise and Fall of Indian Diplomacy in the Arkansas River Valley, 1673–1828" (Ph.D. diss., University of California, Davis, 2001), 204.

7. For a discussion of Jefferson's thinking on the possibilities of "civilizing" the Indians, see Francis Paul Prucha, William T. Hagan, and Alvin M. Josephy Jr., *American Indian Policy* (Indianapolis: Indiana Historical Society, 1971), 6. For laws designed to control white trading, see Prucha, *The Great Father: The United States Government and the American Indians,* vol. 1 (Lincoln: University of Nebraska Press, 1984), 89–98. Prucha also discusses the creation of the trading factories. Ibid., 115–34. For another important source on Indian trade policy, see Anthony F. C. Wallace, *Jefferson and the Indians: The Tragic Fate of the First Americans* (Cambridge, Mass.: Harvard University Press, Belknap Press, 1999), 207–18. Stephen Aron details the interesting clash between white hunters, such as Daniel Boone, and Indians in Kentucky as the middle ground there eroded. Aron, *How the West Was Lost,* 29–57.

8. S. Charles Bolton, "Jeffersonian Indian Removal and the Emergence of Arkansas Territory," *Arkansas Historical Quarterly* 62 (Autumn 2003): 271.

9. For a succinct narrative of the venture, see Trey Berry, "The Expedition of William Dunbar and George Hunter along the Ouachita River, 1804–1805," *Arkansas Historical Quarterly* 62 (Winter 2003): 386–403.

10. For a discussion of the Spanish concerns about the Red River expedition, see Dan L. Flores, ed., *Jefferson and Southwestern Exploration: The Freeman and Custis Accounts of the Red River Expedition of 1806* (Norman: University of Oklahoma Press, 1984), 28–38. For a discussion of the difficulties presented by the Osages, see "Introduction," in "The Western Journals of Dr. George Hunter, 1796–1805," ed. John Francis McDermott, *Transactions of the American Philosophical Society* 53 (July 1963): 11.

11. According to Willard H. Rollings, the Osages, who lived "between the Missouri and the Arkansas Rivers . . . , were in a strategic location that allowed them to control access to the west, while occupying the middle ground between competing European colonial frontiers." Rollings sees the control of the Ozark forests down to the Arkansas River as "vital to their

trade economy, and any threat to it was a serious threat to Osage survival."
Rollings, *The Osage: An Ethnohistorical Study of Hegemony on the Prairie-Plains* (Columbia: University of Missouri Press, 1992), 179, 185. See also
Gilbert C. Din and A. P. Nasatir, *The Imperial Osage: Spanish-Indian Diplomacy in the Mississippi Valley* (Norman: University of Oklahoma Press,
1983). Although Dunbar and Hunter routinely questioned hunters and travelers they encountered on the river as to the activities of the Osages, the expedition was apparently in no danger. William Dunbar, "Journal of a Voyage," in
[Eron Opha Moore] Rowland, ed., *Life, Letters, and Papers of William Dunbar of Elgin, Morayshire, Scotland, and Natchez, Mississippi: Pioneer Scientist of the Southern United States* (Jackson: Mississippi Historical
Society, 1930), Nov. 24 (251), Nov. 26 (252–53), Nov. 28, 1804 (251) [hereafter cited as Dunbar journal]; George Hunter, "Journal of an Excursion from
Natchez on the Mississippi up the River Ouachita, 1804–1805," in
McDermott, "Western Journals of Dr. George Hunter," Nov. 26, 1804 (98)
[hereafter cited as Hunter journal].

12. "William Dunbar," in Rowland, *Life, Letters, and Papers of William Dunbar,* 9–10.

13. McDermott, "Introduction," 5–6.

14. Ibid., 10–12.

15. Hunter journal, Oct. 16 (71), Oct. 17, 1804 (81); Dunbar journal,
Oct. 17, 1804 (216–17).

16. Hunter journal, Oct. 18 (81), Oct. 23 (82), Nov. 6 (87), Nov. 7, 1804
(88); Dunbar journal, Oct. 18 (217), Nov. 6, 1804 (235–36). Dunbar dispatched a letter to Jefferson from the post detailing the problems with the
boat. See McDermott, "Introduction," 13.

17. Hunter journal, Nov. 11 (90), Nov. 14 (91), Nov. 16, 1804 (92);
Dunbar journal, Nov. 11 (238), Nov. 15 (241), Nov. 16, 1804 (242).

18. Dunbar journal, Nov. 13 (239).

19. Ibid., Oct. 22, 1804 (220–21).

20. Hunter journal, Nov. 4, 1804 (86–87). Dunbar praised the soldiers'
exertions on occasion (Dunbar journal, Dec. 3, 1804 [260]). Yet once they
reached the hot springs, he complained of their "dilatory ways" (Dec. 9, 1804
[272]).

21. Hunter made notations about rapids, shoals, or other difficulties on the
river on the following dates: Hunter journal, Oct. 25 (83), Oct. 29 (84), Oct.
31 (85), Nov. 1 (85), Nov. 2 (86), Nov. 3 (86), Nov. 4 (86–87), Nov. 5 (87),
Nov. 13 (90), Nov. 18 (93), Nov. 22 (96), Nov. 23 (96), Nov. 24 (96), Nov.
26 (97), Nov. 27 (97), Nov. 28 (98; he mentions a slight delay), Nov. 29 (99),
Nov. 30 (99), Dec. 1, 1804 (99). On December 2–4, 1804, they reached the
"Great Chute" and encountered some other very difficult obstacles (99–100).
Dunbar was somewhat less attentive in his journal entries to the problems on
the river. In addition to the difficulties of getting the boat and then the barge

over the rapids and shoals, the expedition had two accidents. Their mast was destroyed when they "ran under a projecting tree." Ibid., Nov. 4 (87). They also did damage to their rudder when they came upon a sunken log. Ibid., Nov. 14 (91).

22. Dunbar journal, Nov. 24 (249); Hunter journal, Nov. 22 (96).

23. Dunbar journal, Oct. 25 (226–27), Oct. 29 (228–29), Oct. 30 (229), Oct. 31 (230), Nov. 3 (232–33), Nov. 4 (234), Nov. 5 (234), Nov. 8 (237), Nov. 12 (239), Nov. 13 (240), Nov. 14 (240–41), Nov. 16 (243), Nov. 17 (243–44), Nov. 18 (245), Nov. 19 (246), Nov. 20 (246–47), Nov. 21 (247), Nov. 22 (274–78), Nov. 23 (250), Nov. 26 (252), Nov. 27 (253–54), Nov. 28 (255), Dec. 1 (258), Dec. 2 (259–60), Dec. 4 (263), Dec. 6, 1804 (266); Hunter journal, Oct. 25 (83), Oct. 27 (84), Oct. 28 (84), Oct. 29 (85), Nov. 1 (85), Nov. 2 (86), Nov. 8 (87), Nov. 14 (91), Nov. 15 (92), Nov. 17 (93), Nov. 18 (93), Nov. 20 (94), Nov. 21 (95), Nov. 22 (95), Nov. 24 (96), Nov. 28, 1804 (98).

24. For Jefferson's instructions to Hunter to "ascertain . . . the Latitude & Longitude of the most important sources & courses," see McDermott, "Introduction," 9. For mentions of taking measurements, see Dunbar journal, Oct. 24 (255), Oct. 26 (227), Oct. 28 (228), Oct. 29 (229), Oct. 30 (229), Oct. 31 (230), Nov. 3 (233), Nov. 6 (236), Nov. 7 (236), Nov. 10 (237), Nov. 11 (238), Nov. 12 (239), Nov. 14 (240), Nov. 15 (241), Nov. 17 (244), Nov. 18 (245), Nov. 21 (247), Nov. 23 (249), Nov. 24 (251), Nov. 30 (257), Dec. 2 (260), Dec. 3 (260), Dec. 4, 1804 (263).

25. As Jefferson put it in a communication to Dunbar, "the thing to be guarded against is that an indulgence to his principal qualifications may not lead to a diversion [?] of our mission to a march for gold and silver mines, these are but an incidental object, to be noted if found in their way, as salt, or coal or lime would, but not to be sought after." Quoted in McDermott, "Introduction," 9. For more on Hunter's business reverses as well as his many entrepreneurial activities, see ibid., 6–8.

26. Hunter journal, Nov. 1 (85), Nov. 3 (86), Nov. 27 (97), Nov. 29 (98), Nov. 30, 1804 (99). Dunbar remarked upon Hunter's preoccupation with finding some substance of commercial value. Dunbar journal, Nov. 23 (250), Nov. 24 (251), Nov. 27 (253–54), Nov. 28 (256), Nov. 29 (256), Nov. 30, 1804 (257).

27. Dunbar journal, Nov. 1 (231–32), Nov. 21 (247), Dec. 7 (268), Dec. 11, 1804 (275).

28. For remarks about hunting and fishing, see Dunbar journal, Oct. 30 (229), Nov. 14 (241), Nov. 17 (243), Nov. 21 (247), Nov. 30 (257), Dec. 5, 1804 (266); and Hunter journal, Oct. 28 (84), Nov. 2 (86), Nov. 3 (86), Nov. 5 (87), Nov. 13 (90), Nov. 14 (91), Nov. 15 (92), Nov. 16 (92), Nov. 17 (93), Nov. 21, 1804 (95).

29. Dunbar journal, Nov. 5 (234–35), Nov. 11 (239), Nov. 13 (239), Nov. 17 (243), Nov. 18 (245), Nov. 28, 1804 (255–56). Hunter also reported hunters.

Hunter journal, Nov. 6 (88), Nov. 13 (90), Nov. 16 (92), Nov. 18 (93), Nov. 20 (94), Nov. 21 (95), Nov. 28 (98), Nov. 29, 1804 (98).

30. George E. Lankford, "Almost 'Illinark': The French Presence in Northeast Arkansas," in *Cultural Encounters in the Early South: Indians and Europeans in Arkansas,* comp. Jeannie M. Whayne (Fayetteville: University of Arkansas Press, 1995), 98–99, 111.

31. Hunter journal, Nov. 29, 1804 (98).

32. Le Fevre also gave Dunbar considerable information about the Arkansas River and about the Native Americans in the region. Dunbar journal, Jan. 10, 1805 (306).

33. Ibid., Nov.18, 1804 (245).

34. Interestingly, Morris S. Arnold suggests that "habitants" was a French term applied to agricultural colonists in the eighteenth century. Arnold, *Colonial Arkansas, 1686–1804: A Social and Cultural History* (Fayetteville: University of Arkansas Press, 1991), 11.

35. Hunter journal, Nov. 21, 1804 (95). Neither Dunbar nor Hunter were predisposed to trust a man of Campbell's social standing. Just as Hunter routinely denigrated the soldiers, he dismissed the pilot hired at the Post of Ouachita as a man who was "not remarkable either for his judgment or veracity." Ibid., Nov. 22, 1804 (95–96).

36. Ibid., Nov. 28, 1804 (98).

37. Ibid., Dec. 6 (100–101), Dec. 31, 1804 (109); Dunbar journal, Dec. 6, 1804 (267).

38. See Hunter journal, Dec. 8, 1804 (101).

39. McDermott quotes from Hunter's official report in a footnote. Ibid., 104n.

40. On December 16 Hunter "made an excursion into the mountains and today he goes again; he discovered nothing of importance." Dunbar journal, Dec. 17 (281–82). On the twenty-seventh Hunter indicates that he had taken two short daylong trips and was packing up to take a four-day trip, but he ended up taking only two days "as we saw no appearances of minerals or mettals in this part of the country worth further search." Hunter journal, Dec. 27, 1804 (107–8).

41. Dunbar journal, Dec. 22 (286), Dec. 25, 1804 (292); Hunter journal, Dec. 25, 1804 (106–7). A New Orleans newspaper apparently reported that Hunter indicated to them that the springs "possess extraordinary medical value" (McDermott, "Introduction," 15), but this is not what he confides in his diary. Dunbar writes, the "Doctor has been unable to discover any thing in the water of the hot springs except some weak acid which is probably Carbonic." Dunbar journal, Dec. 19 (283).

42. Hunter journal, Jan. 31, 1805 (116).

43. Jefferson determined to eliminate the Arkansas portion of the Grand Expedition and focus on the Red because of the Osages. As to Hunter's deci-

sion to decline the opportunity to take the Red River trip, Dan Flores specu-lates: "Perhaps the three dollars a day he had been paid the year before [on the Ouachita River excursion] was not enough to keep him away from his business; perhaps, since he was a mineralogist, the deletion of the rockier Arkansas River from the exploration caused him to lose interest. But it seems equally likely that Hunter had some knowledge of what the Spanish reaction would be to the 'Grand Excursion,' and declined primarily on those grounds." Flores, *Jefferson and Southwestern Exploration*, 46–47.

44. Hunter journal, Nov. 28 (98–99); Dunbar journal, Nov. 28 (255–56).

45. Robert A. Myers, "Cherokee Pioneers in Arkansas: The St. Francis Years, 1785–1813," *Arkansas Historical Quarterly* 56 (Summer 1997): 127–57. See also Joseph Patrick Key, "'Masters of This Country': The Quapaws and Environmental Change in Arkansas, 1673–1833" (Ph.D. diss., University of Arkansas, 2001), 138–39.

46. William Dunbar to Henry Dearborn, Feb. 25, 1806, in "William Dunbar's Letterbook from 1805 to 1810," in Rowland, *Life, Letters, and Papers of William Dunbar*, 330; DuVal, "'Faithful Nations' and 'Ruthless Savages,'" 190.

47. Key, "'Masters of This Country,'" 138.

48. John B. Treat to William Davy, Principal Agent for Indian Factories, Oct. 6, 1805, Letter Book of the Arkansas Trading House, 1805–10, Record Group 75, National Archives and Records Administration, Washington, D.C. [hereafter cited as Letter Book].

49. Morris, "Traders and Factories on the Arkansas Frontier," 28–29.

50. Treat to Davy, Nov. 15, 1805, Letter Book. See also Baird, *Quapaw Indians*, 52.

51. Treat to Henry Dearborn, Nov. 15, 1805, Mar. 27, 1806, Letter Book; Treat to Davy, Apr. 15, 1806, ibid. [quotation]; and Davy to Treat, Feb. 14, 1806, ibid.; Myers, "Cherokee Pioneers in Arkansas," 148; Morris, "Traders and Factories on the Arkansas Frontier," 35.

52. Treat to Davy, Feb. 27, 1806, Letter Book; Dearborn to Treat, Apr. 29, 1806, ibid. See also Aloysius Plaisance, "The Arkansas Factory, 1805–1810," *Arkansas Historical Quarterly* 11 (Autumn 1952): 189.

53. White, *Middle Ground*, 53.

54. Baird, *Quapaw Indians*, 51–52.

55. Treat to Dearborn, Mar. 27, 1806, Letter Book.

56. Treat to Dearborn, May 20, 1806, ibid.

57. Treat to Dearborn, Nov. 18, 1806, ibid.

58. In one letter William Davy, the man in charge of all Indian factories when Treat was first appointed, complained, "I am not a little embarrass'd to understand why it is that by the Governor of the Trade of these Waters at this time is prohibited, as you add so much to the injury of your factory by pre-venting the Osage Tribe of 1200 hunting men from coming to, or trading with

you and inducing them to intercept all others from passing by them." Davy to Treat, Feb. 14, 1806, ibid. See also Treat to Dearborn, Nov. 15, 1805, ibid.; and DuVal, "'Faithful Nations' and 'Ruthless Savages,'" 187.

59. Treat to Davy, Nov. 15, 1805, Letter Book.

60. Treat to Dearborn, Nov. 15, 1805, ibid.

61. Treat to John Shee, Jan. 8, 1807, ibid. Shee had replaced Davy as principal agent for Indian factories.

62. Treat to Davy, Apr. 15, 1806, ibid.

63. Myers, "Cherokee Pioneers in Arkansas," 147–53. Connetoo may, in fact, have been a white man adopted into the tribe.

64. Key, "Masters of This Country," 152–53.

65. Baird, *Quapaw Indians,* 53.

66. Shee to Treat, July 20, 1807, Letter Book.

67. Treat first mentions the construction of a building in two letters he wrote in November 1805, one to the secretary of war and the other to the principal agent for Indian factories. Treat to Dearborn, Nov. 15, 1805, ibid.; Treat to Davy, Nov. 15, 1805, ibid. He described the building he hoped to build in mid-1806. Treat to Davy, July 1, 1806, ibid. He reported little progress with the building a year later. Treat to Shee, June 30, 1807, ibid. In early 1808 he reported, too optimistically it turns out, that he hoped to occupy the property by that autumn. Treat to John Mason, Superintendent of Indian Trade, Mar. 21, 1808, ibid. He was still reporting progress in September. John B. Treat to Mason, Sept. 20, 1808, ibid. But the building remained incomplete the following spring. Treat to Mason, Mar. 31, 1809, ibid. For the description of the unfinished building, see Sam Treat, Assistant Factor, to Mason, Sept. 30, 1810, ibid. Aloysius Plaisance suggests that Treat completed his building, but this is clearly a misreading of the correspondence. Plaisance, "Arkansas Factory," 186. For a reference to the closing of the factory, see Mason to Waterman, May 29, 1810, Letter Book.

68. White, *Middle Ground,* x.

5. Jeffersonian Indian Removal and the Emergence of Arkansas Territory

1. On Arkansas and the Trail of Tears, see the extensive documentation and analysis done by the Sequoyah Research Center of the American Native Press Archives at the University of Arkansas at Little Rock. ANPA homepage, http//:www.anpa.ualr.edu.

2. There is a large literature on Jeffersonian Indian removal. The most important work is still Bernard W. Sheehan, *Seeds of Extinction: Jeffersonian Philanthropy and the American Indian* (Chapel Hill: University of North Carolina Press, 1973). But a newer study somewhat more relevant to this essay is Anthony F. C. Wallace, *Jefferson and the Indians: The Tragic Fate of*

the First Americans (Cambridge, Mass.: Harvard University Press, Belknap Press, 1999). Francis Paul Prucha examines federal policy more broadly in *American Indian Policy in the Formative Years: The Indian Trade and Intercourse Acts, 1780–1834* (Cambridge, Mass.: Harvard University Press, 1962) and *The Great Father: The United States Government and the American Indians,* 2 vols. in 1 (Lincoln: University of Nebraska Press, 1984), 1:184–91. More critical is Reginald Horsman, "The Indian Policy of an 'Empire for Liberty,'" in *Native Americans and the Early Republic,* ed. Frederick E. Hoxie, Ronald Hoffman, and Peter J. Albert (Charlottesville: University Press of Virginia, 1999), 37–61. Christian B. Keller argues that Jefferson shifted from a benevolent hope for Indian acculturation to the more negative policy of removal in "Philanthropy Betrayed: Thomas Jefferson, the Louisiana Purchase, and the Origins of Federal Indian Removal Policy," *Proceedings of the American Philosophical Society* 144 (Mar. 2000): 39–66. Roger G. Kennedy discounts the president's concern for Indians and argues that his interest in providing land for small farmers was subverted by his support for the expansion of plantation agriculture. See Kennedy, *Mr. Jefferson's Lost Cause: Land, Farmers, Slavery, and the Louisiana Purchase* (New York: Oxford University Press, 2003), esp. 152–55.

3. Students of Missouri history have noted Jefferson's shift of interest from upper Louisiana in general to the area south of Cape Girardeau as a place to which Indians could be removed, but it has not been closely studied. See William E. Foley, *The Genesis of Missouri: From Wilderness Outpost to Statehood* (Columbia: University of Missouri Press, 1989), 175; and Walter A. Schroeder, *Opening the Ozarks: A Historical Geography of Missouri's Ste. Genevieve District, 1760–1830* (Columbia: University of Missouri Press, 2002), 166. Anthony F. C. Wallace does not distinguish between the two areas. Wallace, *Jefferson and the Indians,* 254–60.

4. Robert A. Myers, "Cherokee Pioneers in Arkansas: The St. Francis Years, 1785–1813," *Arkansas Historical Quarterly* 56 (Summer 1997): 127–57; George E. Lankford, "Shawnee Convergence: Immigrant Indians in the Ozarks," *Arkansas Historical Quarterly* 58 (Winter 1999): 390–413; Joseph Patrick Key, "Indians and Ecological Conflict in Territorial Arkansas," *Arkansas Historical Quarterly* 59 (Summer 2000): 127–46. An exception is Kathleen DuVal's "'Faithful Nations' and 'Ruthless Savages': The Rise and Fall of Indian Diplomacy in the Arkansas River Valley" (Ph.D. diss., University of California, Davis, 2001), which discusses U.S.–Indian relations in Arkansas within the context of Jeffersonian Indian policy. The interpretation of Cherokee migration presented here is similar to her briefer account. Ibid., 223–26.

5. The idea of Indians exercising autonomous power and strategic initiative was developed in James H. Merrell, *The Indians' New World: Catawbas and Their Neighbors from European Contact through the Era of Removal*

(Chapel Hill: University of North Carolina Press, 1989), and became enormously influential as a result of Richard White, *The Middle Ground: Indians, Empires, and Republics in the Great Lakes Region, 1650–1815* (Cambridge: Cambridge University Press, 1991). Their work informs most of the serious scholarship on Native Americans published since that time.

6. Foley, *Genesis of Missouri*, 36; Carl J. Ekberg, *French Roots in the Illinois Country: The Mississippi Frontier in Colonial Times* (Urbana: University of Illinois Press, 1998), 1–2; Nicholas de Finiels, *An Account of Upper Louisiana*, ed. Carl J. Ekberg and William E. Foley, trans. Ekberg (Columbia: University of Missouri Press, 1989), 28 n. 8; Louis Houck, *A History of Missouri from the Earliest Explorations and Settlements until the Admission of the State into the Union* (1908; reprint, 3 vols. in 1, New York: Arno, 1971), 2:62.

7. Finiels, *Account of Upper Louisiana*, 30–31; Morris S. Arnold, *Colonial Arkansas, 1686–1804: A Social and Cultural History* (Fayetteville: University of Arkansas Press, 1991), 8, 20, 145–46.

8. Schroeder, *Opening the Ozarks*, 10–11.

9. Ibid., 79–80, 97–102; Foley, *Genesis of Missouri*, 15–28; James Neal Primm, *Lion of the Valley: St. Louis, Missouri*, 2d ed. (Boulder, Colo.: Pruitt, 1998), 46–52, 54–55, 69–70.

10. Amos Stoddard, *Sketches, Historical and Descriptive, of Louisiana* (Philadelphia: Matthew Carey, 1812), 208, 210; Conevery Bolton Valencius, *The Health of the Country: How American Settlers Understood Themselves and Their Land* (New York: Basic Books, 2002), 86–92.

11. F. Cuming, *Sketches of a Tour to the Western Country*, in *Early Western Travels, 1748–1846*, ed. Reuben Gold Thwaites (1904–7; reprint, New York: AMS, 1966), 4:281–83, 291, 296; Schroeder, *Opening the Ozarks*, 427 n. 33; James L. Penick, *The New Madrid Earthquakes* (Columbia: University of Missouri Press, 1981); Lynn Morrow, "New Madrid and Its Hinterland, 1786–1826," *Bulletin of the Missouri Historical Society* 36, no. 4 (1980): 241–50. Ten months after the initial quake, the rearranged landscape forced Henry Cassidy to give up an attempt to travel overland from Arkansas Post to St. Louis. See Clarence E. Carter and John P. Bloom, eds. *Territorial Papers of the United States* (Washington, D.C.: Government Printing Office, 1934–75), 14:623–24.

12. Bond to James Wilkinson, Aug. 2, 1805, in Carter and Bloom, *Territorial Papers*, 13:176.

13. Daniel H. Usner Jr., *Indians, Settlers, and Slaves in a Frontier Exchange Economy: The Lower Mississippi Valley before 1783* (Chapel Hill: University of North Carolina Press, 1992), 150, 174–76; Arnold, *Colonial Arkansas*, 60–64; Foley, *Genesis of Missouri*, 24–26; William E. Foley and C. David Rice, *The First Chouteaus: River Barons of Early St. Louis* (Urbana:

University of Illinois Press, 1983), 5–9, 37–39; Ekberg, *French Roots in the Illinois Country,* 216–35.

14. Schroeder, *Opening the Ozarks,* 345–58; S. Charles Bolton, *Arkansas, 1800–1860: Remote and Restless* (Fayetteville: University of Arkansas Press, 1998), 5–18, 50–54. Key's "Indians and Ecological Conflict" describes struggles over land use that preceded the arrival of cotton culture.

15. Printed versions of the amendment are available in a number of locations, but the original is in the Thomas Jefferson Papers, Library of Congress, which may be viewed and searched online at the Library of Congress American Memory Project (http://memory.loc.gov/ammen/mtjhtm/mtjhome.html). The quotation is from Jefferson to John C. Breckenridge, Aug. 1803, in *The Jeffersonian Cyclopedia: A Comprehensive Collection of Views of Thomas Jefferson,* ed. John P. Foley (New York: Funk and Wagnalls, 1900), 2:516. See also Jefferson to Dupont de Nemours, Apr. 1802, ibid., 2:515.

16. Donald Jackson, *Thomas Jefferson and the Stony Mountains: Exploring the West from Monticello* (1981; reprint, Norman: University of Oklahoma Press, 1993), 112; Annie Heloise Abel, *The History of Events Resulting in Indian Consolidation West of the Mississippi,* vol. 1, Annual Report of the American Historical Association for the Year 1906 (Washington, D.C.: Government Printing Office, 1908), 246.

17. Published later, Amos Stoddard's sketches indicate that the boundary was the Arkansas River. Stoddard, *Sketches,* 34. A second draft of the amendment is in the Jefferson Papers.

18. The amended version is in the Jefferson Papers. It is not in Jefferson's hand. The author is identified in Abel, *Indian Consolidation,* 247–48.

19. "An Act erecting Louisiana into two territories, and providing for the temporary government thereof," Mar. 26, 1804, in Carter and Bloom, *Territorial Papers,* 9:202, 210.

20. Ibid., 9:202–13. The figures for the Orleans population are taken from Peter John Kastor, "Apprenticeship to Liberty: The Incorporation of Louisiana and the Struggle for Nationhood in the Early American Republic, 1803–1820" (Ph.D. diss., University of Virginia, 1999), 73. The estimate for the population of the District of Louisiana was made by Benjamin Stoddard on June 3, 1804, based on extrapolations from the Spanish census of 1800. See Carter and Bloom, *Territorial Papers,* 13:18 n. 36; and Schroeder, *Opening the Ozarks,* 16. William E. Foley discusses the writing and passage of the act. Foley, *Genesis of Missouri,* 148–49. Sen. William Cocke of Tennessee, quoted by Delaware senator Samuel White, Nov. 2, 1803, in *Annals of Congress,* 8th Cong., 1st sess., 34.

21. "Remonstrance of the People of Louisiana," in *American State Papers: Miscellaneous,* 1:400; "Revision of the Political System Adopted for Louisiana," ibid., 1:417–18. See also Thomas Waters to the President,

Aug. 23, 1804, in Carter and Bloom, *Territorial Papers*, 13:38–39; and Foley, *Genesis of Missouri*, 150–58. On the lead mines report, see David B. Gracy II, *Moses Austin: His Life* (San Antonio: Trinity University Press, 1987), 95–96. The president's message to Congress is available online at the Avalon Project at Yale Law School (http://www.yale.edu/lawweb/avalon/avalon.htm/).

22. The Territory of Orleans law is "Act of March 2, 1805," *Statutes at Large of the United States of America* 2 (1856): 322–23. The Land Claims Board law is "Act of March 2, 1805," ibid., 324–29. The Louisiana Territory law is "Act of March 3, 1805," ibid., 331–22.

23. Dumas Malone, *Jefferson and His Time*, vol. 5, *Jefferson the President: Second Term, 1805–1809* (Boston: Little, Brown, 1974), 227; Foley, *Genesis of Missouri*, 162, 177–78.

24. Wilkinson to [James] Madison, Aug. 24, 1805, in Carter and Bloom, *Territorial Papers*, 13:189; Wilkinson to Jefferson, Nov. 6, 1805, ibid., 13:266.

25. Wilkinson to Madison, Aug. 24, 1805, ibid., 13:189–90.

26. Wilkinson to Jefferson, Nov. 6, 1805, ibid., 13:266; Wilkinson to Madison, Dec. 25, 1805, ibid., 13:317. From the beginning Wilkinson had also made clear that implementation of the president's policy would require peace between the Osages and other Indian nations residing in the territory. See Wilkinson to Dearborn, Sept. 22, 1805, ibid., 13:229. On the concept of encouraging existing white settlers to leave their homes, see the more complete discussion, which does not, however, distinguish between the areas above and below Cape Girardeau, in Wallace, *Jefferson and the Indians*, 254–60.

27. Foley, *Genesis of Missouri*, 159–69; proclamation by Wilkinson, in Carter and Bloom, *Territorial Papers*, 13:540. For Bond's letter, see ibid., 14:16–18. On the relationship between Jefferson and Wilkinson, see Roger G. Kennedy, *Hidden Cities: The Discovery and Loss of Ancient North American Civilization* (New York: Free Press, 1994), 152–56.

28. "Account of Indian Tribes," Sept. 29, 1803, in Carter and Bloom, *Territorial Papers*, 9:62–66. On Clark and the president's quest for information, see Jackson, *Jefferson and the Stony Mountains*, 98–105.

29. Particularly successful in this regard were the twelve hundred Shawnees and six hundred Delawares who had obtained a Spanish grant to 750 square miles in the southeastern portion of Ste. Genevieve District with the assistance of Louis Lorimier, a half-white trader who fought with them on the side of the British in the American Revolution. Agriculturalists as well as hunters, Shawnees and Delawares lived in a manner much like that of white American frontiersmen. The United States recognized the validity of their claim, and Lorimier served as a local official in the government of Louisiana Territory. Wallace, *Jefferson and the Indians*, 274; Schroeder, *Opening the Ozarks*, 371–74; Foley, *Genesis of Missouri*, 64–65; Colin G. Calloway, "The

Continuing Revolution in Indian Country," in Hoxie, Hoffman, and Albert, *Native Americans and the Early Republic,* 20–21. Some of the Shawnees eventually migrated into northern Arkansas. See Lankford, "Shawnee Convergence."

30. Myers, "Cherokee Pioneers," 134–47. Myers appears to think of the Cherokees along the St. Francis as a single unit, though there were Cherokees in the New Madrid area prior to the arrival of Connetoo.

31. Treat to Henry Dearborn, Secretary of War, Dec. 31, 1806, in Carter and Bloom, *Territorial Papers,* 14:56.

32. President's Talk to Chiefs of Cherokee Nation, Jan. 10, 1806, Letters Sent by the Secretary of War Relating to Indian Affairs, 1801–24, Bureau of Indian Affairs, Record Group 75, National Archives and Records Administration, Washington, D.C., M-15, reel 2, 147–48. Jefferson made similar offers to other tribes. See Wallace, *Jefferson and the Indians,* 274.

33. Stanley W. Hoig, *The Cherokees and Their Chiefs: In the Wake of Empire* (Fayetteville: University of Arkansas Press, 1998), 91–94; William G. McLoughlin, *Cherokee Renascence in the New Republic, 1794–1833* (Princeton, N.J.: Princeton University Press, 1986), 84–86, 95–96, 99–100, 104–5.

34. The development of Cherokee nationalism is a major theme of McLoughlin, *Cherokee Renascence,* 109–10, 115, 118–21, 139–43. See also McLoughlin, "Thomas Jefferson and the Beginning of Cherokee Nationalism, 1806 to 1809," *William and Mary Quarterly,* 3d ser., 32 (Oct. 1975): 562–80.

35. McLoughlin, *Cherokee Renascence,* 106–7, 128–29, 132–33, 135, 147–48; Hoig, *Cherokees and Their Chiefs,* 96–99.

36. Jefferson to Cherokees, Jan. 9, 1809, in *American State Papers: Indian Affairs,* 2:125.

37. Meigs to Secretary of War, quoted in *(St. Louis) Louisiana Gazette,* Feb. 1810; McLoughlin, *Cherokee Renascence,* 152–53, 159–60, 163 n. 37, 167; Hoig, *Cherokees and Their Chiefs,* 104–5.

38. *(St. Louis) Louisiana Gazette,* Mar. 21, 1812. Robert A. Myers indicates that the move to the Arkansas River was the result of conflict with white settlers and the effects of the New Madrid earthquakes. Myers, "Cherokee Pioneers," 152–56. These were no doubt factors, but it appears that there were Cherokees along the Arkansas prior to 1811 and that Jefferson's recommendation was the underlying cause of settlement in that area. Myers also estimates the St. Francis population at about two thousand people, which it probably was, but suggests that most of them were in one town that was "four times the size of Arkansas Post." Cherokee towns rarely included more than three hundred people, and the Arkansas population was probably much more widely spread along the St. Francis, White, and upper Arkansas Rivers. See Hoig, *Cherokees and Their Chiefs,* 104; McLoughlin, *Cherokee Renascence,* 56, 163 n. 7, 166; and Meigs to Secretary of War, Feb. 17, 1816, in Carter and Bloom, *Territorial Papers,* 15:121–23.

39. Treaty with the Cherokees, July 8, 1817, in Charles J. Kappler, *Indian Affairs: Laws and Treaties* (Washington, D.C.: Government Printing Office, 1904), 2:140–44. The Cherokees were anxious to have a treaty because of their ongoing conflict with the Osages. See Bolton, *Arkansas, 1800–1860,* 75–77; and the much fuller account in DuVal, "'Faithful Nations' and 'Ruthless Savages,'" 234–48.

40. On the Treaty of 1817, see McLoughlin, *Cherokee Renascence,* 206–20, 228–33; on the struggle over removal, ibid., 234–46; and on the Treaty of 1819, ibid., 247–57. The acreage and population figures are cited in ibid., 256. The number of Cherokees in Arkansas is an elusive figure. Cherokee subagent William Lovely estimated it at thirty-six hundred in 1814, but McLoughlin thinks it was closer to two thousand. Ibid., 220. Gov. William Clark estimated it at six thousand in 1817. See "List of Indian Tribes," in Carter and Bloom, *Territorial Papers,* 15:304–5. Part of the problem is that there was a good deal of movement back and forth across the Mississippi.

41. *Census for 1820* (1821; reprint, New York: Arno, 1976), 41*.

42. Bolton, *Arkansas, 1800–1860,* 69–82. See also DuVal, "'Faithful Nations' and 'Ruthless Savages,'" 227–65; and Arthur H. DeRosier Jr., *The Removal of the Choctaw Indians* (Knoxville: University of Tennessee Press, 1970).

43. Bates to Albert Gallatin, July 22, 1808, in *The Life and Papers of Frederick Bates,* ed. Thomas Maitland Marshall (St. Louis: Missouri Historical Society, 1926), 2:7–11 [quote, 8]; Bates to Land Commissioners, Aug. 15, 1808, ibid., 2:11–13.

44. Proclamation by Governor Clark, Sept. 17, 1814, in Carter and Bloom, *Territorial Papers,* 14:790–91; *Laws of a Public and General Nature of the District of Louisiana, of the Territory of Louisiana, of the Territory of Missouri, and of the State of Missouri: Up to the Year 1824* (Jefferson City, Mo.: W. Lusk and Son, 1842), 299.

45. Resolution of the Territorial Assembly, Jan. 2, 1817, in Carter and Bloom, *Territorial Papers,* 15:224–25; Memorial of the Territorial Assembly, Jan. 8, 1819, ibid., 15:495–98.

46. See Bolton, *Arkansas, 1800–1860,* 25–47, 67–87; and DuVal, "'Faithful Nations' and 'Ruthless Savages,'" 227–65. On the western Cherokees in general, see Hoig, *Cherokees and Their Chiefs;* and Robert Paul Markman, "The Arkansas Cherokees, 1817–1828" (Ph.D. diss., University of Oklahoma, 1972).

6. "Outcasts upon the World"

1. Walter Nugent, *Into the West: The Story of Its People* (New York: Alfred A. Knopf, 1999), 44–45, 49. Nugent uses the phrase "demographic

inundation" in reference to Texas, into which Anglo-Americans had moved even before U.S. acquisition. Between 1492 and 1803 the two most important demographic transitions in Arkansas had involved sudden population declines. The first occurred in the middle to late sixteenth century and has been attributed to drought and/or disease, while the second began with the smallpox epidemic of 1698, which followed the arrival of the French and other Europeans.

2. Clarence E. Carter and John P. Bloom, eds., *Territorial Papers of the United States* (Washington, D.C.: Government Printing Office, 1934–75), 13:164; S. Charles Bolton, *Arkansas, 1800–1860: Remote and Restless* (Fayetteville: University of Arkansas Press, 1998), 5, 10, 17; Morris S. Arnold, *The Rumble of a Distant Drum: The Quapaws and Old World Newcomers, 1673–1804* (Fayetteville: University of Arkansas Press, 2000), 72.

3. Arnold, *Rumble of a Distant Drum;* George Sabo III, "Rituals of Encounter: Interpreting Native American Views of European Explorers," in *Cultural Encounters in the Early South: Indians and Europeans in Arkansas,* comp. Jeannie Whayne (Fayetteville: University of Arkansas Press, 1995), 76–87.

4. Joseph Patrick Key, "Indians and Ecological Conflict in Territorial Arkansas," *Arkansas Historical Quarterly* 59 (Summer 2000): 131–33; W. David Baird, *The Quapaw Indians: A History of the Downstream People* (Norman: University of Oklahoma Press, 1980), 51; Thomas Nuttall, *A Journal of Travels into the Arkansas Territory during the Year 1819* (1980; reprint, Fayetteville: University of Arkansas Press, 1999), 101, 310. In the years just before and after the purchase, travelers commented on the presence of several Indian camps, including a Choctaw village, along the Arkansas between the Quapaw villages and the Arkansas Post. See Victor Collot, *A Journey in North America* (1826; reprint, Firenze: O. Lange, 1924), 2:41; and Thomas Ashe, *Travels in America* (London: William Sawyer, 1808), 305. For a similar situation in Missouri, see John Mack Faragher, "'More Motley than Mackinaw': From Ethnic Mixing to Ethnic Cleansing on the Frontier of the Lower Missouri, 1783–1833," in *Contact Points: American Frontiers from the Mohawk Valley to the Mississippi, 1750–1830,* ed. Andrew R. L. Cayton and Fredrika J. Teute (Chapel Hill: University of North Carolina Press, 1998); and Daniel H. Usner Jr., "An American Indian Gateway: Some Thoughts on the Migration and Settlement of Eastern Indians around Early St. Louis," *Gateway Heritage* 11 (Winter 1990–91): 42–51.

5. John B. Treat to Henry Dearborn, Secretary of War, May 20, Nov. 18, 1806, Letter Book of the Arkansas Trading House, 1805–10, Record Group 75, National Archives and Records Administration, Washington, D.C. [hereafter cited as Letter Book].

6. Treat to William Davy, Principal Agent for Indian Factories, Oct. 6, Dec. 27, 1805, Letter Book. Treat and the agent for the Chickasaws did

intervene to prevent a dispute between the Quapaws and the Chickasaws. See
Treat to Henry Dearborn, Apr. 4, 1807, ibid.

7. Carter and Bloom, *Territorial Papers,* 13:280, 464, 14:165; John
Sibley, "Historical Sketches of the Several Indian Tribes in Louisiana, South of
the Arkansas River, and between the Mississippi and River Grand," in *Travels
in the Interior Parts of America* (London: J. G. Barnard, 1807), 53. For
Quapaw hunting, see Arnold, *Rumble of a Distant Drum,* 30–42. For French
hunters in Arkansas during the colonial era, see Daniel H. Usner Jr., *Indians,
Settlers, and Slaves in a Frontier Exchange Economy: The Lower Mississippi
Valley before 1783* (Chapel Hill: University of North Carolina Press, 1992),
174–76; Gilbert Din, "Between a Rock and a Hard Place: The Indian Trade in
Spanish Arkansas," in Whayne, *Cultural Encounters,* 112–15; and Joseph
Patrick Key, "'Masters of This Country': The Quapaws and Environmental
Change in Arkansas, 1673–1833" (Ph.D. diss., University of Arkansas, 2001),
68–77.

8. Myra Vaughan, "Genealogical Notes of the Valliere-Vaugine Families,"
Arkansas Historical Quarterly 15 (Winter 1956): 313–16. On American settlers
and their family connections, see Elliott West, "Families," in *The Way to the
West: Essays on the Central Plains* (Albuquerque: University of New Mexico
Press, 1995), 85–125; Richard White, "The Altered Landscape: Social Change
and the Land in the Pacific Northwest," in *Regionalism and the Pacific
Northwest,* ed. William G. Robbins, Robert J. Frank, Richard E. Ross
(Corvallis: Oregon State University Press, 1983), 111–12.

9. Bolton, *Arkansas, 1800–1860,* 28–29.

10. Conevery Bolton Valencius, *The Health of the Country: How American
Settlers Understood Themselves and Their Land* (New York: Basic Books,
2002), 17.

11. Ibid., 229ff.

12. On the contrast between policy and reality on the frontier, see Reginald
Horsman, *Expansion and American Indian Policy, 1783–1812* (East Lansing:
Michigan State University Press, 1967); and Anthony F. C. Wallace, *The
Long, Bitter Trail: Andrew Jackson and the Indians* (New York: Hill and
Wang, 1993).

13. Baird, *Quapaw Indians,* 56–60. The Quapaws refer to the president as
"Father" in John B. Treat to Secretary of War, Mar. 27, 1806, in Carter and
Bloom, *Territorial Papers,* 13:464. They address Cherokee agent William
Lovely as "Friend and Brother" in a speech recorded in William L. Lovely to
Secretary of War, Oct. 1, 1813, ibid., 14:705.

14. Horsman, *Expansion and American Indian Policy,* vii–x, 53–59.
Reading Jefferson's official letters, Christian B. Keller argues that Jefferson
considered Indian land cessions and removal as a way to pay for the
Louisiana Purchase by opening up eastern territory to sell to white settlers.
Keller, "Philanthropy Betrayed: Thomas Jefferson, the Louisiana Purchase,

and the Origins of Federal Indian Policy," *Proceedings of the American Philosophical Society* 144 (Mar. 2000): 39–66. Keller's view has found support in recent works on the Louisiana Purchase. See Roger G. Kennedy, *Mr. Jefferson's Lost Cause: Land, Farmers, Slavery, and the Louisiana Purchase* (New York: Oxford University Press, 2003), 152–54; and Jon Kukla, *A Wilderness So Immense: The Louisiana Purchase and the Destiny of America* (New York: Alfred A. Knopf, 2003), 301–3.

15. William Clark, Ninian Edwards, and Auguste Chouteau to William Crawford, Dec. 7, 1816, Missouri Historical Society, photocopy, W. David Baird Papers, Box 3 (1804–18), Special Collections Division, University of Arkansas Libraries, Fayetteville; Carter and Bloom, *Territorial Papers,* 15:87–88; "Treaty with the Quapaw, [Aug. 24,] 1818," http://digital.library. okstate.edu/kappler/Vol2/treaties/qua0160.htm. On the development of the American legal system in Arkansas, see Morris S. Arnold, *Unequal Laws unto a Savage Race: European Legal Traditions in Arkansas, 1686–1836* (Fayetteville: University of Arkansas Press, 1985), 130–202.

16. See Arnold, *Rumble of a Distant Drum;* and Kathleen DuVal, "The Education of Fernando de Leyba: Quapaws and Spaniards on the Borders of Empires," *Arkansas Historical Quarterly* 60 (Spring 2001): 1–29.

17. Nuttall, *Journal,* 104.

18. For more on the influence of the civilization program with respect to gender, see Theda Perdue, *Cherokee Women: Gender and Culture Change, 1700–1835* (Lincoln: University of Nebraska Press, 1998), 109ff.

19. For the gender division of labor among other Indian societies, see Perdue, *Cherokee Women;* Ramón A. Gutiérrez, *When Jesus Came, the Corn Mothers Went Away: Marriage, Sexuality, and Power in New Mexico, 1500–1846* (Stanford: Stanford University Press, 1991), 13–21; Carolyn Merchant, *Ecological Revolutions: Nature, Gender, and Science in New England* (Chapel Hill: University of North Carolina Press, 1989); and Carolyn Merchant, "Gender and Environmental History," *Journal of American History* 76 (Mar. 1990): 1117–21.

20. On the complementary nature and reciprocal obligations of Quapaw social divisions, see Sabo, "Rituals of Encounter," 79–80.

21. Carter and Bloom, *Territorial Papers,* 14:129, 165.

22. Ibid., 13:464.

23. Ibid., 14:705.

24. William Clark, Ninian Edwards, and Auguste Chouteau to William Crawford, Dec. 7, 1816, Baird Papers.

25. Ibid.; Horsman, *Expansion and American Indian Policy,* 114.

26. Baird, *Quapaw Indians,* 86–87; Perdue, *Cherokee Women,* 115–16.

27. Key, "Indians and Ecological Conflict," 141–43.

28. David W. Bizzell, ed., "A Report on the Quapaw: The Letters of Governor George Izard to the American Philosophical Society, 1825–1827,"

Pulaski County Historical Review 29 (Winter 1981): 72; Baird, *Quapaw Indians,* 64–69. The Choctaws had already negotiated a removal treaty in 1820, though they would not actually move until 1830. The treaty signaled the federal government's increasing insistence on removal. Unlike earlier cessions of tribal territory, removal meant the sale of all tribal land in the East and, in most cases, migration to the Indian Territory, which was being created in the 1820s. See Wallace, *Long, Bitter Trail,* 39–54. Writing to Calhoun, Crittenden displayed his ignorance of the Quapaws' long history of negotiations with newcomers when he noted that he had them "in training for a Treaty." Carter and Bloom, *Territorial Papers,* 19:549–50.

29. "Treaty with the Quapaw, [Nov. 15,] 1824," http://digital.library.okstate.edu/kappler/Vol2/treaties/qua0210.htm; Arnold, *Unequal Laws,* 160–93. Sarasin's decision to go with his people has been overlooked by contemporaries and historians who have criticized him for his alleged concern with financial gain. See, for example, Baird, *Quapaw Indians,* 71.

30. George Sabo III, "Inconsistent Kin: French-Quapaw Relations at Arkansas Post," in *Arkansas before the Americans,* ed. Hester A. Davis, Research Series 40 (Fayetteville: Arkansas Archeological Survey, 1991), 105–30; Sabo, "Rituals of Encounter," 76–87.

31. Baird, *Quapaw Indians,* 68.

32. Ibid., 69–71.

33. On the Great Raft, see Dan L. Flores, ed., *Jefferson and Southwestern Exploration: The Freeman and Custis Accounts of the Red River Expedition of 1806* (Norman: University of Oklahoma Press, 1984), 126–35.

34. Baird, *Quapaw Indians,* 70–72.

35. The Chiefs, Head men and Warriors of the Quapaw Tribe to the President, July 10, 1831, Letters Received, Office of Indian Affairs, Neosho Agency, Record Group 75, National Archives and Records Administration, M-669; Carter and Bloom, *Territorial Papers,* 20:497; Arnold, *Rumble of a Distant Drum,* 146–48.

36. Quapaw Chiefs to Secretary of War, Oct. 15, 1831, Letters Received, Office of Indian Affairs, Neosho Agency, M-669.

37. Ibid.; Chiefs, Head men, and Warriors of the Quapaw Tribe to the President, July 10, 1831; Carter and Bloom, *Territorial Papers,* 20:466, 477, 496–97, 708, 21:45, 356; Bobbie Jones McLane, Charles William Cunning, and Wendy Bradley Richter, comps., *Observations of Arkansas: The 1824–1863 Letters of Hiram Abiff Whittington* (Hot Springs, Ark.: Garland County Historical Society, 1997), 23. Primary sources do not specify the gender of the Quapaw cotton-pickers, but we might assume that they were women, who remained primarily responsible for agriculture. Daniel H. Usner Jr., *American Indians in the Lower Mississippi Valley: Social and Economic Histories* (Lincoln: University of Nebraska Press, 1998), 80–81, 106. George Gray also

noted that, in addition to the Quapaws, "Lawless Fellows" stole horses from Indians to bring east. Carter and Bloom, *Territorial Papers,* 20:743. Dan L. Flores discusses the horse trade from the plains to the East in *Horizontal Yellow: Nature and History in the Near Southwest* (Albuquerque: University of New Mexico Press, 1999), 88–92, 103–19.

38. Heckaton to Secretary of War, Sept. 26, 1831, Letters Received, Office of Indian Affairs, Neosho Agency, M-669.

39. Chiefs, Head men, and Warriors of the Quapaw Tribe to the President, July 10, 1831; Ronald N. Satz, *American Indian Policy in the Jacksonian Era* (1975; reprint, Norman: University of Oklahoma Press, 2002), 249–51.

40. Carolyn Thomas Foreman, "The Choctaw Academy," *Chronicles of Oklahoma* 9 (Dec. 1931): 408–9. The students were named most often after leading American politicians and, probably, benefactors of the school. In 1834 one Choctaw student was named Ambrose Severe.

41. Satz, *American Indian Policy,* 246–48.

42. Ibid., 251.

43. Baird, *Quapaw Indians,* 76.

44. Heckaton to Ambrose Sevier, Sept. 21, 1831, Letters Received, Office of Indian Affairs, Neosho Agency, M-669; Baird, *Quapaw Indians,* 76–78; "Treaty with the Quapaw, [May 13,] 1833," http://digital.library.okstate.edu/kappler/Vol2/treaties/qua0395.htm.

45. Baird, *Quapaw Indians,* 78–79.

7. The Louisiana Purchase and the Black Experience

1. "State Announces Major Tourism Initiative—Louisiana Purchase Bicentennial Celebration Runs throughout 2003," http://www.crt.state.la.us/pressarchive/20020424.htm.

2. Jerry W. Knudson, "Newspaper Reaction to the Louisiana Purchase: This New, Immense, Unbounded World," *Missouri Historical Review* 63 (Jan. 1969): 197.

3. Thomas A. Bailey, *A Diplomatic History of the American People* (Englewood Cliff, N.J.: Prentice-Hall, 1980), 110.

4. James Morton Smith, ed., *The Republic of Letters: The Correspondence between Thomas Jefferson and James Madison, 1776–1826,* vol. 2 (New York: W. W. Norton, 1995), 1287.

5. Thomas N. Ingersoll, "Free Blacks in a Slave Society: New Orleans, 1718–1812," in *The African American Experience in Louisiana: Part A: From Africa to the Civil War,* ed. Charles Vincent (Lafayette: Center for Louisiana Studies, University of Southwestern Louisiana, 1999), 155; Ira Berlin, *Many Thousands Gone: The First Two Centuries of Slavery in North America* (Cambridge, Mass.: Harvard University Press, 1998), 81.

6. Gilbert C. Din, *Spaniards, Planters, and Slaves: The Spanish*

Regulation of Slavery in Louisiana, 1763–1803 (College Station: Texas A&M University Press, 1999), 8; Berlin, *Many Thousands Gone*, 83, 87.

7. Din, *Spaniards, Planters, and Slaves*, 9.

8. Ibid., 241; Berlin, *Many Thousands Gone*, 86, 197–201, 345–48.

9. Gwendolyn Midlo Hall, *Africans in Colonial Louisiana: The Development of Afro-Creole Culture in the Eighteenth Century* (Baton Rouge: Louisiana State University Press, 1992), 150–52.

10. Din, *Spaniards, Planters, and Slaves*, 23.

11. Ibid., 10.

12. Ingersoll, "Free Blacks in a Slave Society," 157.

13. Frank Tannenbaum, *Slave and Citizen: The Negro in the Americas* (New York: Knopf, 1946).

14. David Brion Davis, *The Problem of Slavery in Western Culture* (Ithaca, N.Y.: Cornell University Press, 1966), 223–43, 262–88.

15. Jack D. Holmes, "The Abortive Slave Revolt at Pointe Coupee, Louisiana, 1795," *Louisiana History* 11 (Fall 1970): 341–62.

16. Ira Berlin, *Slaves without Masters: The Free Negro in the Antebellum South* (New York: Pantheon, 1974), 109; Berlin, *Many Thousands Gone*, 213.

17. Berlin, *Slaves without Masters*, 109; Berlin, *Many Thousands Gone*, 331.

18. Kimberly S. Hanger, "'Almost All Have Callings: Free Blacks at Work in Spanish New Orleans,'" *Colonial Latin American Historical Review* 3, no. 2 (1994): 141–64.

19. Kimberly S. Hanger, "A Privilege and Honor to Serve: The Free Black Militia of Spanish New Orleans," *Military History of the Southwest* 21 (Spring 1991): 59–86.

20. Berlin, *Slaves without Masters*, 110.

21. Ibid., 110–11.

22. Berlin, *Many Thousands Gone*, 342–45.

23. Roger G. Kennedy, *Mr. Jefferson's Lost Cause: Land, Farmers, Slavery, and the Louisiana Purchase* (New York: Oxford University Press, 2003), 210–14.

24. Paul F. Lachance, "The Politics of Fear: French Louisianians and the Slave Trade, 1706–1809," in Vincent, *African American Experience in Louisiana*, 135.

25. David Patrick Geggus, *Haitian Revolutionary Studies* (Bloomington: Indiana University Press, 2002), 9–25.

26. Lachance, "Politics of Fear," 173–75.

27. Ingersoll, "Free Blacks in a Slave Society," 168.

28. Berlin, *Slaves without Masters*, 118.

29. Ibid., 122–23.

30. Ibid., 120.

31. Donald E. Everett, "Émigrés and Militiamen: Free Persons of Color in New Orleans, 1803–1815," in Vincent, *African American Experience in Louisiana*, 271.

32. Ibid., 276.

33. Ibid.

34. Benard C. Nalty, *Strength for the Fight: A History of Black Americans in the Military* (New York: Free Press, 1986), 25.

35. Junius P. Rodriguez, "'Always En Garde': The Effects of Slave Insurrection upon the Louisiana Mentality, 1811–1815," in Vincent, *African American Experience in Louisiana*, 306; Everett, "Émigrés and Militiamen," 277–78.

36. Rodger A. Fisher, "Racial Segregation in Antebellum New Orleans," in Vincent, *African American Experience in Louisiana*, 331–34.

37. Orville Taylor, *Negro Slavery in Arkansas* (Durham, N.C.: Duke University Press, 1958), 244–58.

38. Paul F. Lachance, "The Limits of Privilege: Where Free Persons of Color Stood in the Hierarchy of Wealth in Antebellum New Orleans," in Vincent, *African American Experience in Louisiana*, 428–46.

39. Joe Gray Taylor, *Negro Slavery in Louisiana* (Baton Rouge: Louisiana Historical Association, 1963), 195–96; Berlin, *Many Thousands Gone*, 333, 356.

40. Taylor, *Negro Slavery in Louisiana*, 106–32.

41. Ira Berlin, Marc Favreau, and Steven F. Miller, eds., *Remembering Slavery: African Americans Talk about Their Personal Experiences of Slavery and Emancipation* (New York: New Press, 1998), 19–20.

42. Ibid., 114.

43. Marie Jenkins Schwartz, *Born in Bondage: Growing Up Enslaved in the Antebellum South* (Cambridge, Mass.: Harvard University Press, 2000), 89–90.

44. Berlin, Favreau, and Miller, *Remembering Slavery*, 147–48.

45. Taylor, *Negro Slavery in Louisiana*, 106–32.

46. Ibid.

47. Jeannie Whayne et al., *Arkansas: A Narrative History* (Fayetteville: University of Arkansas Press, 2002), 70–73; Morris S. Arnold, *Colonial Arkansas, 1686–1804: A Social and Cultural History* (Fayetteville: University of Arkansas Press, 1991), 65, 66, 69; Taylor, *Negro Slavery in Arkansas*, 3–17.

48. On the spread of plantation slavery in Arkansas, see Donald P. McNeilly, *The Old South Frontier: Cotton Plantations and the Formation of Arkansas Society* (Fayetteville: University of Arkansas Press, 2000); and S. Charles Bolton, *Arkansas, 1800–1860: Remote and Restless* (Fayetteville: University of Arkansas Press, 1998), 125–44.

49. W. E. B. DuBois, *The Souls of Black Folk* (1903; reprint, New York: Knopf, 1993), 79–95, 274–76.

8. The First Years of American Justice

1. Anton-Hermann Chroust, "The Legal Profession on the Frontier," chap. 2 in *The Revolution and Post-Revolutionary Era,* vol. 2 of *The Rise of the Legal Profession in America* (Norman: University of Oklahoma Press, 1965), 92. For other discussions of law on the frontier, see Lawrence M. Friedman, "Outposts of the Law: The Frontier and the Civil Law Fringe," chap. 2 in *A History of American Law,* 2d ed. (New York: Simon and Schuster, 1985), 157–76; and William Francis English, *The Pioneer Lawyer and Jurist in Missouri,* University of Missouri Studies vol. 21, no. 2 (Columbia: University of Missouri, 1947).

2. The record books of these courts were kept by the clerks. Each day the clerk would enter the proceedings: for example, when the court convened; the names of the presiding judges; the names of the grand jurors summoned, those who failed to appear, and how they were sanctioned; the outcome of each complaint brought before the grand jury; and in the case of a trial, the names of the jurors and the verdict. For each case called, the clerk noted its disposition, such as whether it was continued to a later day or term, or whether it was dismissed. The books also contain other business of the courts, such as admitting attorneys to practice, granting licenses to ferry operators, commissioning surveys for roads, and approving reimbursements to the sheriff. Between 1808 and 1814, separate books were kept for the Courts of Quarter Sessions and of Common Pleas. The court files consist of pleadings (statements of the parties), writs and orders (commands of the court), motions (requests of the parties), and returns (responses the sheriffs would make after serving process) as well as depositions, affidavits, deeds, contracts, and other instruments submitted as evidence.

3. S. Charles Bolton's two treatises, *Territorial Ambition: Land and Society in Arkansas, 1800 to 1840* (Fayetteville: University of Arkansas Press, 1993) and *Arkansas, 1800–1860: Remote and Restless* (Fayetteville: University of Arkansas Press, 1998), provide general treatments of territorial Arkansas. Morris S. Arnold, *Unequal Laws unto a Savage Race: European Legal Traditions in Arkansas, 1686–1836* (Fayetteville: University of Arkansas Press, 1985) is the authoritative work on law in both colonial and territorial Arkansas and is the foundation on which much of this article stands. Judge Arnold's work, however, was written before the discovery of the Arkansas Post case files, which contain significant information about some of the cases handled by the territorial courts.

4. *Statutes at Large of the United States of America* 2 (1856): 283 (enacted Mar. 26, 1804), 331 (enacted Mar. 3, 1805), 743 (enacted June 4, 1812), 3 (1856):493 (enacted Mar. 2, 1819). Throughout this article, "Arkansas" refers to the area that is the state of Arkansas today. Similarly "Missouri" refers to the area that constitutes contemporary Missouri and not

the Missouri Territory, which originally stretched west to the Rockies and north to Canada.

5. The districts bore the same names as their Spanish predecessors. From north to south, they were: St. Charles, St. Louis, Ste. Genevieve, Cape Girardeau, and New Madrid. Proclamation of Gov. William Henry Harrison, Oct. 1, 1804, in *Territorial Papers of the United States,* ed. Clarence E. Carter and John P. Bloom (Washington, D.C.: Government Printing Office, 1934–75), 13:51–52.

6. Proclamation, Jan. 1, 1806, in Carter and Bloom, *Territorial Papers* 13:540; Proclamation, July 7, 1807, in *The Life and Papers of Frederick Bates,* ed. Thomas Maitland Marshall (St. Louis: Missouri Historical Society, 1926), 1:152–53; Proclamation, Aug. 20, 1808, ibid., 2:15–16.

7. A court of record is required by law to keep a record of its proceedings. This suffices as evidence in another court without further proof.

8. Proclamation, Oct. 1, 1812, in Carter and Bloom, *Territorial Papers,* 14:599–600. In November 1809 Bates wrote the judges: "I send you blank commissions, and ask, that you employ your best efforts in filling them worthily. On your success in this attempt will probably depend the existence of your Settlements as a *Separate District.*" To the Judges of the District of Arkansas, in Marshall, *Life and Papers of Bates,* 2:115–16.

9. Arnold writes, "Though the Arkansas judicial records for 1808 to 1814 several times refer to the files of the court, no files have in fact survived." *Unequal Laws,* 170.

10. This distinction should not be confused with the "civil/criminal" dichotomy. France and Spain are "civil law" countries as contrasted with Great Britain and the United States, which are "common law" countries.

11. Arnold, *Unequal Laws,* 49, 54.

12. English, *Pioneer Lawyer,* 37.

13. For a discussion of these "unwritten norms," see Stuart Banner, *Legal Systems in Conflict: Property and Sovereignty in Missouri, 1750–1860* (Norman: University of Oklahoma Press, 2000), 51–66. On Spanish and French law at the Post and the transition to American jurisprudence, see Arnold, *Unequal Laws.*

14. Louis Houck, *A History of Missouri from the Earliest Explorations and Settlements until the Admission of the State into the Union* (Chicago: R. R. Donnelly and Sons, 1908), 2:387.

15. *Laws of a Public and General Nature of the District of Louisiana, of the Territory of Louisiana, of the Territory of Missouri, and the State of Missouri: Up to the Year 1824,* (Jefferson City, Mo.: W. Lusk and Son, 1842) [hereafter cited as *Laws*], chap. 38, sec. 2 (enacted July 3, 1807).

16. English, *Pioneer Lawyer,* 66.

17. *Laws,* chap. 13, sec. 16. A plea of assize, which is no longer used, concerned the possession of real property. Scire facias, still used today, concerns a

previous matter of record, such as a plea to revive a judgment after it has expired. Arkansas Code Annotated Sec. 16-65-501. Replevin, also in use today, is an action to recover personal property. Arkansas Code Annotated Secs. 18-60-801 et seq. Real actions concern rights in land, personal actions concern personal obligations and duties, and mixed actions are those with elements of both.

18. Literally, "to hear and to determine."

19. *Laws,* chap. 38, sec. 13.

20. Ibid., chap. 65, sec. 2.

21. Ibid., chap. 65, sec. 8. The first case in Hempstead's *Reports,* the earliest bound compilation of Arkansas territorial and federal cases, concerns an incestuous rape. The defendant was sentenced to castration, but territorial governor James Miller commuted the sentence. Samuel H. Hempstead, *Reports of Cases Argued and Determined in the United States Superior Court for the Territory of Arkansas, from 1820 to 1836* (Boston: Little, Brown, 1856), 1–3.

22. *Laws,* chap. 65, sec. 32.

23. Ibid., chap. 65, sec. 39. For a discussion of the evolution of the benefit of clergy doctrine, see Friedman, *History of American Law,* 71.

24. *Laws,* chap. 65, sec. 35.

25. A quorum court is akin to what many states call a "county commission," a board of elected representatives that handles county administrative matters. Although originally Arkansas quorum courts had a few judicial functions, today they have none.

26. Court of General Quarter Sessions, District of Arkansas, Record Book 43, Arkansas History Commission, Little Rock [hereafter cited as Quarter Sessions].

27. *Laws,* chap. 65, sec. 1.

28. Ibid., chap. 65, secs. 1–2, 5.

29. Ibid., chap. 2.

30. Ibid., chap. 143. The courts met at the house of Mary Moore, who presented a bill every session. On August 8, 1810, she billed the court one dollar for use by the Orphans Court. But the court, without stating any reasons, refused payment.

31. *Laws,* chap. 51.

32. The Spanish had established Hopefield as El Campo de la Esperanza, across the Mississippi from Chickasaw Bluffs. Hopefield does not exist today but was at the approximate site of present-day West Memphis. Chickasaw Bluffs became Memphis.

33. To the Land Commissioners, n.d., in Marshall, *Life and Papers of Frederick Bates,* 2:12–13. Like many an early traveler, Bates had nothing kind to say about the inhabitants of the Post. "The People are for the most part so entirely unacquainted with every kind of business, except of that of the chase,

it is not at all to be wondered at that affairs requiring method, order and an observance of legal forms, should be totally unintelligible to them." Ibid., 8.

34. Arnold, *Unequal Laws,* 30, 158.

35. John B. Treat, the Indian factor at Arkansas Post between 1805 and 1810, wrote that the population consisted of "between sixty and seventy families, nine, or ten of which are from the three states Virginia, Maryland, and Pennsylvania; the others (one or two excepted) are all French, either natives; or those who emigrated from the Illinois, New Orleans, and two or three from Europe." Treat to Secretary of War, Nov. 15, 1805, in Carter and Bloom, *Territorial Papers,* 13:278–79. Both the French and Americans owned slaves, of whom Treat estimated there to be about sixty. The population of the Post fluctuated as hunters, trappers, and traders, a significant portion of the inhabitants, came and went. For more information on the population at Arkansas Post, see Arnold, *Unequal Laws,* 151–52.

36. For a discussion of the Cherokees in northeastern Arkansas during this time period and estimates of the size of the St. Francis settlements, see Robert A. Myers, "Cherokee Pioneers in Arkansas: The St. Francis Years, 1785–1813," *Arkansas Historical Quarterly* 56 (Summer 1997): 127–57.

37. "Most of the inhabitants of that village [the Post] are of mixed blood, and the same mixture is observable among the Indians, who are now reduced to a very few in number." Amos Stoddard, *Sketches, Historical and Descriptive, of Louisiana* (Philadelphia: Matthew Carey, 1812), 206. For a discussion of Quapaw and French intermarriage, see also Morris S. Arnold, *The Rumble of a Distant Drum: The Quapaws and the Old World Newcomers, 1673–1804* (Fayetteville: University of Arkansas Press, 2000), 7–14. For a discussion of European and American intermarriage with Cherokees, see Stanley W. Hoig, *The Cherokees and Their Chiefs: In the Wake of Empire* (Fayetteville: University of Arkansas Press, 1998).

38. Arnold, *Unequal Laws,* 158.

39. Ibid.; Dallas T. Herndon, *Centennial History of Arkansas* (Chicago: S. J. Clarke, 1922), 1:126–27. Stillwell was one of the few successful Spanish-land-grant claimants, in part because he settled and improved his land. An arpen, or arpent, was the French and Spanish measure for land commonly used in grants. It could refer either to a distance or an area. Lengthwise, an arpent is 63.75 yards long; a square arpent is 0.85 acre. Paul W. Gates, *History of Public Land Law Development* (Washington, D.C.: Government Printing Office, 1968), 89 n. 4.

40. Appointments to Civil Offices by Governor Lewis, Sept. 30, 1808, in Marshall, *Life and Papers of Frederick Bates,* 2:30.

41. Court of Common Pleas, District of Arkansas, Record Book, Arkansas History Commission, [hereafter cited as Common Pleas], 1.

42. Ibid., 2; Appointments to Civil Offices by Governor Lewis, 30.

43. *Laws,* chap. 60, sec. 2.

44. Ibid.

45. The grand jurors were John Henry (this may have been John Hendrez or Hendry), Joseph Bougy (or Bogy, or Bougie), Daniel Mooney, Frederick Hagen, William Glass, Benjamin Fowler, Samuel Carter, Christian Pringle, Leonard Rush, François Michel (or Mitchel), Baptiste Desruisseaux, Raffilel Brinsback, Michel Pringle, John Hadley, Charles Forenash (or Fallanash), Anthony Woolf, Jacob Greenawault, Isaac Rider, August De Surville, Jean Baptiste Duchassine, James Scull, Peter Lefevre Junior, Tanas Racine, and Robert Algou (or Algoe, or Aljou). Spelling of all words in the record books varies wildly, but particularly the spelling of names. I have spelled names in a particular way either because 1) the name is spelled in that form most of the time, e.g., "Hewes Scull" versus "Hugh Scull"; 2) the person signed his name in that form, e.g., "Benjamin Fooy" versus "Benjamin Foy"; or 3) in particularly hard cases, the way the name has been spelled by contemporary historians, e.g. "Desruisseaux." In quotations from the record books, I have preserved the original text exactly as it appears in the book with regard to spelling, capitalization, and punctuation.

46. Arnold, *Unequal Laws,* 162–63.

47. Quarter Sessions, 1. The court was informed that Brinsback was deceased; it remitted his fine.

48. Ibid., 1–2.

49. English, *Pioneer Lawyer,* 48–49.

50. *Laws,* chap. 38, sec. 58.

51. Common Pleas, 2.

52. We know that Armistead held court because of Wallis's letter (see below) and because the record book of the Court of Common Pleas mentions him as "late judge." As early as January 1, 1806, Governor Wilkinson appointed John B. Treat, Charles Refeld, François Vaugine, Leonard Repler, Joseph Bougy, and François Valliere justices of the Common Pleas and Quarter Sessions Court. Proclamation, Jan. 1, 1806, in Carter and Bloom, *Territorial Papers,* 13:540. There is no evidence that this court ever met, but if it did, Wallis may have tried cases before it. Alternatively he could have practiced in Benjamin Fooy's 1808 justice-of-the-peace court at Hopefield.

53. Wallis to Bates, Sept. 1, 1808, in Marshall, *Life and Papers of Frederick Bates,* 2:23–24. Wallis writes: "we have had serious work and hard swearing here last week capt Armistead has had his hands head & heart full Burnet has been apprehended for the murder of Patterson and many others have been arraigned for felony and bound to the Peace Burnet is sent to New Madrid gaol."

54. Arnold, *Unequal Laws,* 167–68.

55. To the Land Commissioners, Aug. 15, 1808, in Marshall, *Life and Papers of Frederick Bates,* 2:13. The Post of Ouachita was located at the site of present-day Monroe, Louisiana.

56. English, *Pioneer Lawyer,* 67–68.

57. Debt was the most common cause of action during this period. No federal bankruptcy laws or courts existed; instead, debtors were adjudicated insolvent, usually at the instigation of creditors, and legal questions were adjudicated by state courts. Debtor's prison came to an end in the United States during this time. Trespass on the case was a rather amorphous cause of action, not used today, involving injuries not caused by force or by direct result of the defendant's act. An injury caused by negligence would be considered trespass on the case. Trespass on the case could also encompass actions considered to be separate today, such as slander. *Black's Law Dictionary,* 5th ed. (St. Paul: West, 1979), 1347.

58. Common Pleas, 4–14.

59. Quarter Sessions, 6.

60. Attorneys in fact were not admitted to the bar and could not practice as attorneys at law, though some of them (e.g., Darby, Kirpatrick, and Henderson) seemed to make a living as attorneys in fact.

61. Common Pleas, 22–34. During the August 1810 term, William Mabbett had a number of lawsuits against various men, including three against Christopher Kauffman. Kauffman also sued Mabbett in debt, and one of the trial jurors was Richard Melton, who was a defendant in another suit by Mabbett. Common Pleas, 41–52. These sorts of situations come up again and again in the record books.

62. "Indian factories" were simply trading houses established by the federal government. For a discussion of the three factories in Arkansas, see Wayne Morris, "Traders and Factories on the Arkansas Frontier, 1805–1822," *Arkansas Historical Quarterly* 28 (Spring 1969): 18–48.

63. Wallis v. Treat, Complaint to the Grand Jury, Apr. 1809 [reproduced as part of the record in the later *Wallis v. Treat* slander case], Missouri Supreme Court Collection, Missouri State Archives, Jefferson City.

64. Others seem to have shared Treat's low opinion of Wallis. In 1819 Wallis ran against five other candidates for the office of territorial delegate to Congress. The official count states that Wallis received four votes out of a total of more than one thousand cast. Lonnie J. White, *Politics on the Southwestern Frontier: Arkansas Territory 1819–1836* (Memphis: Memphis State University Press, 1964), 22.

65. Wallis v. Treat, Complaint to the Grand Jury, Apr. 1809. This refers to *Hook v. Treat,* a debt case in which Wallis represented the plaintiff and Treat was the defendant. Treat ultimately lost.

66. "No person shall take upon himself to exercise or officiate in any office or place of authority in this territory, without being lawfully authorized thereto; and if any person shall presume so to do, he shall upon conviction thereof be fined in a sum not exceeding one hundred dollars." *Laws,* chap. 65, sec. 26.

67. Quarter Sessions, 26.

68. Ibid., 14.

69. Ibid., 4, 14.

70. Ibid., 26–28.

71. Wallis v. Treat, Declaration, Capias, Apr. 1809, Missouri Supreme Court Collection. Literally, "capias" means "you shall seize." Capias writs were issued to take the defendant into custody to ensure his presence in court to defend a suit, or to jail a defendant who owed a judgment. In either case the defendant could avoid imprisonment by posting a bond or paying the judgment. *Black's Law Dictionary,* 188–89.

72. Treat v. Wallis, Declaration, Apr. 1809, Missouri Supreme Court Collection.

73. *Laws,* chap. 38, sec. 32.

74. Common Pleas, 17.

75. Ibid., 20.

76. Ibid., 19.

77. Ibid.

78. Ibid., 22.

79. Ibid., 22–21 [the second page is misnumbered]. Statutes entitled persons accused of crimes to counsel "learned in the law," but no such right inhered to civil defendants. *Laws,* chap. 65, sec. 37.

80. Common Pleas, 23–24, 35–36.

81. Treat v. Wallis and Wallis v. Treat, Certification of Records, Apr. 1809, Missouri Supreme Court Collection.

82. Common Pleas, 35–36.

83. Ibid., 137.

84. Quarter Sessions, 44–45. Defendants who put themselves "upon the Court" received a bench trial.

85. Darby's jurors were Sherad Hadley, Sylvanus Phillips, Peter Edwards, Henry Cassidy, Martin McWilliams, Christopher Kauffmann, William Mabbett, Willis Lemons, William H. Glass, Abraham Casey, William Gates, and John Madox. Ibid., 45. Note the complete absence of any French names on this jury. Morris Arnold attributes such absences both to French reluctance to become involved with the legal system and American desires to exclude the French. Arnold, *Unequal Laws,* 162–63. At the same time, juror Kauffmann, represented by Perly Wallis, was suing juror Mabbett, represented by Darby, in a completely unrelated lawsuit.

86. Quarter Sessions, 44–45.

87. Ibid., 49.

88. Ibid.

89. Ibid., 50.

90. Common Pleas, 53.

91. The Cassidy brothers, Henry and Patrick, probably came to Arkansas Post from Missouri. A Patrick Cassidy is listed as a resident of New Madrid in

1797. Houck, *History of Missouri*, 2:156. Henry Cassidy was commissioned as a justice of the peace in the District of Cape Girardeau in 1806. Carter and Bloom, *Territorial Papers*, 13:546. In 1807 John B. Treat complained when Henry Cassidy was appointed deputy surveyor for the Wachita District that "the bestowing of a place, requiring any confidence on a person generally thought to be wholly undeserving of trust: may cause unsuitable impressions. and I feel confident would never have been the case had his character been truly known—." John B. Treat to Secretary of War, Oct. 29, 1807, ibid., 14:150.

92. Common Pleas, 54. Anthony Haden had previously served as captain in the District of Cape Girardeau. Carter and Bloom, *Territorial Papers*, 13:549. Walker is mentioned in that venerable source, William F. Pope, *Early Days in Arkansas* (Little Rock: Frederick W. Allsopp, 1895), 68–70. John Miller probably came from Missouri since he presented a license from Judge John B. C. Lucas of the General Court at St. Louis.

93. Presumably because the General Court had refused to hear it.

94. Common Pleas, 64, 67.

95. Charles Bougie and Pierre Lefevre were the only French jurors.

96. Common Pleas, 67, 74, 76.

97. *Black's Law Dictionary*, 149.

98. Common Pleas, 79–80.

99. Ibid., 103–5. The trial actually was two trials. At the end of the first trial, when the jury returned the morning after to give its verdict, juror Christopher Kauffman was missing. The court ordered a new trial immediately with the same jury, with James Crafts replacing Kauffman. The defense unsuccessfully objected.

100. Aloysius Plaisance, "The Arkansas Factory, 1805–1810," *Arkansas Historical Quarterly* 11 (Autumn 1952): 200.

101. Myers, "Cherokee Pioneers," 129, 141, 148, 155–56.

102. Quarter Sessions, 57, 62. The record book does not state the alleged crime for the other trial.

103. Common Pleas, 71, 89.

104. Quarter Sessions, 69.

105. Common Pleas, 89, 90–91, 126–27. John Miller, Isaac's attorney, presented a bill of exceptions that the judges refused to sign because it "embraced more matter" than was contained in their decision. At the August 1812 term, Miller presented a writ of error from the General Court, and the Common Pleas Court ordered a transcript to be made out for appeal. The outcome of the appeal is not known.

106. Myers, "Cherokee Pioneers," 151.

107. Quarter Sessions, 12, 17, 22, 26. During that term he was also appointed assessor for a road from Arkansas Post to "a place called the Bay." Ibid., 29. Assessors determined the number of days "each able bodied male person of full age" was required to "labour on the public roads." *Laws*, chap. 28, sec. 3.

108. Quarter Sessions, 40, 53, 64; Common Pleas, 103.

109. For information on John D. Chisholm's life, and the sources used, see Myers, "Cherokee Pioneers," 131; and "John D. Chisholm," http://www.ctc. volant.org/home/genea/chis/html/I049.html. He is mentioned in a number of books about the Cherokees, notably Hoig, *Cherokees and Their Chiefs.*

110. At this point not much is known about Robert Clary, though Thomas Nuttall, who visited Arkansas in 1819, mentions a "Clary" who led a gang of "swindling robbers" around the mouth of the Arkansas up till the year 1811. Nuttall, *A Journal of Travels into the Arkansas Territory during the Year 1819* (1980; reprint, Fayetteville: University of Arkansas Press, 1999), 251.

111. The files for these two suits survive in the University of Arkansas at Little Rock/Pulaski County Law Library's collection. The case files, transcripts, and abstracts can be viewed at http://arcourts.ualr.edu/case-006/6.1t.htm; and http://arcourts.ualr.edu/case-007/7.1t.htm.

112. The list can be viewed at http://arcourts.ualr.edu/case-007/7.3S4.pdf.

113. Quarter Sessions, 61, 69.

114. Arnold, *Unequal Laws,* 9.

115. John B. Treat to Secretary of War, Nov. 15, 1805, in Carter and Bloom, *Territorial Papers,* 13:279.

116. *Laws,* chap. 35. Records from freedom suits in Missouri are available at "Freedom Suits Case Files, 1814–1860," St. Louis Circuit Court Historical Records Project, http://stlcourtrecords.wustl.edu/about-freedom-suits-series.php.

117. Common Pleas, 60.

118. See Carol Wilson, *Freedom at Risk: The Kidnapping of Free Blacks in America, 1780–1865* (Lexington: University Press of Kentucky, 1994).

119. Peeler v. Phillips, Declaration, Plea, Missouri State Supreme Court Collection, Missouri State Archives. The outcome of the appeal is not known.

120. Common Pleas, 93, 95, 115.

121. On the Winter grant, see Arnold, *Unequal Laws,* 98; and Bolton, *Arkansas, 1800–1860,* 14–15.

122. Miller v. Cassidy, Declaration of Sept. 12, 1812, Missouri State Supreme Court Collection, Missouri State Archives. The wording of the declaration demonstrates the "elaborate and absurd jargon of recitals and explanations which obscure the real issues to be tried almost as effectually as if the pleadings were still drawn in Latin." Benjamin J. Shipman, *Handbook of Common-Law Pleading,* 3d ed., rev. by Henry Winthrop Ballentine (St. Paul: West, 1923), 219. A declaration of slander had to contain an inducement, a colloquium, publication, innuendoes, and damages to meet the technical pleading requirement. Ibid. The declaration is also available online at http://arcourts.ualr.edu/case-020/20.2S1.pdf through 20.2S8.pdf; a transcription is online at http://arcourts.ualr.edu/case-020/20.2t.htm.

123. At this time nothing further is known about the Peter Walker whose deeds were said to have been stolen. He does not appear on various lists of settlers.

124. Miller v. Cassidy, Declaration of Oct. 4, 1813, Missouri State Supreme Court Collection.

125. Quarter Sessions, 71.

126. Ibid., 73, 76.

127. Ibid., 77–79.

128. Common Pleas, 109.

129. Ibid., 124.

130. Banner, *Legal Systems,* 107 n. 44.

131. Ibid., 107 n. 45.

132. Quarter Sessions, 81.

133. Miller v. Cassidy, Affidavit, Missouri State Supreme Court Collection, Missouri State Archives.

134. Ibid., Return of the Sheriff.

135. Ibid.

136. English, *Pioneer Lawyer,* 25, 27.

137. Common Pleas, 150.

138. *Statutes at Large of the United States of America* 3 (1856):95 (enacted Jan. 27, 1814).

139. General Court, 150. The page numbering picks up where Common Pleas leaves off because the courts used the same book.

140. Ibid., 171.

141. See, for instance, Bolton, *Arkansas, 1800–1860,* 30–35.

9. Dancing into the Past

1. James Mooney, *The Ghost-Dance Religion and the Sioux Outbreak of 1890* (Washington, D.C.: Fourteenth Annual Report of the Bureau of Ethnology, 1892–93, 1896), 1093–94. In the early colonial era, separate communities of Caddos were organized into three regional alliances: the Kadohadacho, the Hasinai, and the Natchitoches. Archeologists locate the beginnings of their settled, agriculturally based economy, hierarchically organized social structure, and distinctive material culture around A.D. 1000. For a recent summary of Caddo precontact and early historic development, see Ann M. Early, "The Caddos of the Trans-Mississippi South," in *Indians of the Greater Southeast: Historical Archaeology and Ethnohistory,* ed. Bonnie G. McEwan (Gainesville: University Press of Florida, 2000), 122–41. The basic ethnographic source is John R. Swanton, *Source Material on the History and Ethnology of the Caddo Indians,* Bureau of American Ethnology Bulletin 132 (Washington, D.C.: Smithsonian Institution, 1942).

2. See, for example, Cecile Elkins Carter, *Caddo Indians: Where We Come From* (Norman: University of Oklahoma Press, 1995).

3. Peter Nabokov, *A Forest of Time: American Indian Ways of History* (Cambridge: Cambridge University Press, 2002), 21.

4. Marshall Sahlins, *Islands of History* (Chicago: University of Chicago Press, 1985); Robert Borofsky, *Making History: Pukapukan and Anthropological Constructions of Knowledge* (Cambridge: Cambridge University Press, 1987); John Comaroff and Jean Comaroff, *Ethnography and the Historical Imagination* (Boulder, Colo.: Westview, 1992).

5. Most Caddos understand the distinction between conventional and traditional historical knowledge perfectly well but consider it unimportant in applying that knowledge to the task of dealing with present-day circumstances. What is important is the moral or thematic significance that can be attached to events and circumstances in which their ancestors were involved.

6. Vynola Beaver Newkumet and Howard L. Meredith, *Hasinai: A Traditional History of the Caddo Confederacy* (College Station: Texas A&M University Press, 1988).

7. Ibid., 102. See also Irving Whitebead and Howard L. Meredith, "Nuh-Ka-Oashun: Hasinai Turkey Dance Tradition," in *Songs of Indian Territory: Native American Music Traditions of Oklahoma,* ed. Willie Smyth (Oklahoma City: State Arts Council of Oklahoma and the Center for the American Indian, 1989), 25–31; and Cecile E. Carter, "Caddo Turkey Dance," in *Remaining Ourselves: Music and Tribal Memory,* ed. Dayna Bowker Lee (Oklahoma City: State Arts Council of Oklahoma, 1995), 31–36.

8. To supplement my own observations, the following description of the Turkey Dance uses Newkumet and Meredith, *Hasinai,* 102–5; and Carter, "Caddo Turkey Dance."

9. Claude Medford Jr., "Southeastern Drums," *American Indian Crafts and Culture* 6 (Nov. 1972): 14–16. My thanks to Dr. Jason Baird Jackson, Sam Noble Oklahoma Museum of Natural History, for supplying this reference.

10. Carter, *Caddo Indians,* 40.

11. The most accessible English translations of primary sources related to this venture are found in Robert Weddle, Mary Christine Morkovsky, and Patricia Galloway, eds., *La Salle, the Mississippi, and the Gulf: Three Primary Documents* (College Station: Texas A&M University Press, 1987); and William C. Foster, ed., *The La Salle Expedition to Texas: The Journal of Henri Joutel, 1684–1687* (Austin: Texas State Historical Association, 1998).

12. Foster, *La Salle Expedition,* 226.

13. Ibid., 228.

14. Ibid., 263.

15. Fray Francisco Céliz, *Diary of the Alarcón Expedition into Texas, 1718–1719* (New York: Arno, 1967), 75; Fray Isidro Félix de Espinosa, *Cronica apostolica, y seraphica de todos los colegios de propaganda fide de*

esta Nueva-España, de Missioneros Franciscanos observantes: Erigidos con autoridad pontifica, y regia, para la reformacion de los fieles y conversion de los gentiles (Mexico City: Hogal, 1746), 433.

16. Newkumet and Meredith, *Hasinai,* 104.

17. Carter, "Caddo Turkey Dance," 31.

18. Espinosa, *Cronica apostolica,* 420.

19. George A. Dorsey, *Traditions of the Caddo* (1905; reprint, Lincoln: University of Nebraska Press, 1967), 86.

20. Ibid., 102.

21. George A. Hurst and James G. Dickson, "Eastern Turkey in Southern Pine-Oak Forests," in *The Wild Turkey: Biology and Management,* ed. James G. Dickson (Harrisburg, Pa.: Stackpole, 1992), 265–85; Samuel L. Beasom and Don Wilson, "Rio Grande Turkey," ibid., 306–30.

22. Julia E. Hammett, "Ethnohistory of Aboriginal Landscapes in the Southeastern United States," in *Biodiversity and Native America,* ed. Paul E. Minnis and Wayne J. Elisens (Norman: University of Oklahoma Press, 2000), 248–99. See also J. Ned Woodall, "Cultural Ecology of the Caddo" (Ph.D. diss., Southern Methodist University, 1969).

23. Richard E. McCabe and Thomas R. McCabe, "Of Slings and Arrows: An Historical Retrospection," in *White-Tailed Deer Ecology and Management,* ed. Lowell K. Halls (Harrisburg, Pa.: Stackpole, 1984), 19–72.

24. In the discussion of Turkey Dance songs that follows, Caddo phrases along with their English translations are taken from the master list unless otherwise specified. Caddo Turkey Dances: Master List, typescript on file, Caddo Heritage Museum, Binger, Okla. There are variations in the spelling and accenting of certain Caddo words in the transcripts. This seems odd, but there is an explanation. Each song is "owned" by a singer, so that he possesses sole right to perform it or to give permission for another to do so. Moreover, ownership may be inherited, so many singers today own songs passed down from a grandfather, an uncle, or some other elder. In some cases the songs have descended through several generations and represent earlier dialects. In a few cases, in fact, a modern version consists of fragments from several earlier songs, each representing a slightly different dialect. The lyrics are given here exactly as rendered in the sources.

25. Notes on Turkey Dance Song Translation, typescript on file, Caddo Heritage Museum.

26. W. W. Newcomb Jr., *The Indians of Texas: From Prehistoric to Modern Times* (Austin: University of Texas Press, 1961), 133–53.

27. Mattie Austin Hatcher, "Descriptions of the Tejas or Asinai Indians, 1691–1722," *Southwestern Historical Quarterly* 30 (Apr. 1927): 287; F. Todd Smith, *The Caddo Indians: Tribes at the Convergence of Empires, 1542–1854* (College Station: Texas A&M University Press, 1995), 57. I am indebted to Cecile Elkins Carter for pointing out the antiquity of the Tonkawa songs.

28. Smith, *Caddo Indians,* 14. The best modern treatments of Osage Indians during the colonial era are Gilbert C. Din and Abraham P. Nasatir, *The Imperial Osages: Spanish-Indian Diplomacy in the Mississippi Valley* (Norman: University of Oklahoma Press, 1983); and Willard H. Rollings, *The Osage: An Ethnohistorical Study of Hegemony on the Prairie-Plains* (Columbia: University of Missouri Press, 1992).

29. Din and Nasatir, *Imperial Osages,* 51–86.

30. Herbert Eugene Bolton, ed., *Athanase de Mézières and the Louisiana-Texas Frontier, 1768–1780: Documents Published for the First Time, from the Original Spanish and French Manuscripts, Chiefly in the Archives of Mexico and Spain* (Cleveland: Arthur H. Clark, 1914), 1:167.

31. Ibid., 1:193–94, 2:131, 141–42; Din and Nasatir, *Imperial Osages,* 73–74, 107–8; Smith, *Caddo Indians,* 66, 75.

32. The Norteños, or "Nations of the North," was the term Spanish officials used to refer collectively to Comanches, Wichitas, and Wichita-speaking Iscanis, Tonkawas, and Taovayas. For an excellent discussion of the Norteños' emergence, see Gary Clayton Anderson, *The Indian Southwest, 1580–1830: Ethnogenesis and Reinvention* (Norman: University of Oklahoma Press, 1999), 145–65.

33. Smith, *Caddo Indians,* 67–70.

34. Lawrence Kinnaird, ed. and trans., *Spain in the Mississippi Valley, 1765–1794* (Washington, D.C.: Government Printing Office, 1946–49), 3:259, 316; Din and Nasatir, *Imperial Osages,* 139–45; Rollings, *The Osage,* 143–46; Smith, *Caddo Indians,* 76–77.

35. Richard A. Barrett, *Culture and Conduct: An Excursion in Anthropology,* 2d ed. (Belmont, Calif.: Wadsworth, 1991), 87–96.

36. Anderson, *Indian Southwest,* 251–65.

37. Newkumet and Meredith, *Hasinai,* 103.

38. Lowell "Wimpy" Edmonds, videotape [interview] by Mary Cecile Carter and John Davis, typescript on file, Caddo Heritage Museum.

39. Mircea Eliade, *The Myth of the Eternal Return or, Cosmos and History* (Princeton, N.J.: Princeton University Press, 1954). On "epitomizing events" that condense, encapsulate, and represent key cultural meanings, see Raymond D. Fogelson, "The Ethnohistory of Events and Nonevents," *Ethnohistory* 36 (Spring 1989): 133–47.

40. Carter, *Caddo Indians;* Smith, *Caddo Indians;* F. Todd Smith, *The Caddos, the Wichitas, and the United States, 1846–1901* (College Station: Texas A&M University Press, 1996); David LaVere, *The Caddo Chiefdoms: Caddo Economics and Politics, 700–1835* (Lincoln: University of Nebraska Press, 1998); Dayna Bowker Lee, "A Social History of Caddoan Peoples: Cultural Adaptation and Persistence in a Native American Community" (Ph.D. diss., University of Oklahoma, 1998).

41. Smith, *Caddo Indians,* 120–24.

42. Ibid., 143–67.
43. Ibid., 167–68.
44. Anderson, *Indian Southwest*, 179–203.
45. Newkumet and Meredith, *Hasinai*, 51–52.

Index